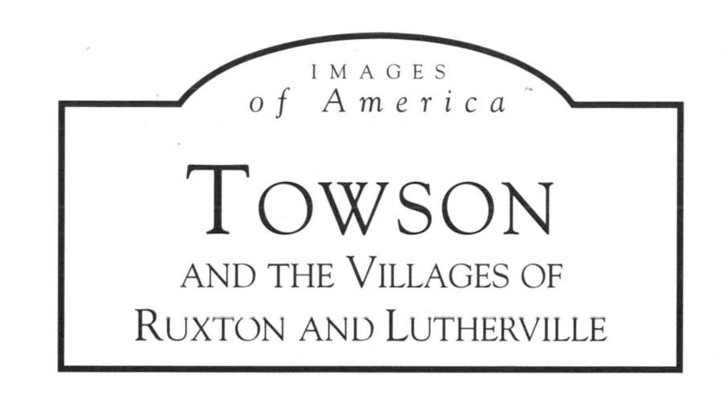
IMAGES
of America
TOWSON
AND THE VILLAGES OF
RUXTON AND LUTHERVILLE

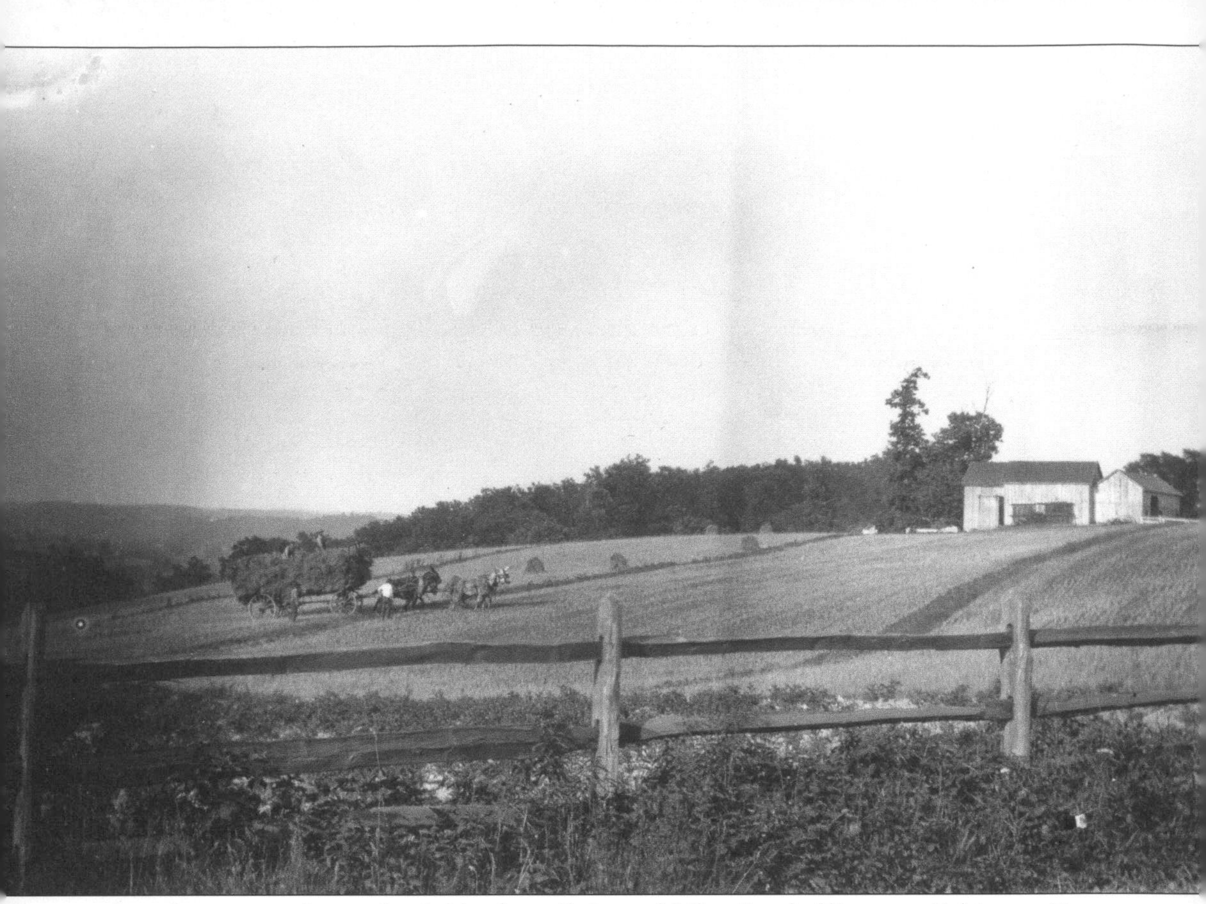

A mule team works in the fields along Dulaney Valley Road. (Courtesy Baltimore County Historical Society.)

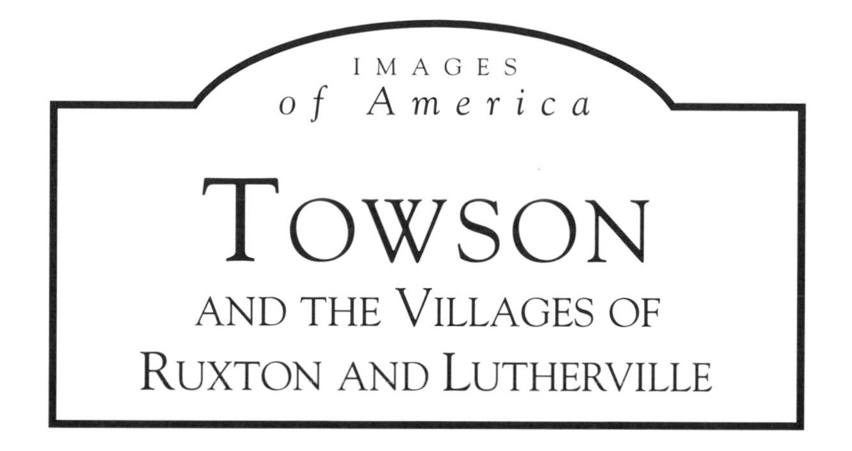

Molly O'Donovan
and Brooke Gunning

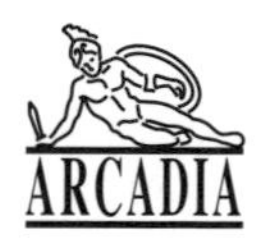

ISBN 0-7385-0226-X

First published in 1999.

Published by Arcadia Publishing,
an imprint of Tempus Publishing, Inc.
2 Cumberland Street
Charleston, SC 29401

Printed in Great Britain.

Library of Congress Catalog Card Number: 99-65672

For all general information contact Arcadia Publishing at:
Telephone 843-853-2070
Fax 843-853-0044
E-Mail sales@arcadiapublishing.com

For customer service and orders:
Toll-Free 1-888-313-2665

Visit us on the internet at http://www.arcadiaimages.com

To our wonderful husbands, René and Charlie, with love, affection, and thanks for their support, suggestions, and patience.

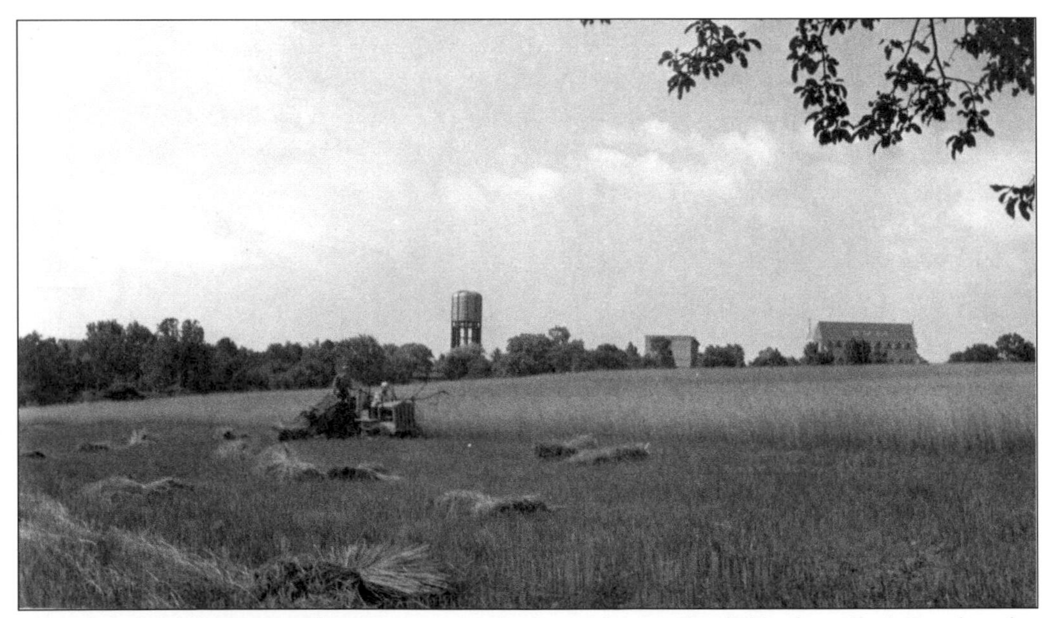

The Church of the Immaculate Conception kept watch over the fields along York Road in the early 1930s. (Courtesy Baltimore County Historical Society.)

Contents

Acknowledgments

Our heartfelt thanks go out to the following individuals and organizations, among others, for their invaluable assistance and time: Winslow and Peter Barlow, Adelaide Bentley, Lee and Holly Brent, Doug and Ellen Brinkley, Marguerite Brown, Kathy Calvert, Dallahan Casey, Andrew Clemens, Lewis Diggs, Harry Gesser, Pat Gibbons, David Goodman, Nancy Gonce, Mary Gunning, René Gunning Sr., René Gunning Jr., George Houghton Huppman, Beth Jordan, Joan Kaltenbach, Marian and Jim Kurapka, Sarah Galloway Larrabee, Andrea and Jonathan Leavitt, Milton Loizeaux, Beatrice Hooker Marty, John W. McGrain, Mindy Miller, Dick and Betsy Mooney, Julie Murphy, Charlie O'Donovan, Gail O'Donovan, Richard Parsons, Dod Poe, Sydney Roby, Sue Ryan, Carlton Seitz, Marge Shipley, Anne Strott, Suzanne Waller, Marilyn and David Warshawsky, Dedi and Hal Whitaker, Joann Winterle, Ada Woods, Baltimore County Historical Society, Loyola Blakefield, Goucher College, Towson Public Library, and Towson University.

Special thanks go to our daughters, Winslow, Kate, and Eliza, who are too young to know how much help they have been by being so good throughout all of this, or just how much we love them.

To the best of our ability, we have attempted to ensure accuracy, given the antiquated and often obscure nature of the subject matter and materials.

Finally, we would like to acknowledge that this book would not have been possible if we hadn't followed the advice of Proverbs 3:5-6 and Colossians 3:23.

References

Brooks, Neal A. and Eric G. Rockel. *A History of Baltimore County*. Towson, MD: Friends of the Towson Library, Inc., 1979.

Brooks, Neal A. and Richard Parsons. *Baltimore County Panorama*. Towson, MD: Baltimore County Public Library, 1988.

Coale, Joseph M., III. *Middling Planters of Ruxton 1694-1850*. Baltimore, MD: Maryland Historical Society, 1996.

Hahn, H. George and Carl Behm III. *Towson: A Pictorial History of a Maryland Town*. Norfolk, VA: The Donning Company/Publishers, 1977.

INTRODUCTION

Before there was a TowsonTown Center, there was a Towsontown. Before there were beltways and byways, there were fields and farms, and before there was a Towsontown, there was a family named Towson. William and Thomas Towson are generally credited with founding Towson, upon their settlement there in 1752. However, the land had already been divided into grants, and they were not the first to discover the area. In 1768, William's enterprising son Ezekial established a combination tavern/inn, which became a landmark for many generations, strategically situated on the increasingly busy route used by farmers, travelers, and merchants heading to and from the port of Baltimore.

For many years, there were relatively few residents in the area, which consisted mainly of farmland. All that began to change when the local populace voted Towson the new seat of Baltimore County in 1854. In addition, the advent of the railroad, horse-drawn streetcars, and Towson's rising popularity as a summer retreat lead to increased growth. As the city of Baltimore grew and spread toward Towson, Towson also grew. And when the city stopped growing, Towson grew even more. This growth continued, as it still does today, with the tremendous increase in people and businesses, schools, and houses.

Prior to its present name, the area which comprises Ruxton was known by a collection of quite colorful names, such as Young Man's Adventure, Carr's Pleasure, Hector's Hopyard, Samuel's Hope, Hooker's Prosperity, Bosley's Adventure, and Beale's Discovery. The eager reader might suspect, quite reasonably, that all these hopes, discoveries, and adventures would indicate a history rife with intrigue and assignations. In fact, Ruxton's history has, in general, been rather placid and comfortable.

Originally, the land was farmed; the first documented settlement was in the early 1700s. However, it was not until the late 1800s that the community began to grow and transform appreciably. After the 1885 construction of a train station, the name Ruxton came into use, in honor of former resident Nicholas Ruxton Moore, who was a veteran of both the American War for Independence and the War of 1812. Improved accessibility encouraged prosperous Baltimoreans to build beautiful summer homes, many of which are still standing. Ruxton and Lake Roland provided a cool and healthy alternative to city life. Over the following decades, Ruxton made the successful shift from seasonal community to suburb. Today, it retains its quiet dignity and unannounced affluence.

The village of Lutherville's origins are a wonderful blend of the practical and the creative, which so typifies the American spirit of the 19th century. Doctors Benjamin Kurtz and John

Gottlieb Morris were two Lutheran ministers whose dream was to found a school for women. To achieve this end, they purchased a 2,000-acre farm in 1852. The revenues from the sale of 119 lots, carved from the original parcel, enabled the good doctors to build the Lutheran Female Seminary in 1853.

Lutherville soon became a popular summer resort, easily accessible to Baltimore, particularly after it received its own railroad station. Wholesome family activities and environment led to a growing number of year-round residents. Their legacy is a charming and widely renowned assortment of houses and buildings in the Victorian, Gothic, and Downing-Vaux styles. In 1972, the National Park Service added Lutherville to its National Register of Historic Places. Baltimore County followed suit in 1988 by designating the area as a historic district. Although the bucolic surroundings it once enjoyed are gone, the heart of Lutherville remains much the same as it was in those tree-shaded summer days of long ago.

Come with us as we take a fond, but, of sad necessity, all-too-brief journey to look back on Towson and its neighbors, Ruxton and Lutherville, as they were before 1960. Some of these glimpses from the past may be familiar because the name rings a bell or the building still stands. For those of you to whom all this is new, we say welcome to your past. Here are some of the people and places, events, and organizations that have helped shape your community. And to those of you who have helped with the building and shaping and preserving, we say thank you.

One
TOWSON

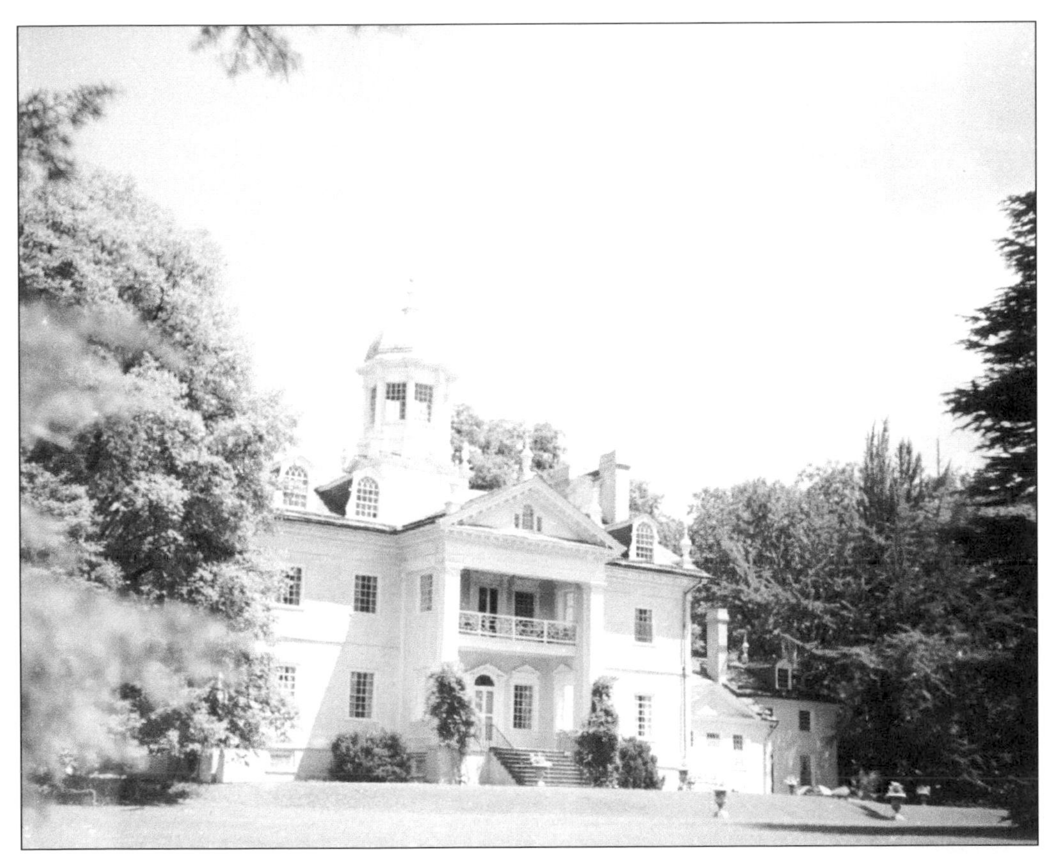

Historic Hampton was the home of the wealthy Ridgley family. The house was built between 1783 and 1790 and remained in the family until 1948. The Ridgley holdings reached 10,000 acres at one point. The estate is now operated by the National Park Service and is open to the public. (Courtesy Baltimore County Historical Society.)

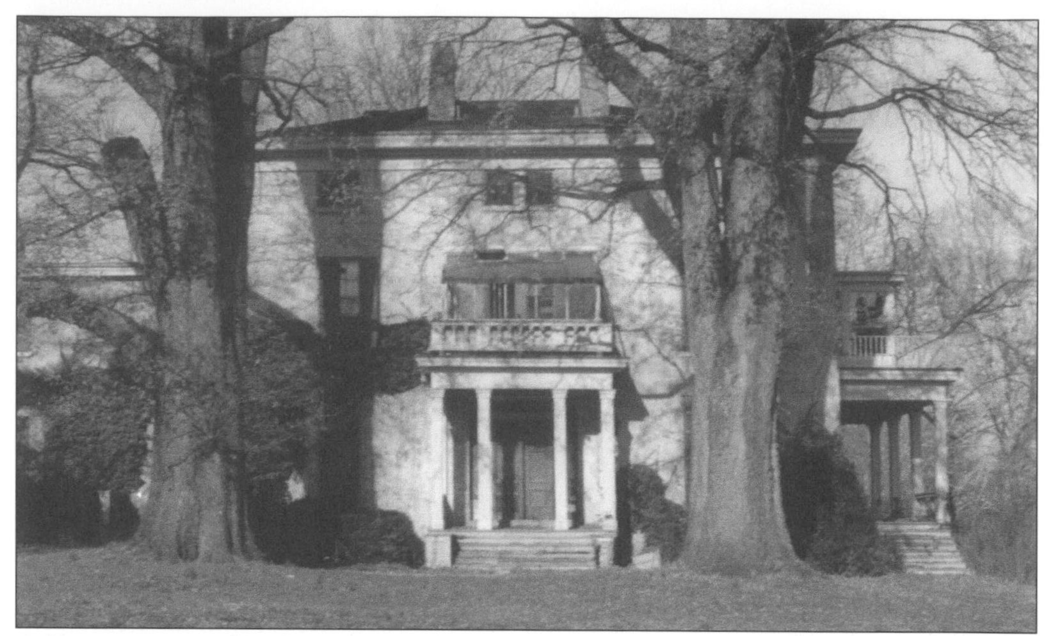

Auburn was originally the home of Rebecca Dorsey who, upon the death of her husband, Charles Ridgley, lost her beloved Hampton to her nephew Charles Carnan. (Carnan legally changed his surname to Ridgley to ensure the continuation of the family name.) In an attempt to appease his aunt, Carnan built Auburn, where Dorsey resided until 1812. The historic elms, the "Bride" and "Groom," flank the gracious entry. (Courtesy Baltimore County Historical Society.)

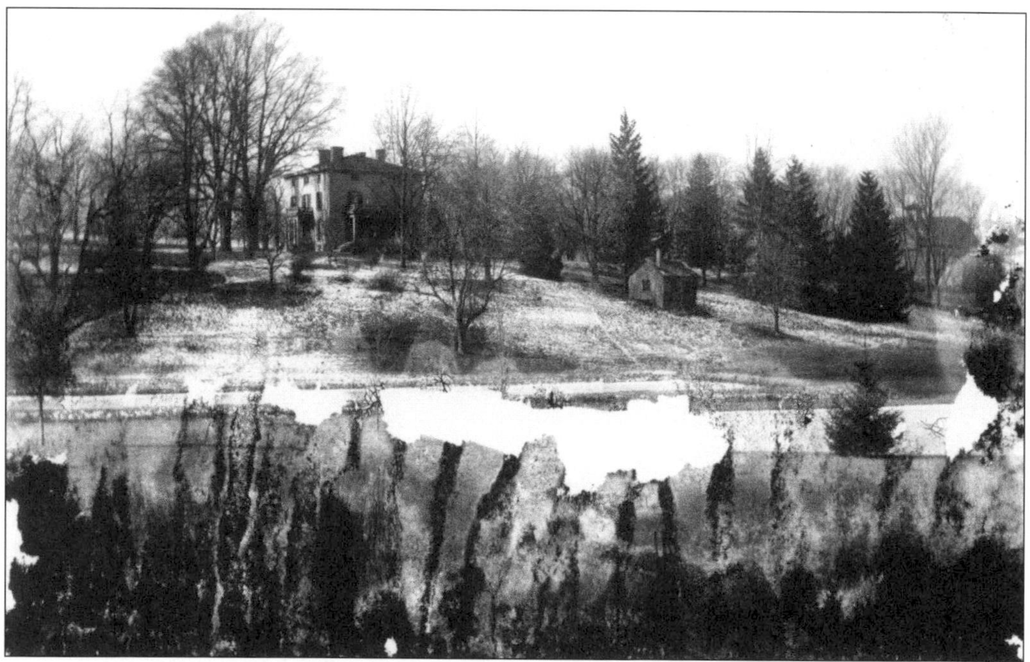

After a succession of illustrious owners, Auburn was saved from the brink of destruction when Towson University restored it and established Auburn as its Alumni House. (Courtesy Baltimore County Historical Society.)

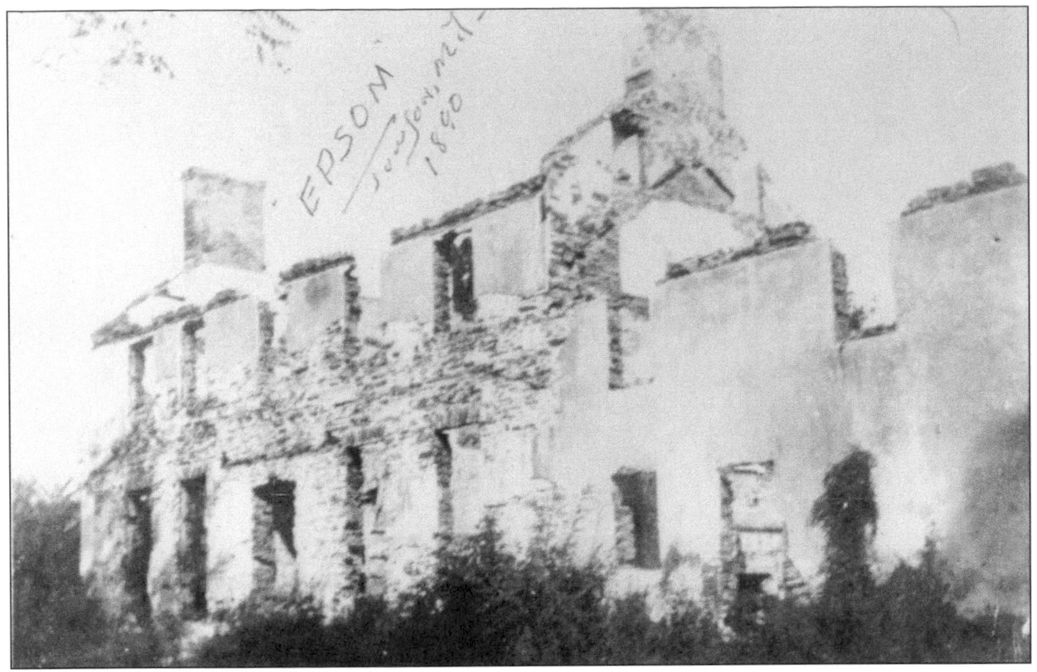

Epsom was built by Henry Chew in the 1850s on over 600 acres east of Dulaney Valley Road. He received the land from John Ridgley of Hampton upon his marriage to Harriet Ridgley. The house was destroyed by fire in 1886. Goucher College's Julia Rodgers Library was built on the footprint of this once beautiful house. (Courtesy Baltimore County Historical Society.)

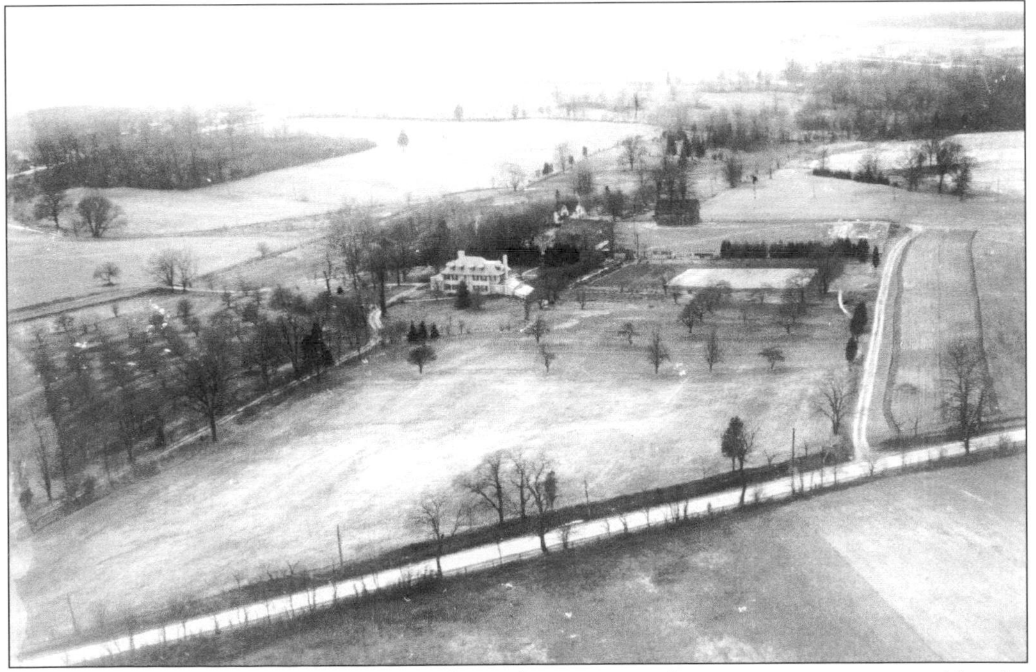

This aerial photograph, taken in 1937, shows the estate on the property now occupied by the Dulaney Towers. The road in the foreground is Dulaney Valley Road, and York Road can be seen in the upper left corner. (Courtesy Baltimore County Historical Society.)

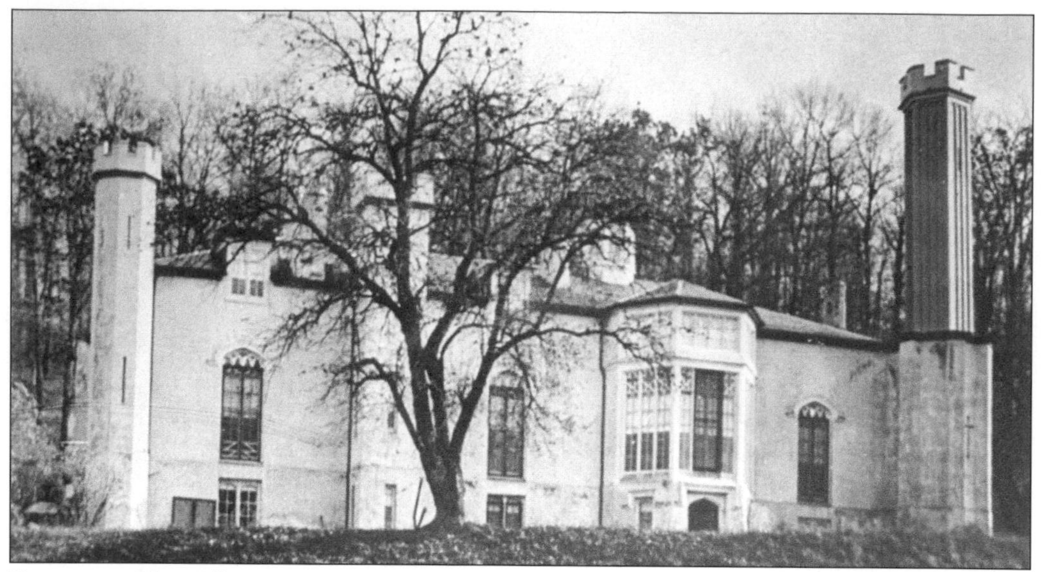

Known as Glen Ellen or the "Castle," Robert Gilmor, inspired by Sir Walter Scott's home during a trip to Scotland, built this fanciful house on the banks of Loch Raven in the 1830s. (Courtesy Baltimore County Historical Society.)

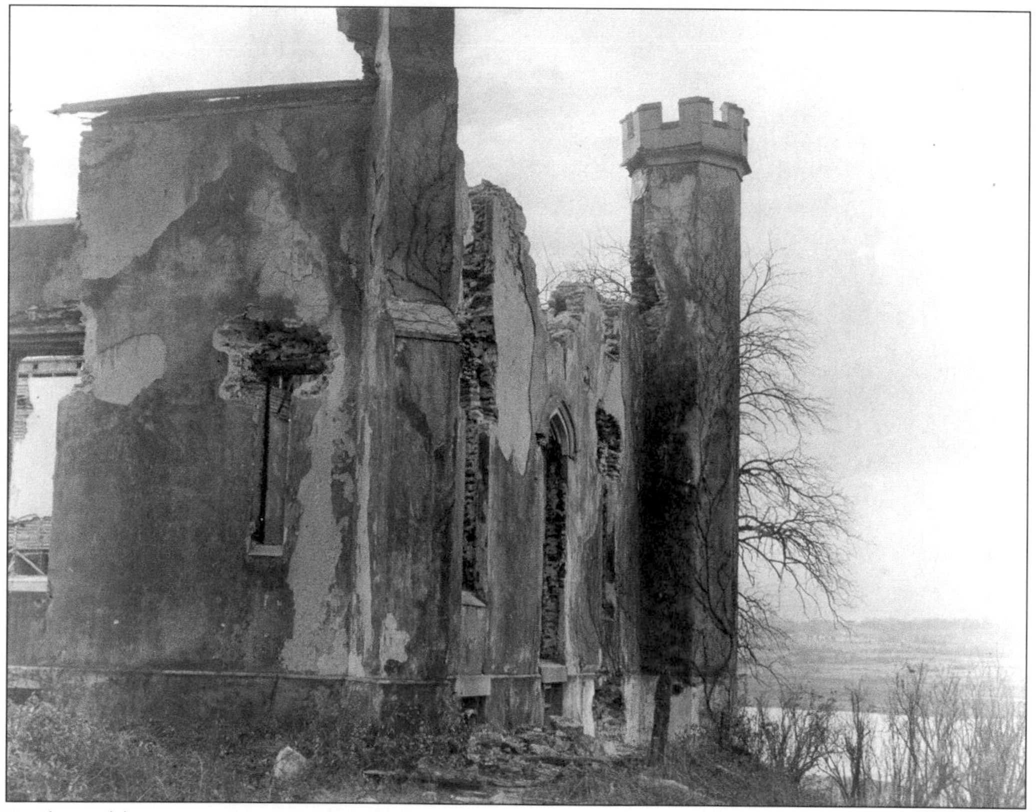

Looking like a set for a gothic horror movie, Glen Ellen's dramatic ruins loom over the encroaching waters of Loch Raven. The foundations can still be found by intrepid hikers. (Courtesy Baltimore County Historical Society.)

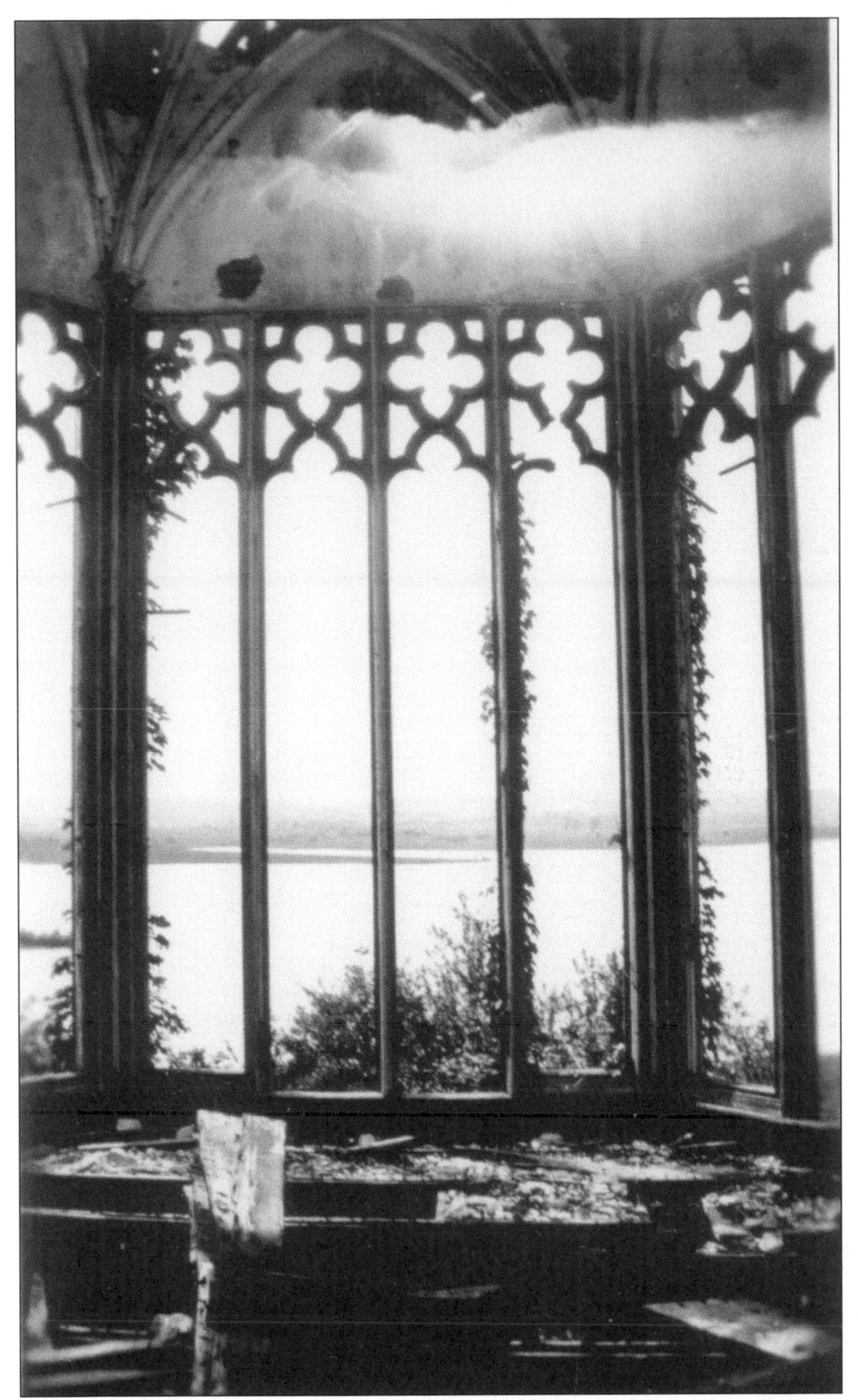

Sunlight pours through the once beautiful gothic windows at Glen Ellen. Baltimore City purchased the estate for the Loch Raven watershed in 1920. Sadly, the estate was allowed to deteriorate over the years, and it became a target for vandals. (Courtesy Baltimore County Historical Society.)

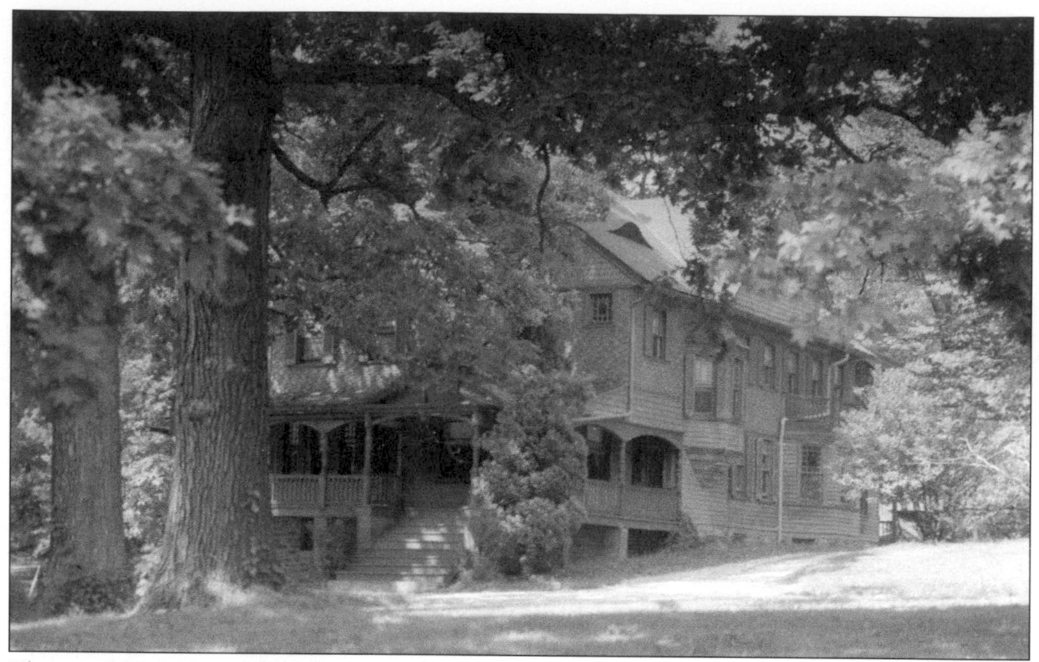

This rambling Victorian known as La Paix was built in 1885 as a summer retreat for the Turnbull family. The once elegant home had fallen into disrepair by the 1950s. In 1961, it was razed and replaced by a parking lot for St. Joseph's Hospital. (Courtesy Baltimore County Historical Society.)

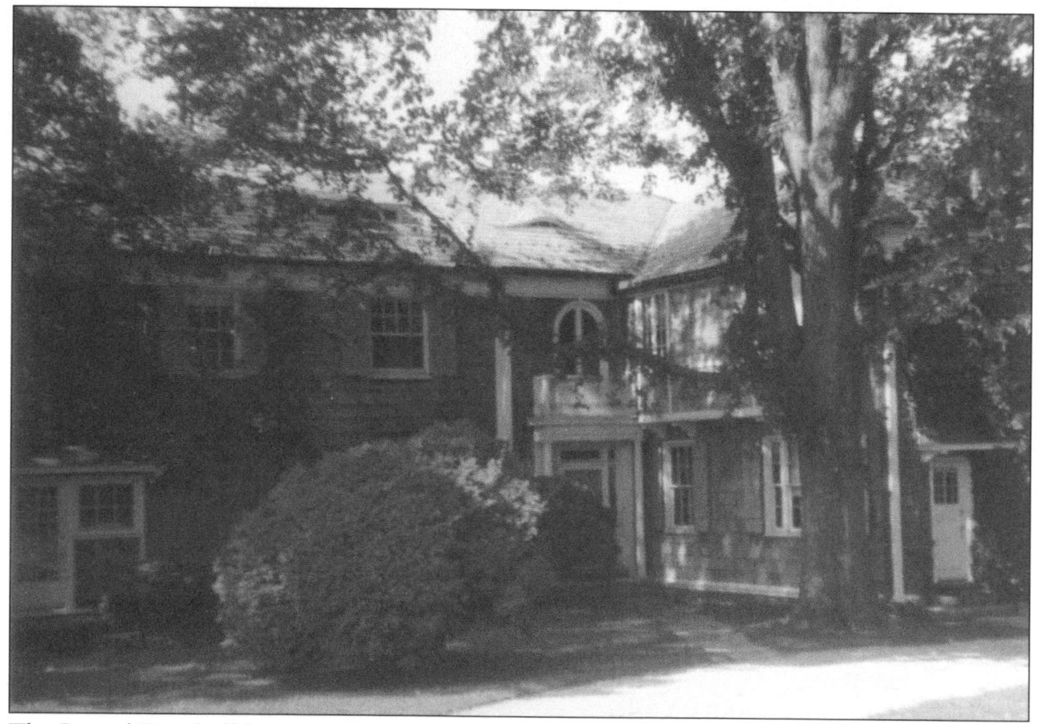

The Bayard Turnbull house, built near La Paix , was demolished recently, when the expense of restoring it discouraged buyers. (Courtesy John W. McGrain.)

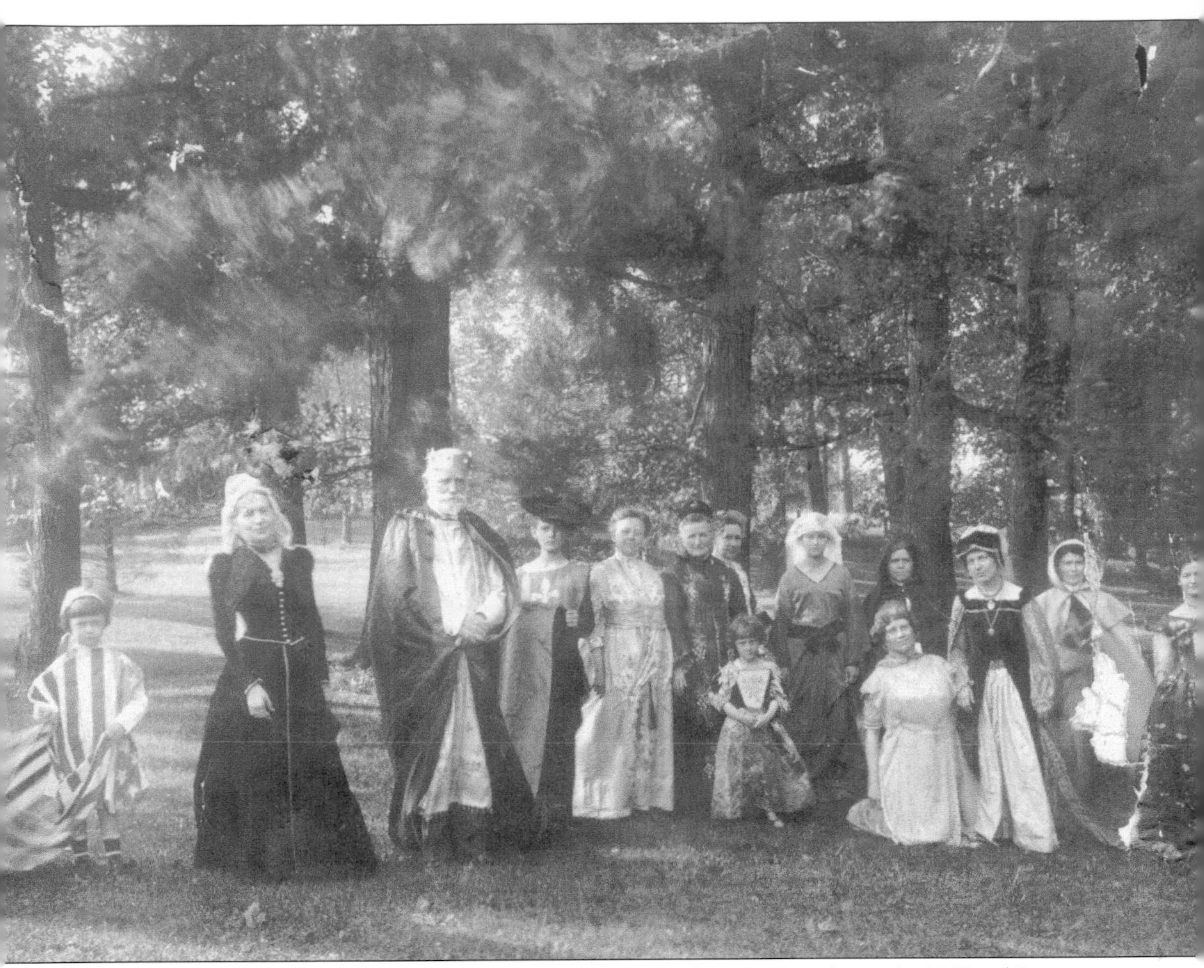

Revelers, in fancy dress, are seen here on the grounds of La Paix in the early 1900s. (Courtesy Anne T. Strott.)

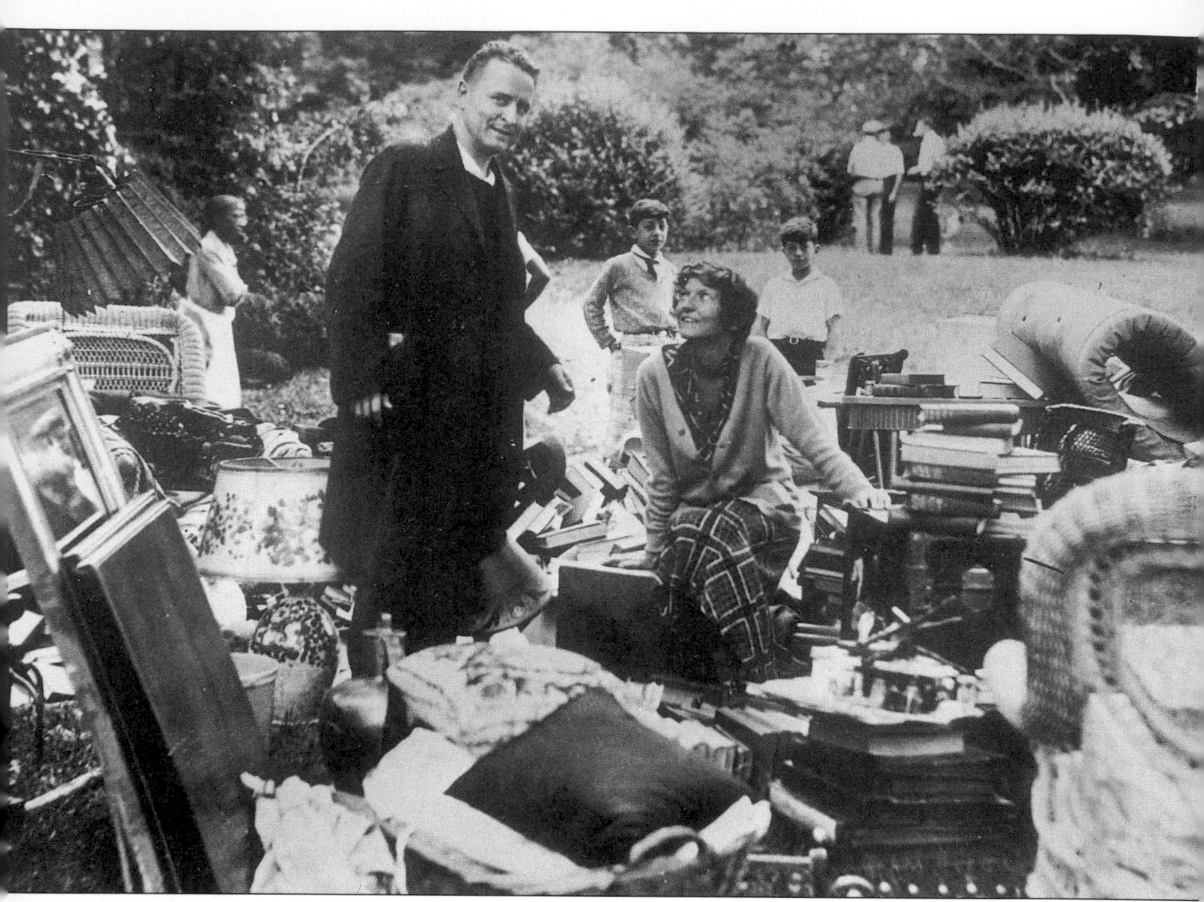

From 1932 to 1933, F. Scott Fitzgerald rented La Paix, while his beloved wife, Zelda, received psychiatric treatment at the nearby Sheppard Pratt Hospital. It was here that the scion of the Jazz Age was able to complete *Tender is the Night*, in spite of the difficult times in his marriage. This photograph captures both Fitzgeralds in a stressful moment, surrounded by possessions rescued from a fire at La Paix, possibly set by Zelda. (Courtesy Baltimore County Public Library.)

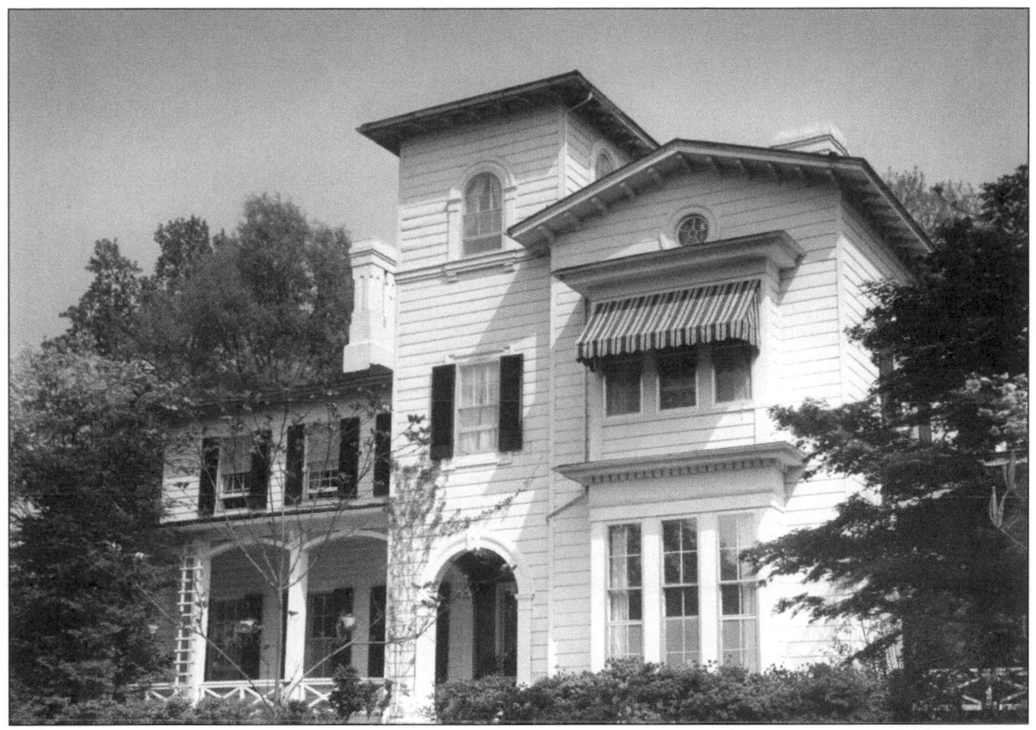

Anneslie was built as a summer home in 1855 by Frederick Harrison. The Italian-Revival mansion remained in the family for 120 years. Most of the estate had been sold in 1921, creating one of the area's first planned communities, which was named for the land upon which it was built. (Courtesy Baltimore County Historical Society.)

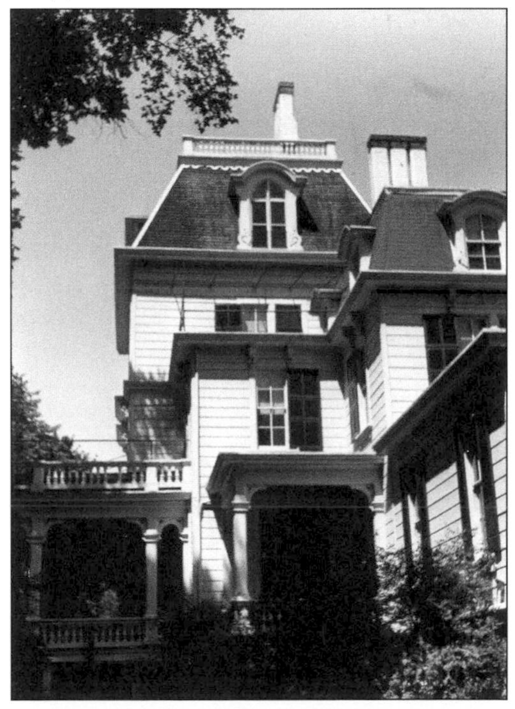

Aigburth Vale was regarded as one of the most beautiful estates in Baltimore County during the mid-19th century. John E. Owens, the wealthy and world-renowned comic actor, purchased property south of Towson and transformed the farm, at great expense, into a beautiful, if not profitable, farm. After Owens's death in 1886, the house was used as a summer boarding home, an adult hospital, and finally, in 1950, the house was occupied by the Baltimore County School Board. (Courtesy Baltimore County Historical Society.)

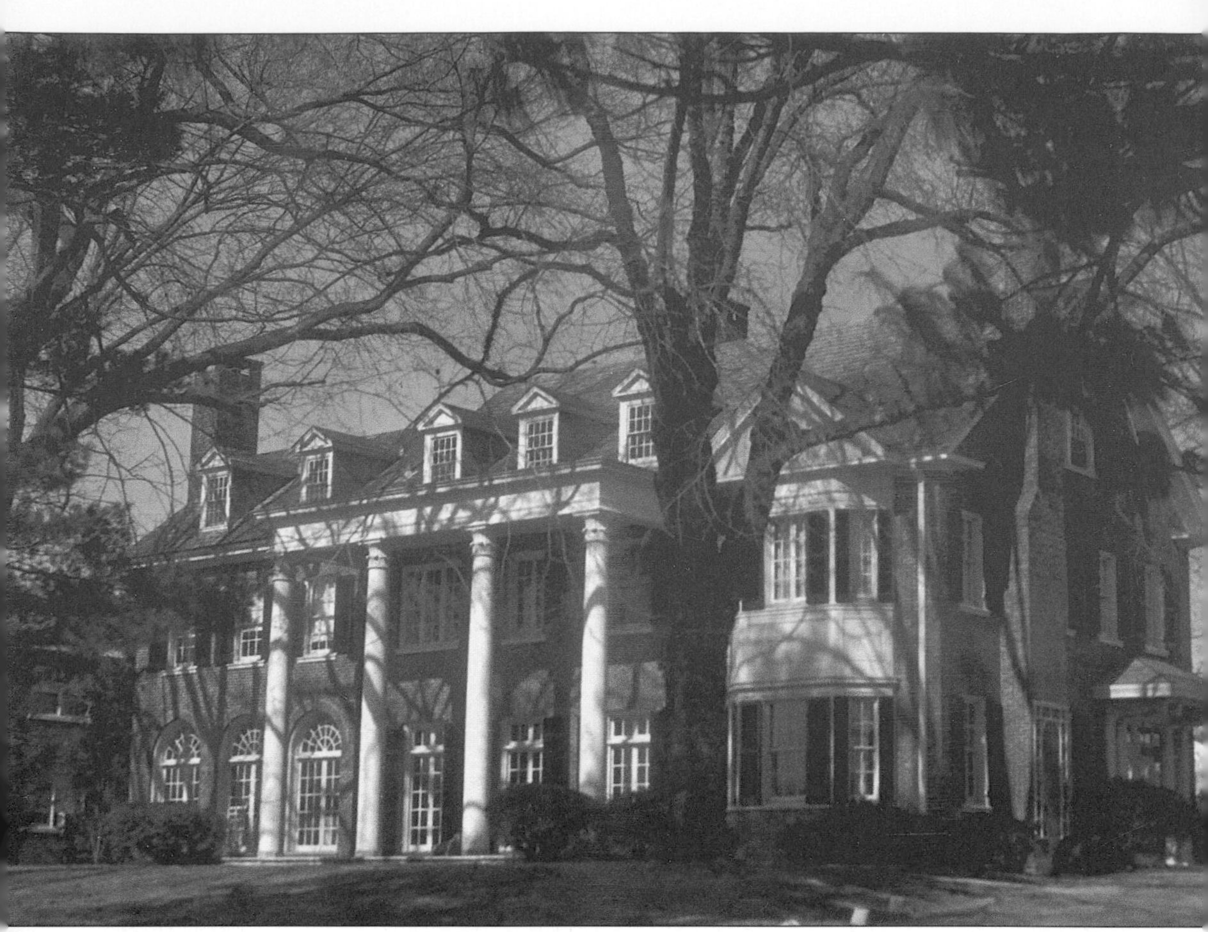

Originally called Briarfield, this house's name was changed to Blakefield in honor of the Blake family, who donated the property used for Loyola-Blakefield's campus. (Courtesy John W. McGrain.)

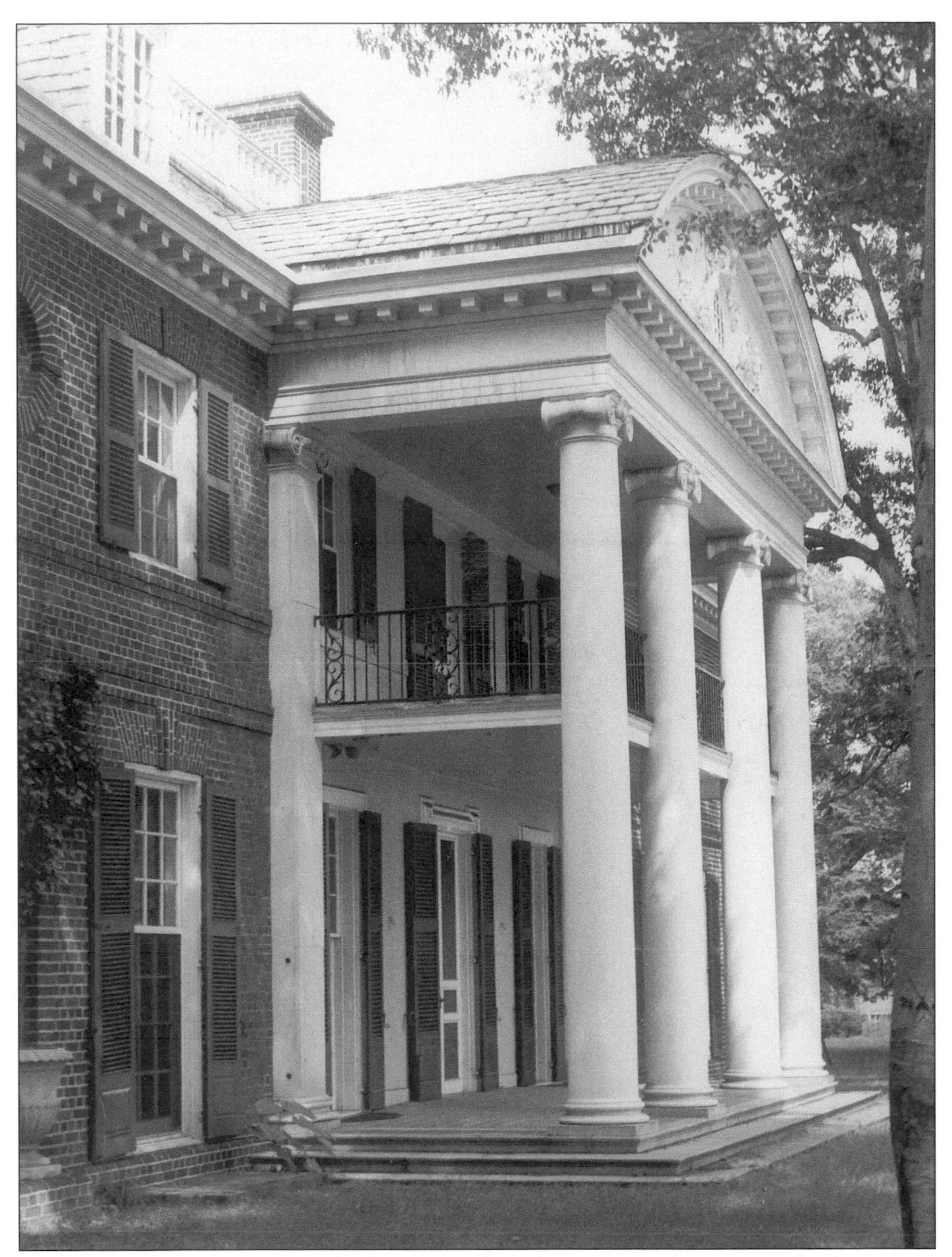

The Greenwood mansion was built in 1915 by John E. DeFord. In 1927, the house was transformed into the Greenwood School. Young ladies who attended enjoyed a variety of activities, including horse shows and hunts, as the school owned hounds. On Saturdays, the seniors were permitted to go into Towson, while the juniors had to content themselves with the attractions of Ruxton. In 1966, the school and grounds were purchased by Baltimore County and became the headquarters for the board of education. (Courtesy John W. McGrain.)

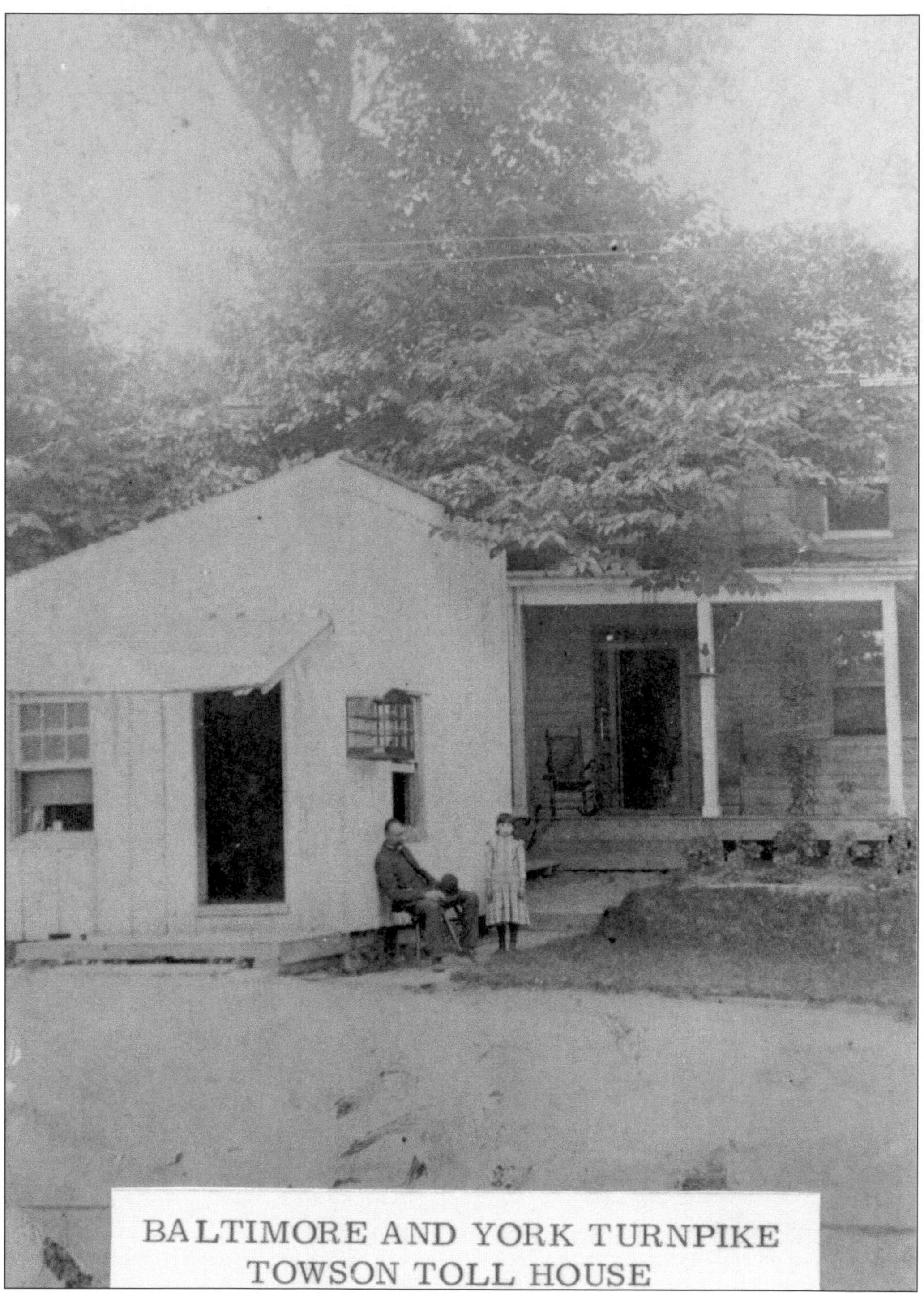

The toll collector and a young girl pose outside of the Towson Tollhouse in 1889. Crucial to commerce between farmlands and the port of Baltimore, York Road was owned by the Baltimore and Yorktown Turnpike Company, which collected tolls and maintained the road until 1908. (Courtesy Baltimore County Historical Society.)

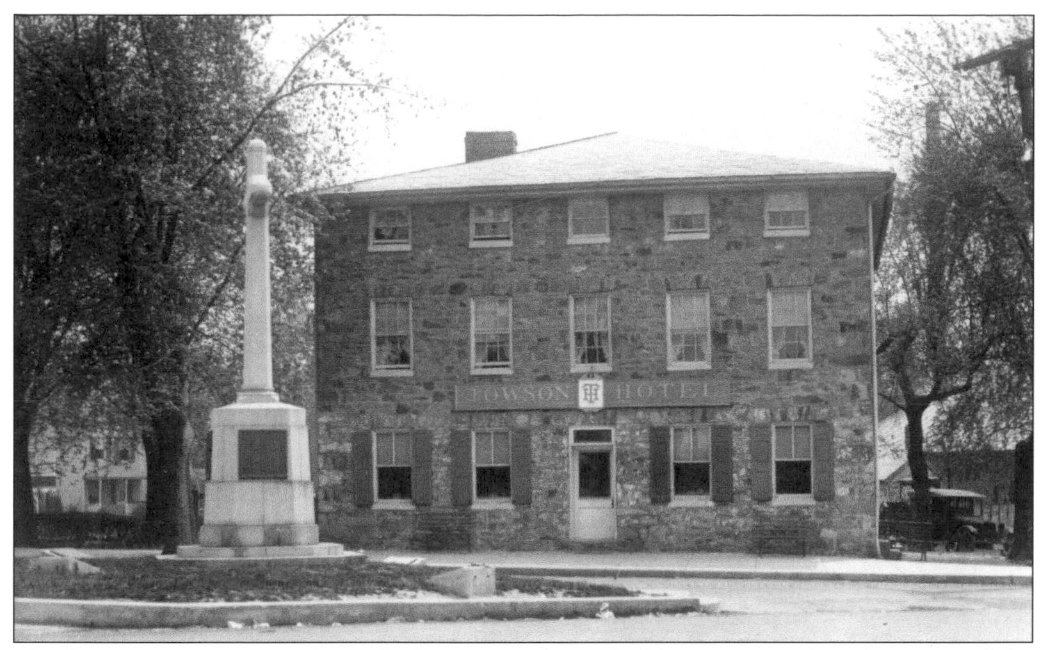

The historic Towson Hotel was built in 1768 by Ezekial Towson to take advantage of the steadily increasing traffic on the York and Joppa Roads. The tavern's 160 years of success were ensured when Towson "bribed" the state with land donations to keep the York Turnpike at the inn's doorstep. Edward Ady was the inn's proprietor during the second half of the 1800s. Mr. Ady provided comfort for farmers on their way south to the Baltimore markets and a meadow for their livestock. It could be said that many a head of cattle enjoyed its last meal at the Towson Tavern. The Towson Inn played a crucial role in Towson's social scene until 1929, when it was demolished. (Courtesy Baltimore County Historical Society.)

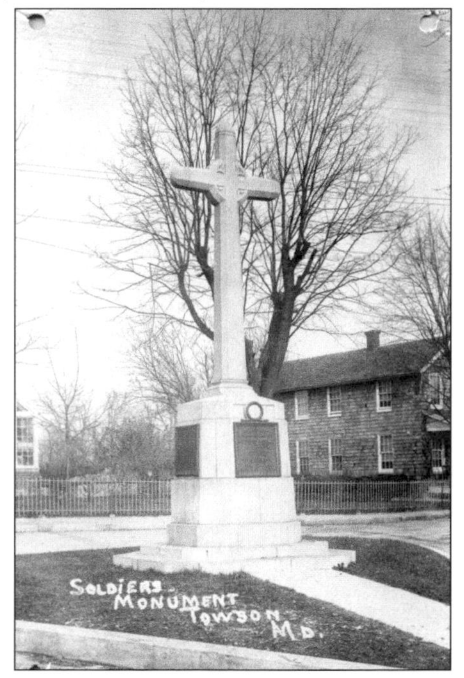

The Wayside Cross stands at the intersection of York Road and Shealy Avenue. It commemorates the lives lost in the Great War. (Courtesy Baltimore County Historical Society.)

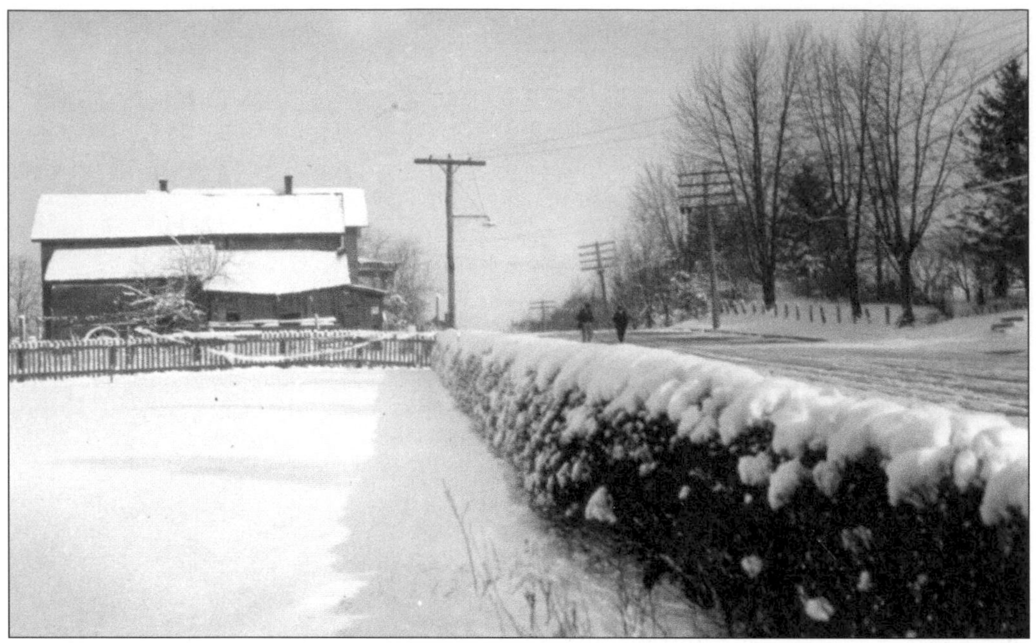

Two men trudge south on a snowy York Road in 1917. They have just passed the Pennington Forge, which stood on land just north of today's traffic oval. (Courtesy Baltimore County Historical Society.)

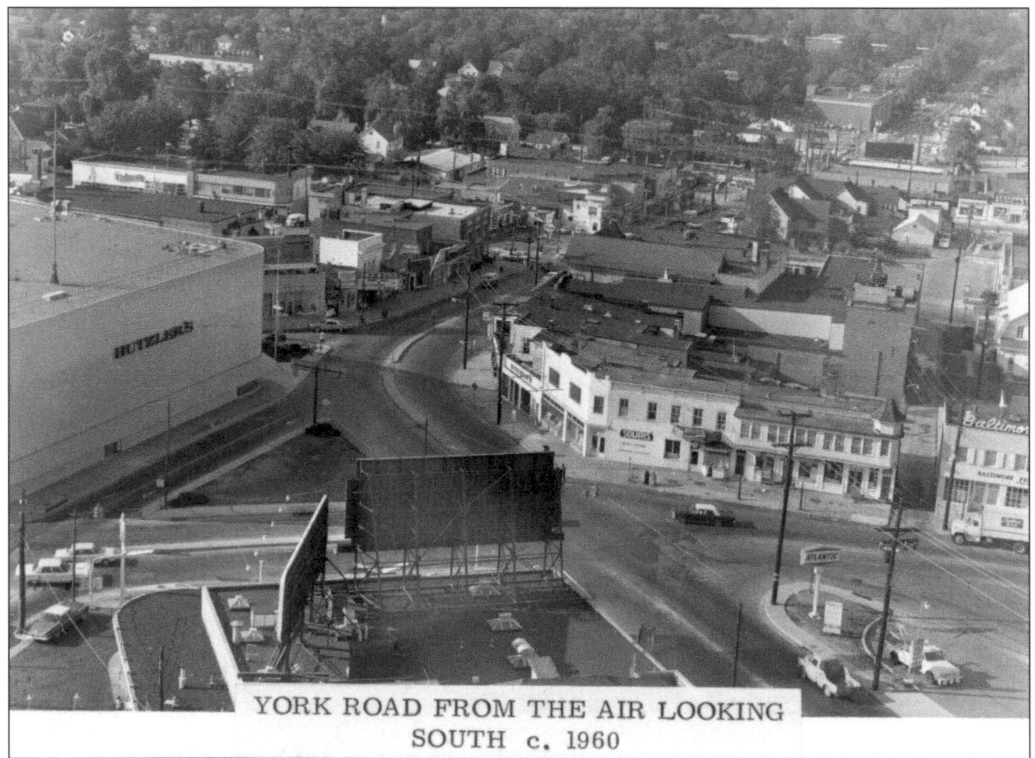

This aerial photo shows some of Towson's business district, including the famous Hutzler's department store. (Courtesy Baltimore County Historical Society.)

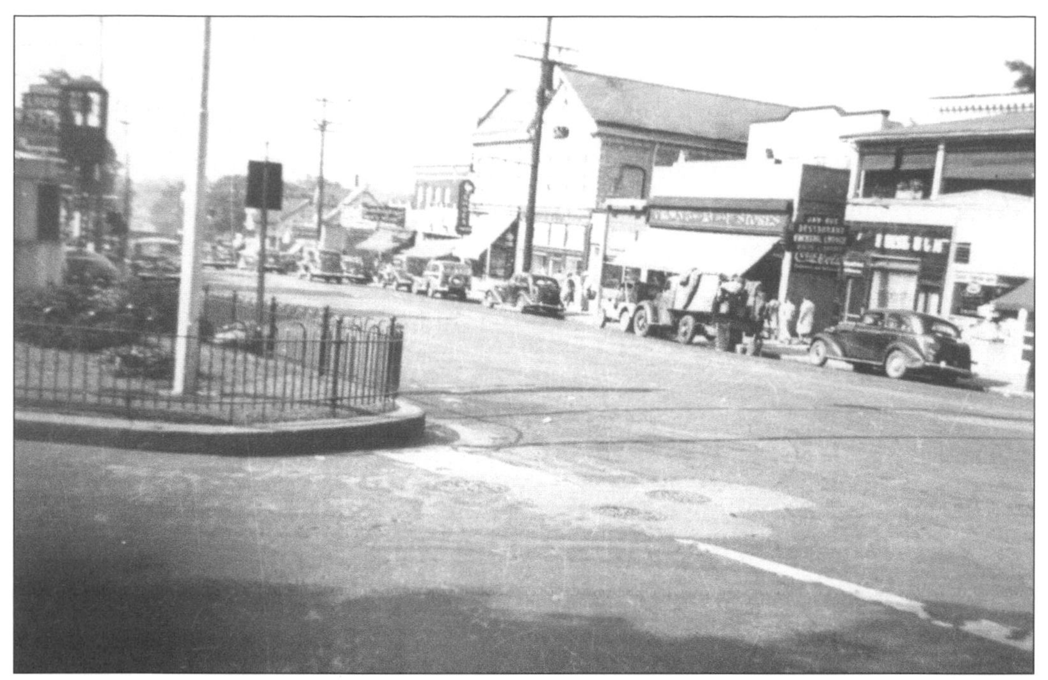

York Road is pictured here in the 1940s, looking south from the Bosley Hotel, which was on the same corner as the present-day Barnes & Noble Bookstore (the former Hutzler's department store). (Courtesy Baltimore County Historical Society.)

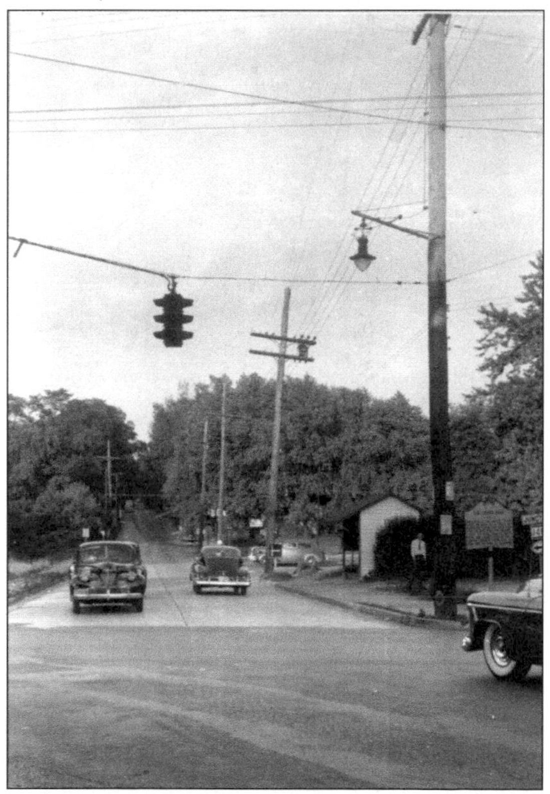

Joppa Road is seen here in the 1940s, looking east from Dulaney Valley Road. (Courtesy Baltimore County Historical Society.)

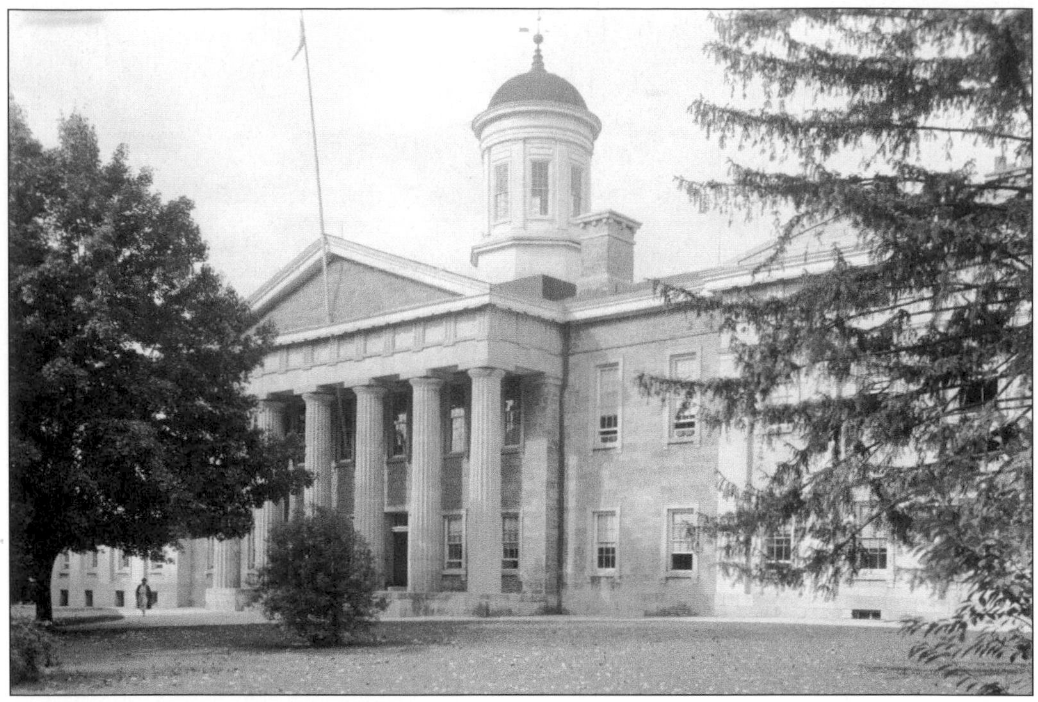

The Towson Court House was built with stone donated by the Ridgleys and on land donated by Grafton M. Bosley, who also donated land for the jail. On February 13, 1854, Towson became the county seat of Baltimore County. (Courtesy Baltimore County Historical Society.)

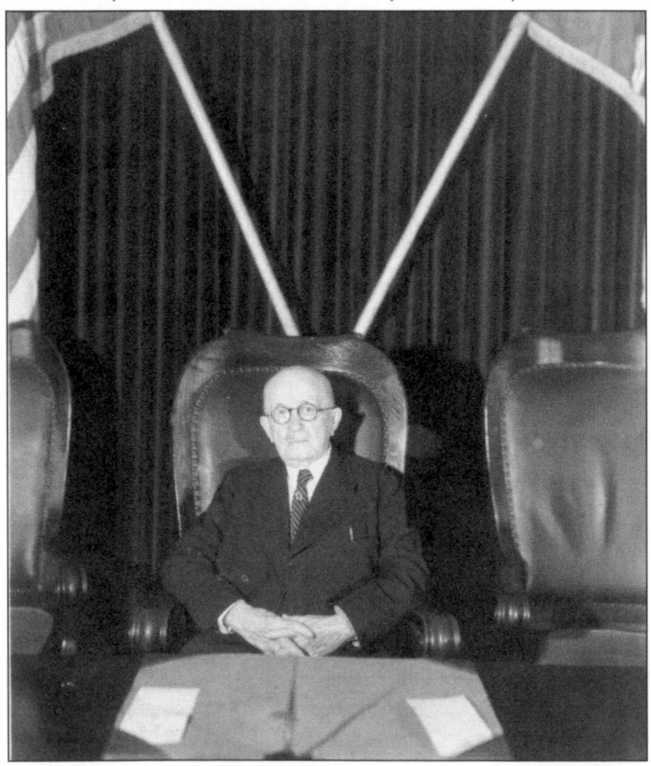

The Honorable Frank Duncan was a judge in the Baltimore County courts, c. 1920. (Courtesy Baltimore County Historical Society.)

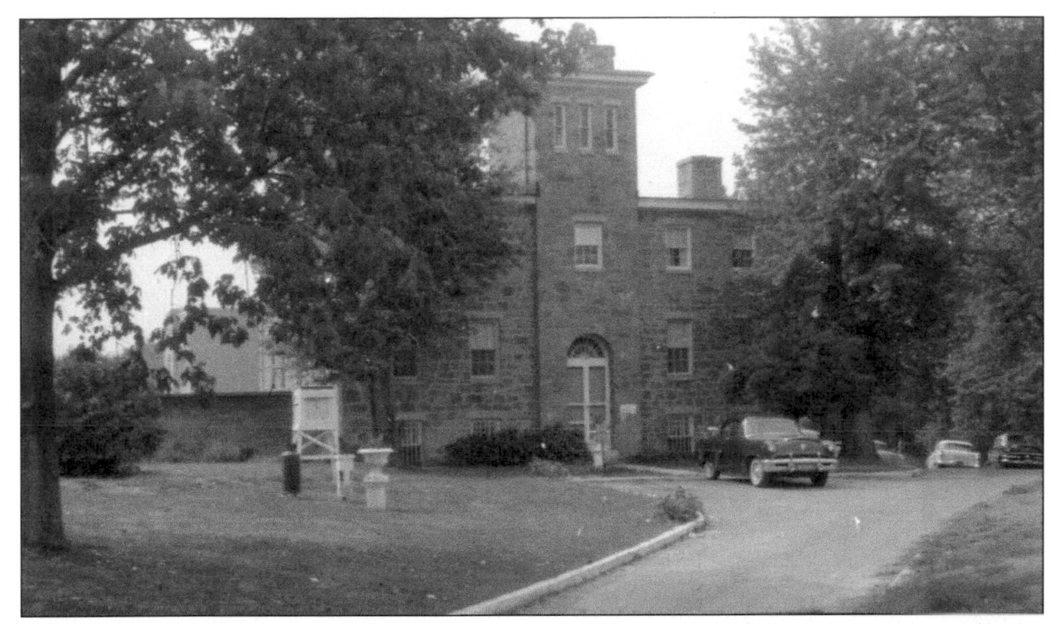

Built in 1854, the Towson Jail's peaceful appearance in 1957 belies the serious role the institution played in Baltimore County's justice system. Public hangings were popular events in Towson, and if it were a particularly noteworthy criminal, spectators would spend the night in the Courthouse Square! In 1885, an angry mob lost confidence in proper judicial proceedings and broke into the jail to forcefully remove Howard Cooper. In spite of the efforts of the jailer's daughter to prevent it, the unfortunate prisoner was lynched on a tree nearby. (Courtesy Baltimore County Historical Society.)

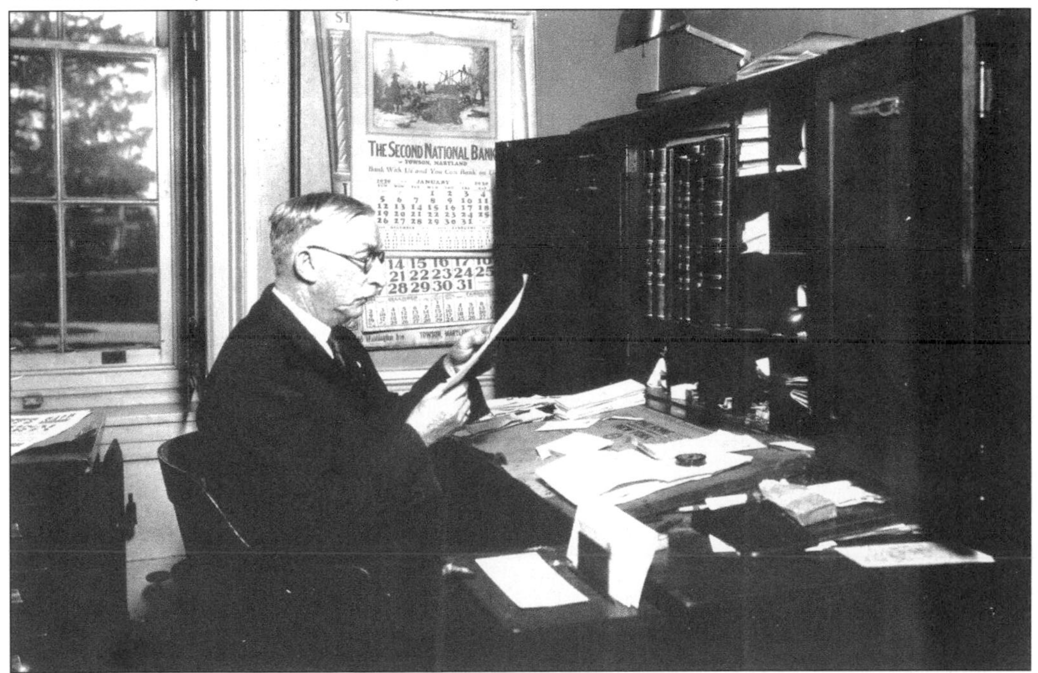

Chief Deputy Sheriff George Morely is pictured here in 1931. (Courtesy Baltimore County Historical Society.)

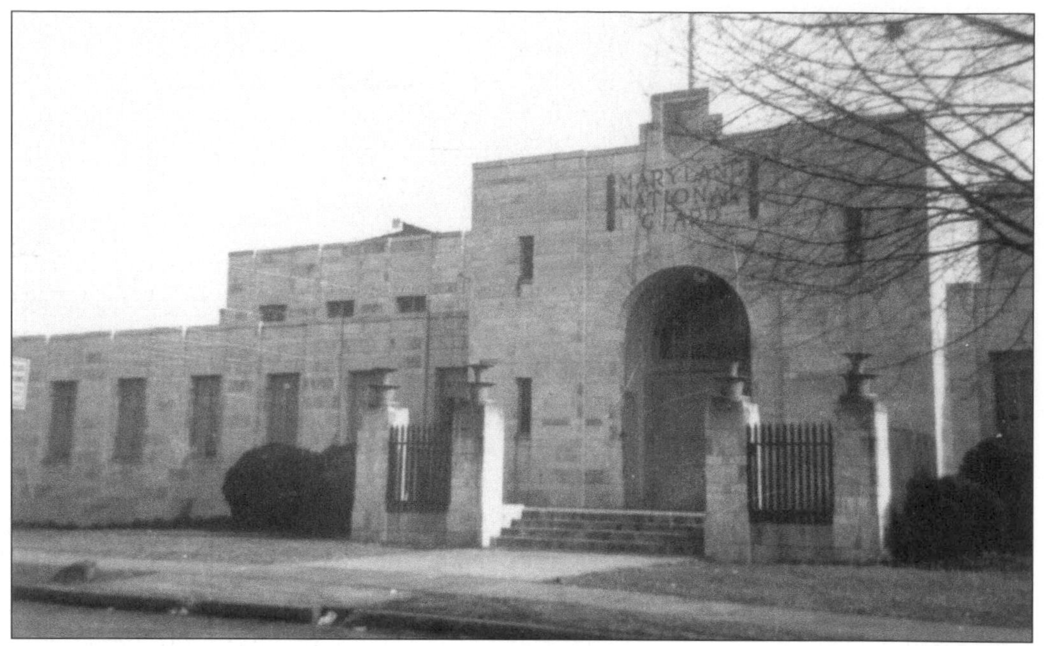

The Maryland National Guard's armory was built at the corner of Washington and Chesapeake Avenues in 1933. (Courtesy Baltimore County Historical Society.)

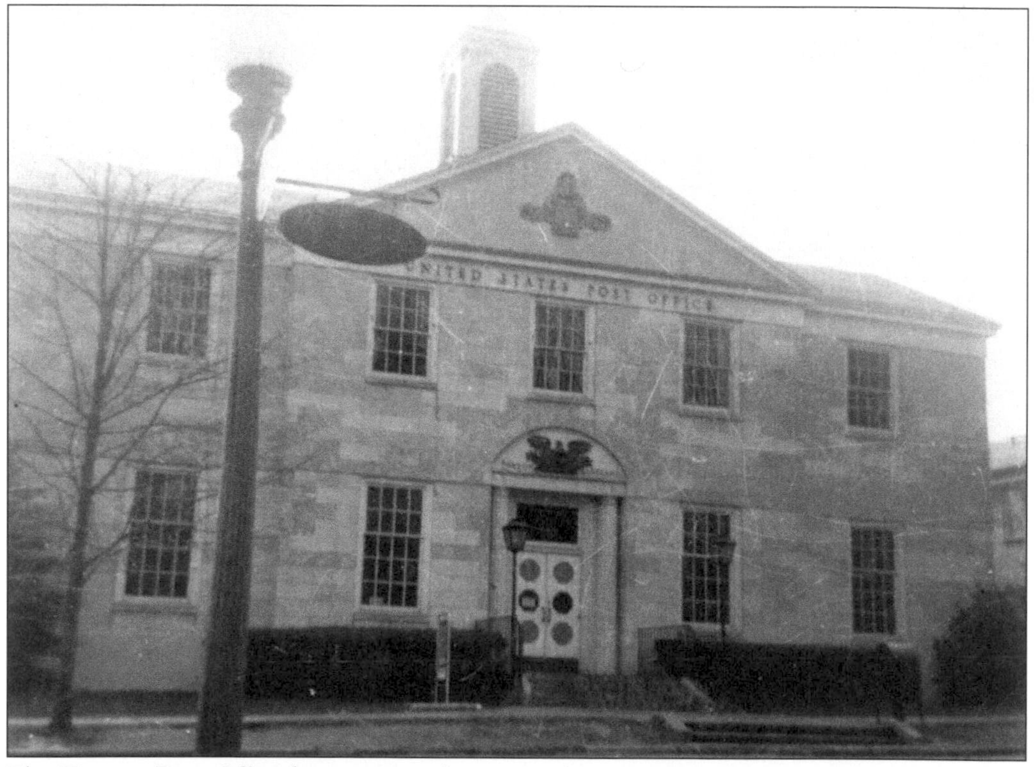

The Towson Post Office has continued to serve the community since it was built in 1938; however, the price of stamps has increased a bit since then. (Courtesy Baltimore County Historical Society.)

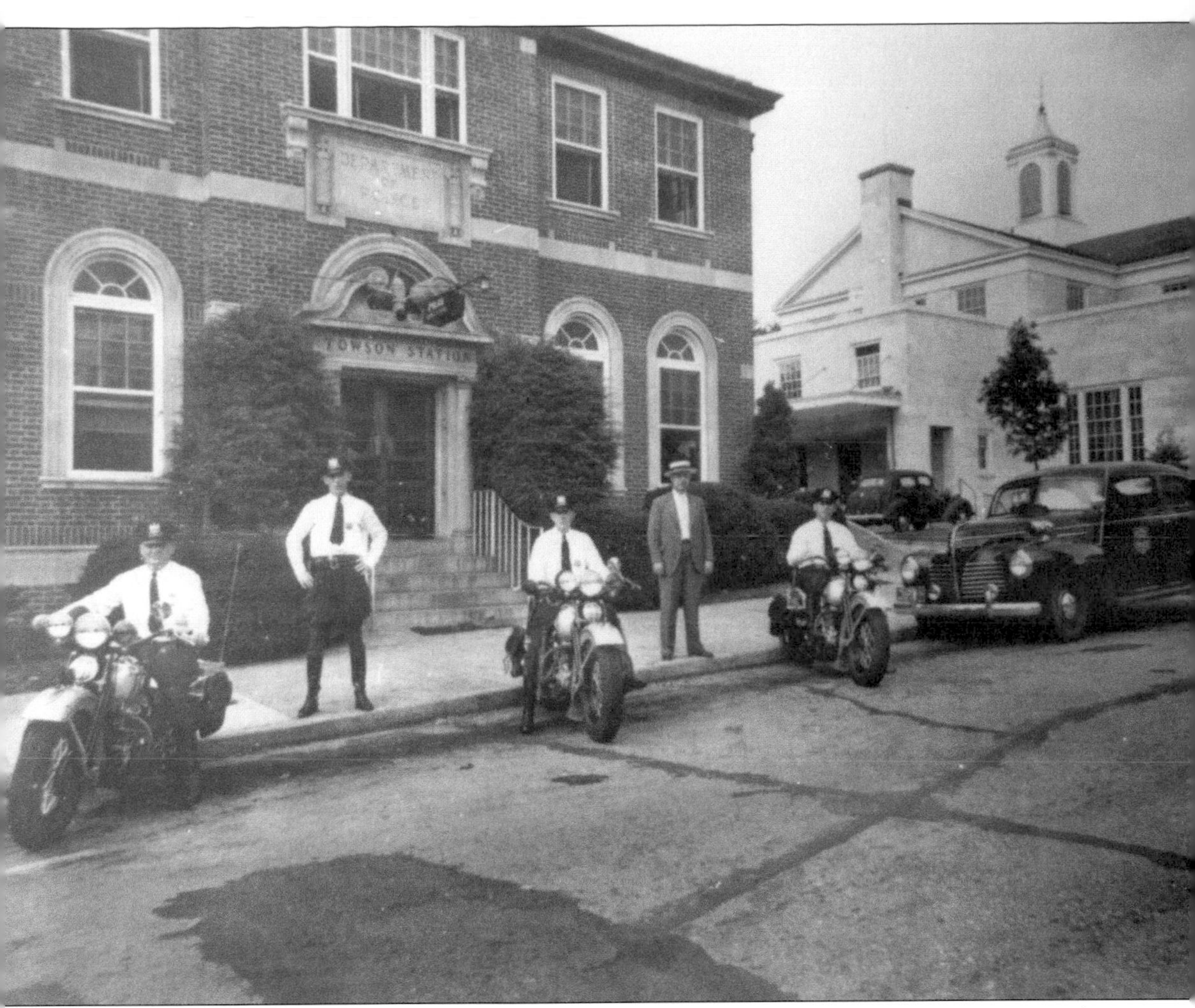

Towson established a police force in 1874. The patrolmen earned $2 per day, while mounted officers earned $3. The Towson police precinct on Washington Avenue was built in 1926. Here, Towson's "Men In Blue" pose with their motorcycles, a far cry from the mounted officers who were required to provide their own horses! (Courtesy Baltimore County Historical Society.)

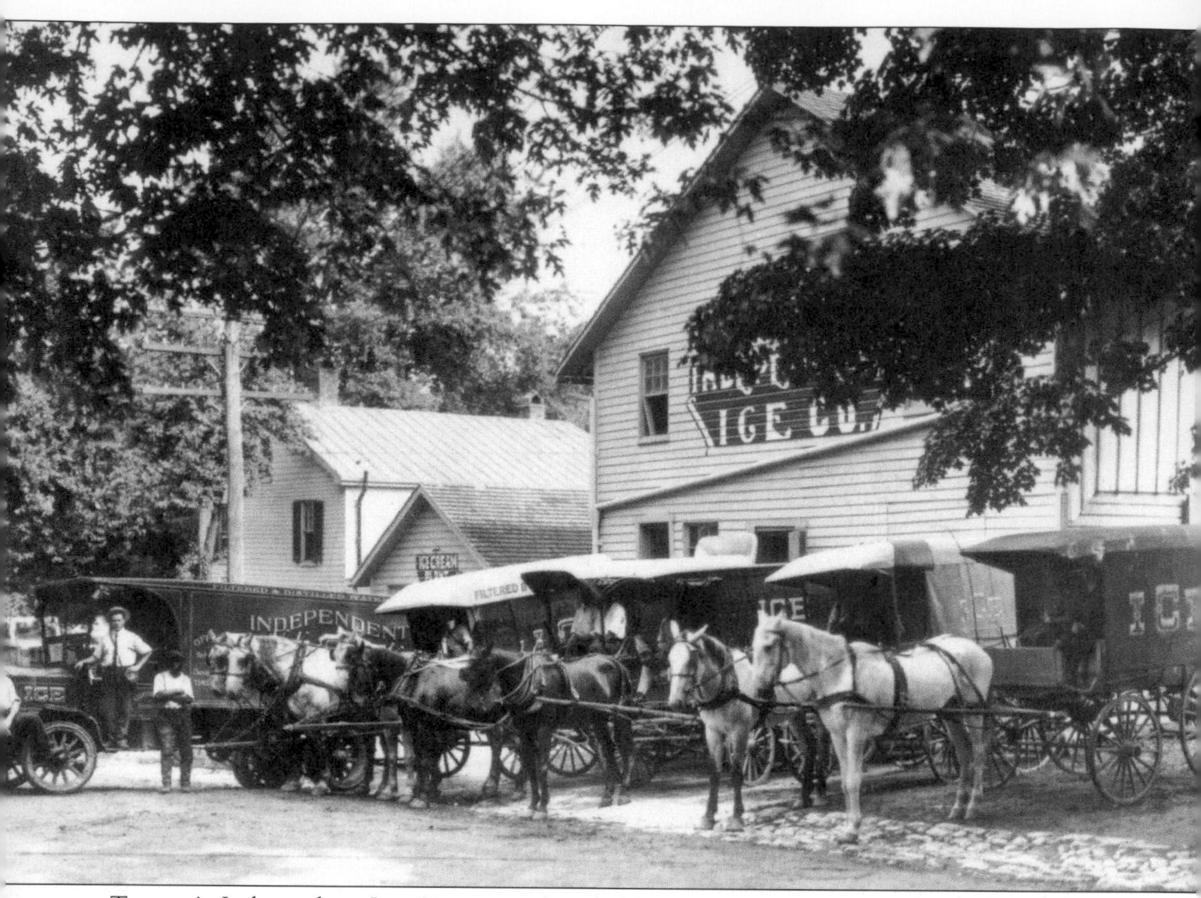

Towson's Independent Ice Company, founded by S.C. Seitz in 1909, was located on West Chesapeake Avenue. Formerly, ice had been shipped from Maine, but in 1920, the company began manufacturing the ice using giant compressors in their Towson plant. The ice was then delivered door to door in Towson, as well as in Ruxton, with the company's fleet of horse-drawn wagons. In 1929, a delivery truck was added, which would spare the horses from the dangerous hills in Ruxton. (Courtesy Carleton Seitz.)

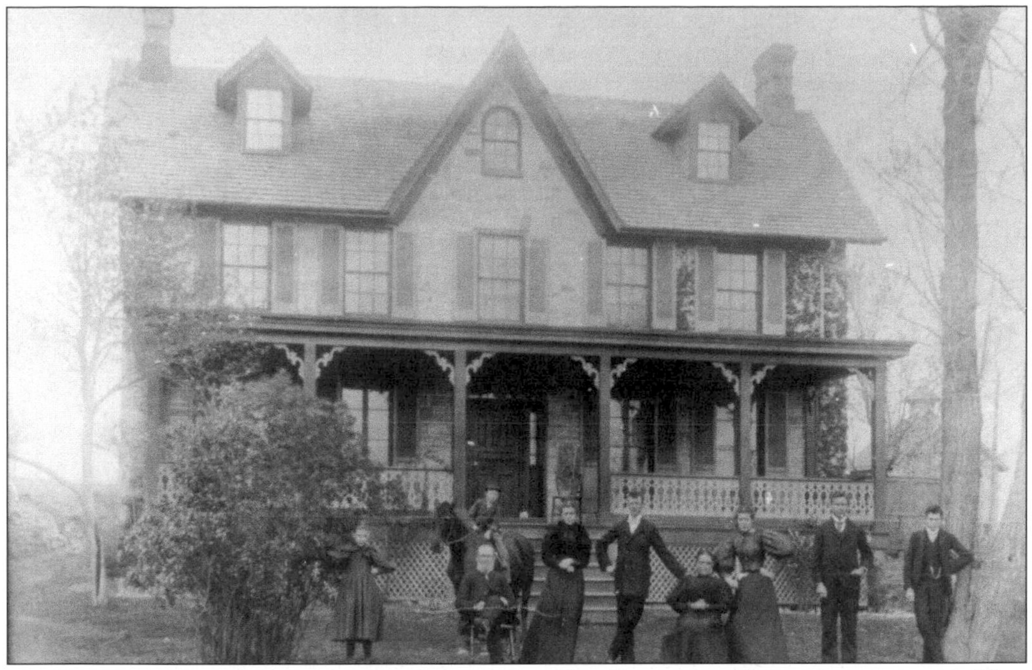

The Lees, a prominent Towson family, posed on the front steps of their home at 100 West Pennsylvania Avenue. The site is now occupied by the Campbell Building. (Courtesy Baltimore County Historical Society.)

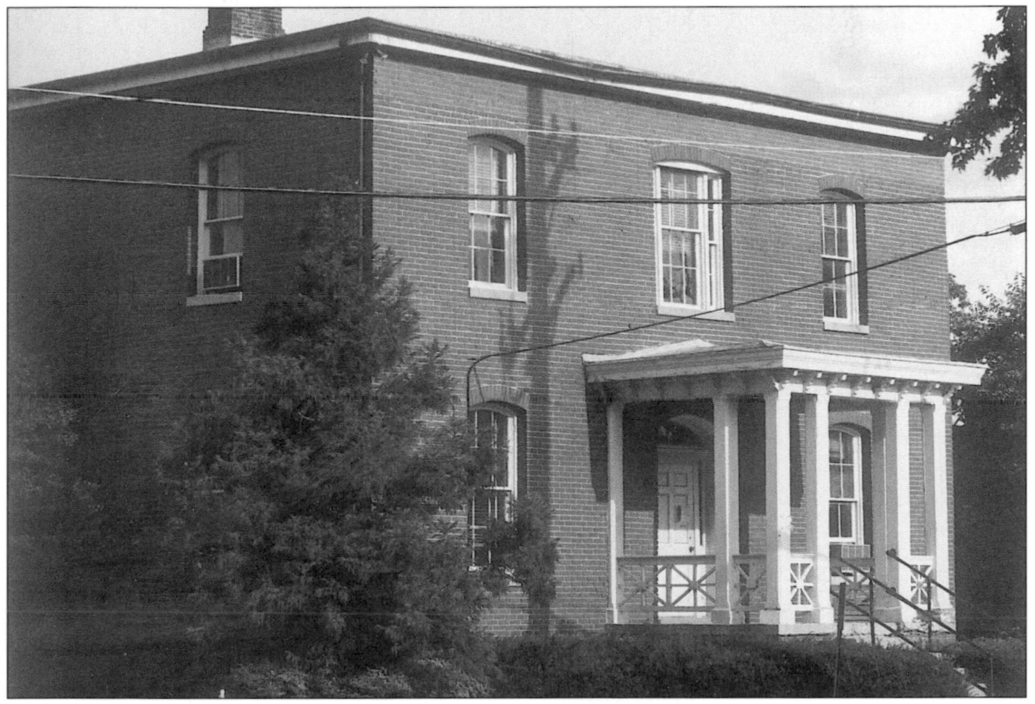

Another prominent Towson family, the Slingluffs, built this brick federal home at 209 Washington Avenue. The house was razed in the 1980s. (Courtesy Baltimore County Historical Society.)

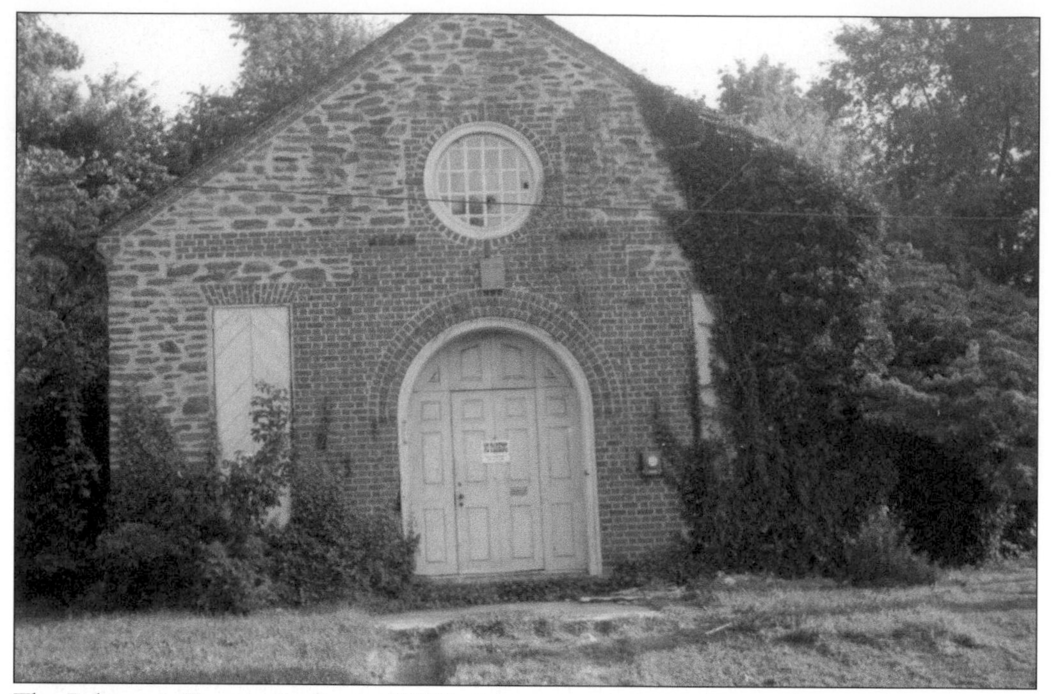

The Baltimore Transit Company (BTC) Substation on Susquehanna Avenue features lovely architectural details that belie the structure's relatively recent construction in 1947. The building is a wonderful example of the merits of adaptive use. It was preserved and is currently used by Wilson Lighting. (Courtesy Baltimore County Historical Society.)

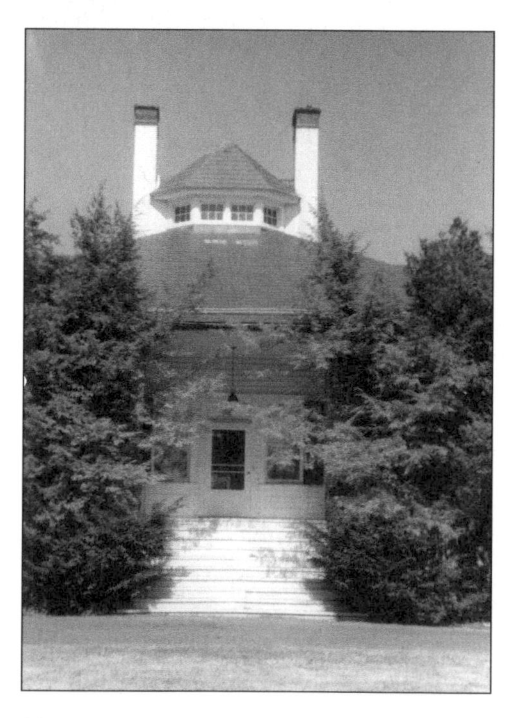

The office building at 7400 York Road, just north of Stevenson Lane, replaced this unusual home. (Courtesy Baltimore County Historical Society.)

The Beeches belonged to the Passano family in 1911. Located on Susquehanna Avenue adjacent to the Ma & Pa tracks, the building later became the Towson YMCA. The house was eventually torn down. (Courtesy John W. McGrain.)

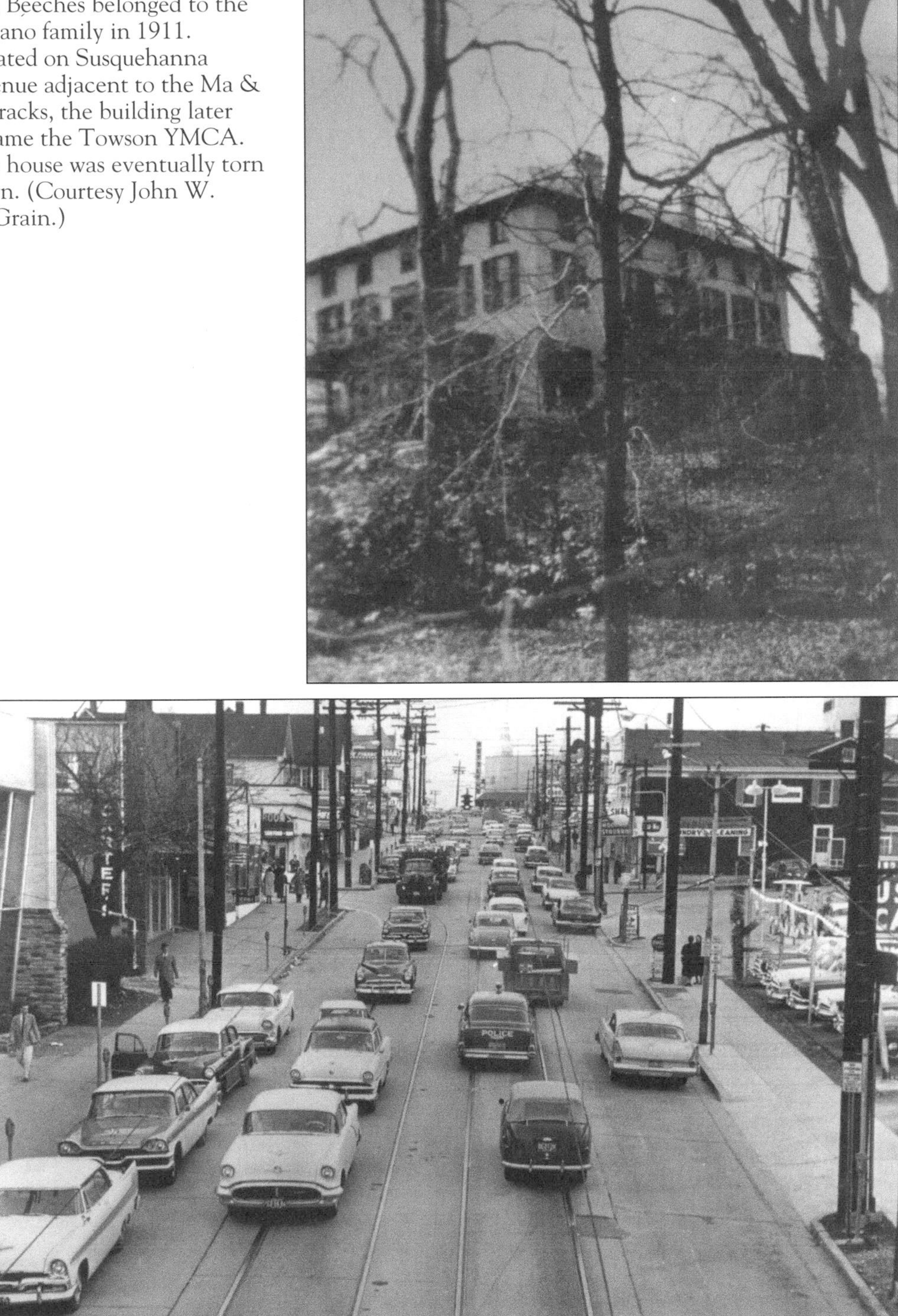

By the 1950s, York Road had become a bustling commercial district. There are streetcar tracks visible in the road, and Hutzler's, a recent addition to the community, can be seen in the distance. (Courtesy Baltimore County Historical Society.)

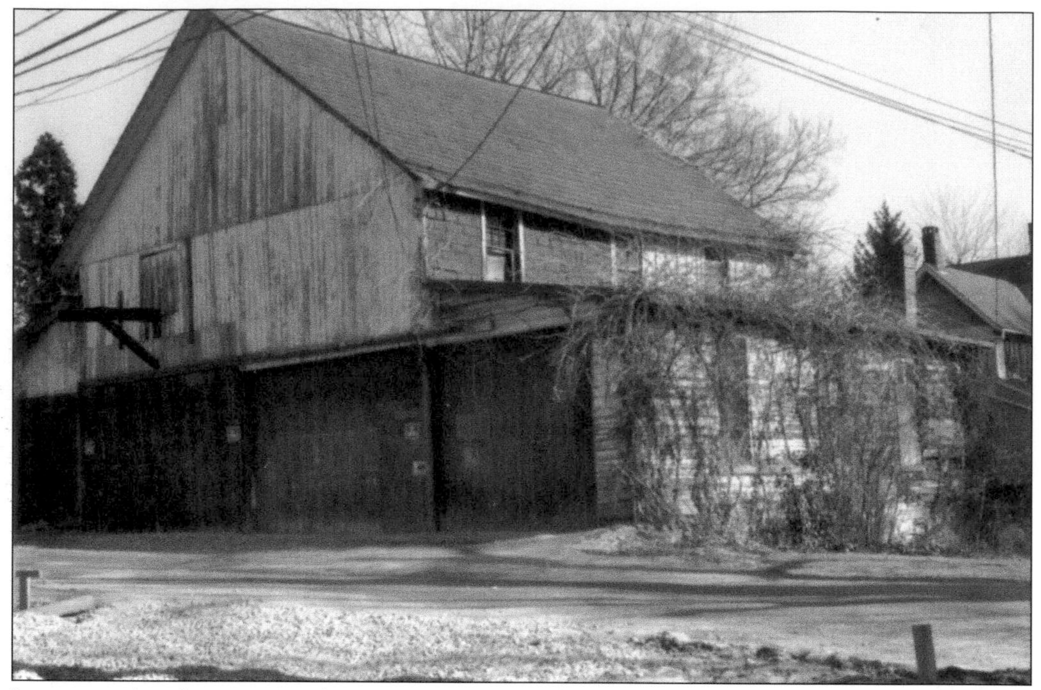

In an era when horses were the primary mode of transportation, livery stables were the parking garages of the day. This stable was located in the rear of 602 Baltimore Avenue, which is now occupied by an office tower. (Courtesy John W. McGrain.)

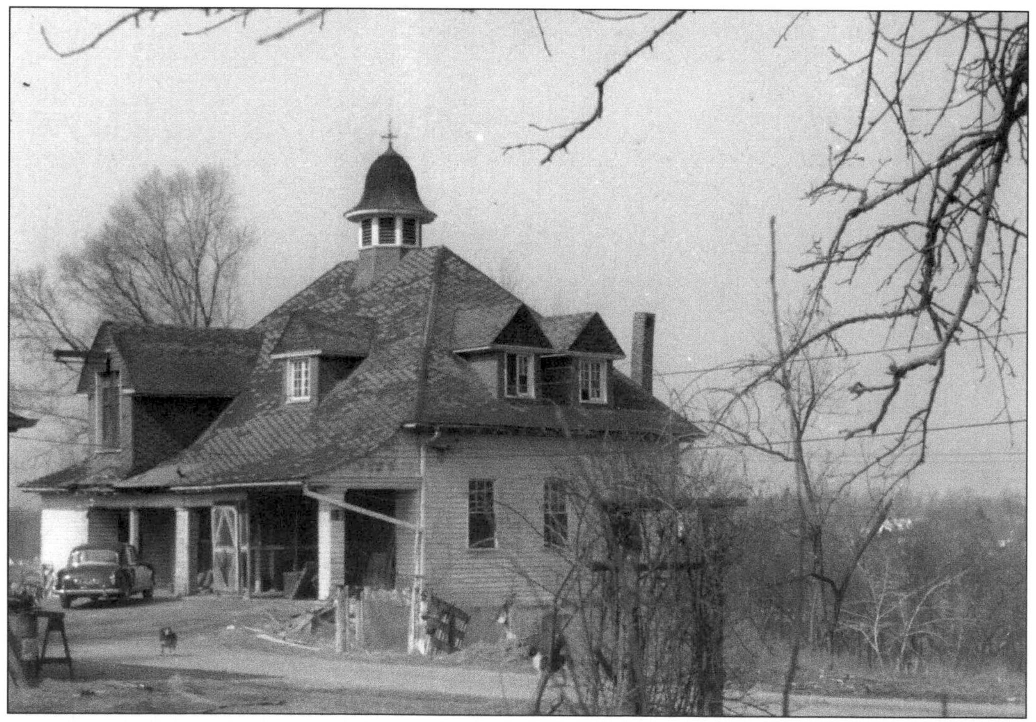

The Fiore's barn stood on York Road south of Towson University. (Courtesy John W. McGrain.)

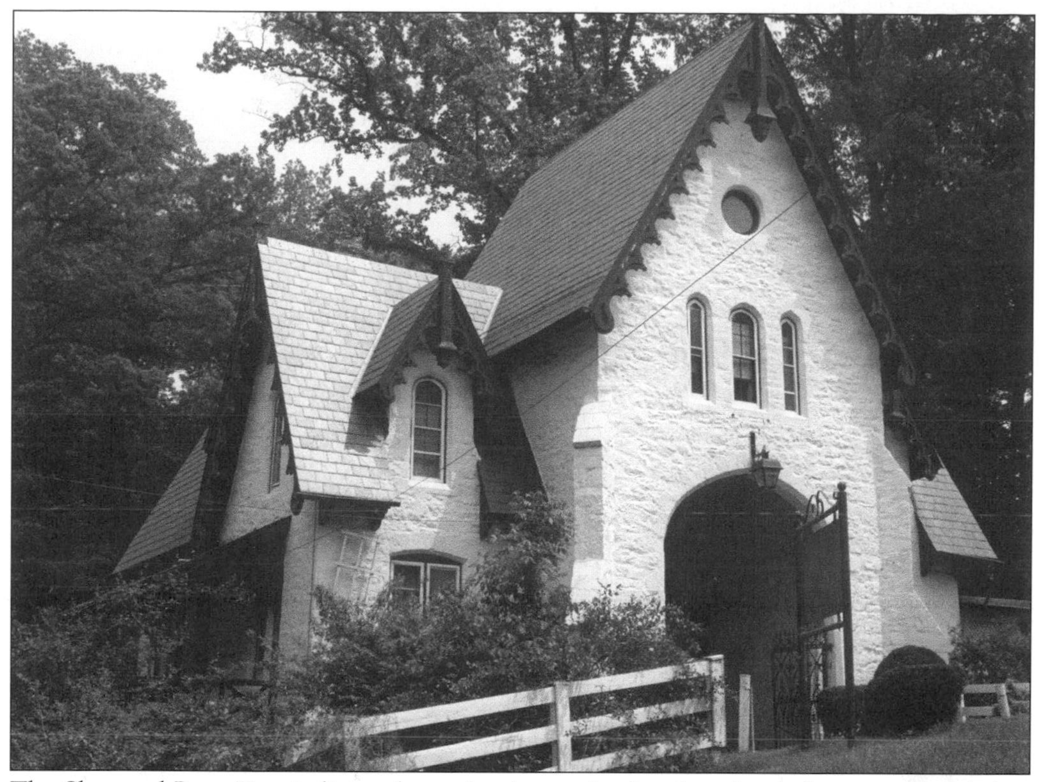

The Sheppard Pratt Hospital's gatehouse has been a landmark to locals for years. Founded in 1860, the institution's mission was to provide humane treatment for the mentally ill. Still regarded as one of the foremost hospitals of its kind, the Sheppard Pratt Hospital is also architecturally significant. The main buildings are unique examples of Victorian institutional architecture, and the lovely Casino, built in 1901, resembles the shingle-style summer homes built by the leisure class. (Courtesy Baltimore County Historical Society.)

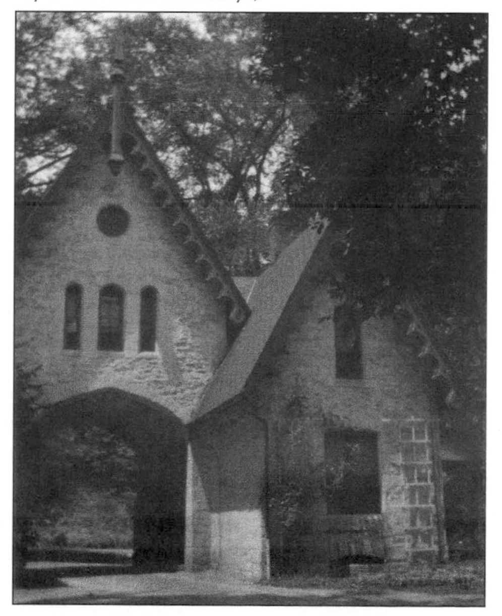

A view through the gatehouse archway shows North Charles Street in 1950. (Courtesy John W. McGrain.)

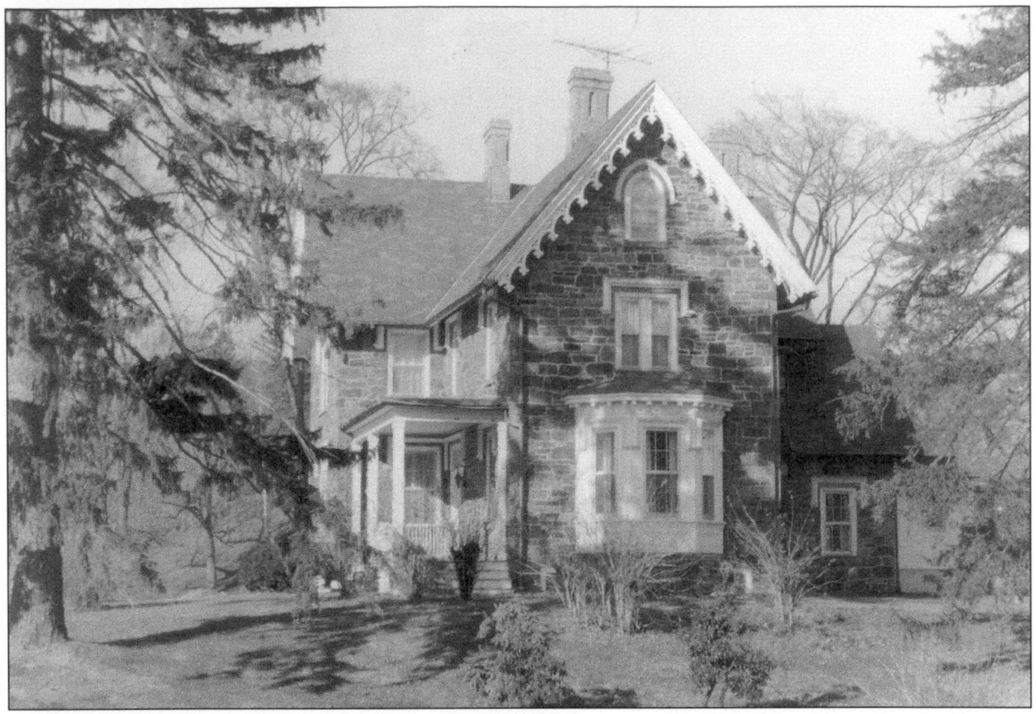

The Norris Cottage was built on the hospital grounds by the family of a patient. It stands near the Osler Drive entrance. (Courtesy John W. McGrain.)

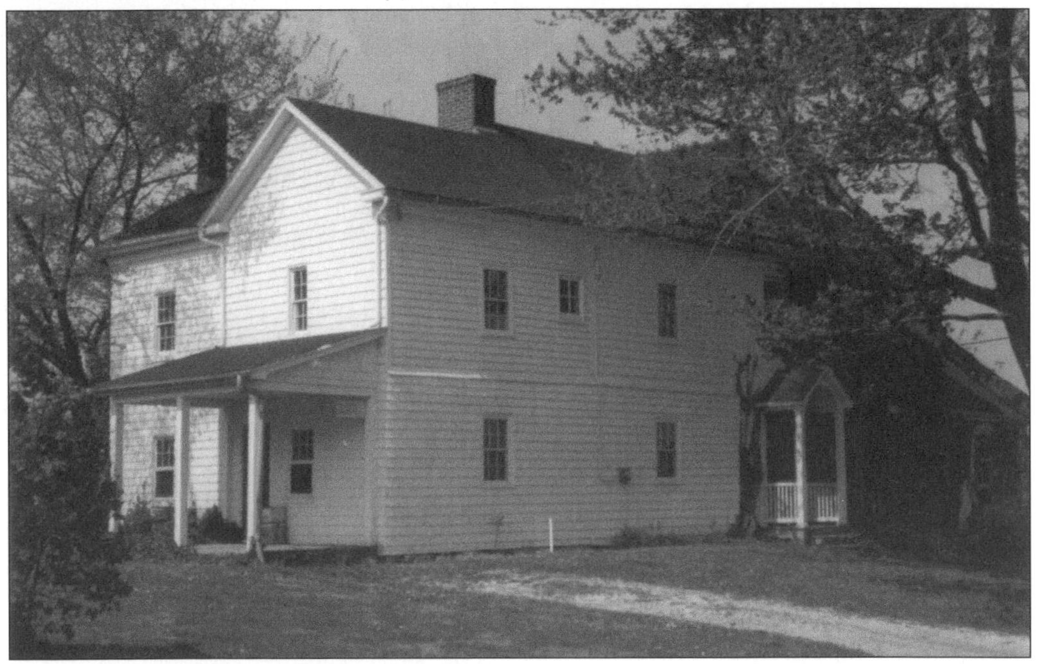

Samuel Bowen built this house in 1767. One of the early landholders, Bowen held title to property in what are now Towson and Ruxton. This house still stands on the grounds of the Greater Baltimore Medical Center and is used for the annual "Nearly New Sale." (Courtesy John W. McGrain.)

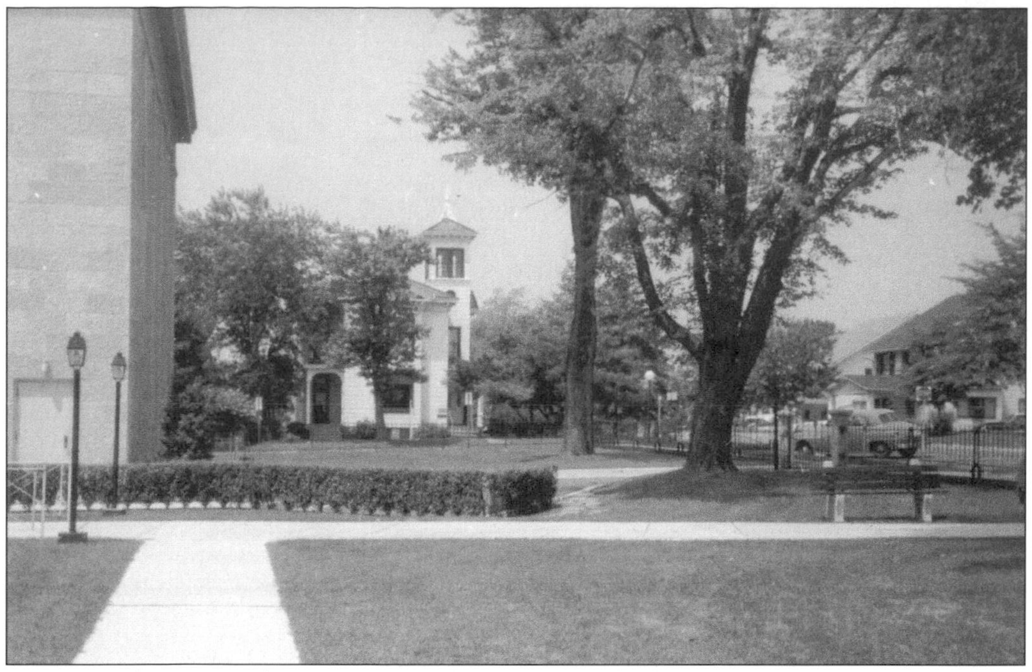

Known as the Longnecker House, the white Italianate building was used as a dentist's office from the 1940s until the building was razed to make way for the Courthouse Plaza in 1970. (Courtesy John W. McGrain.)

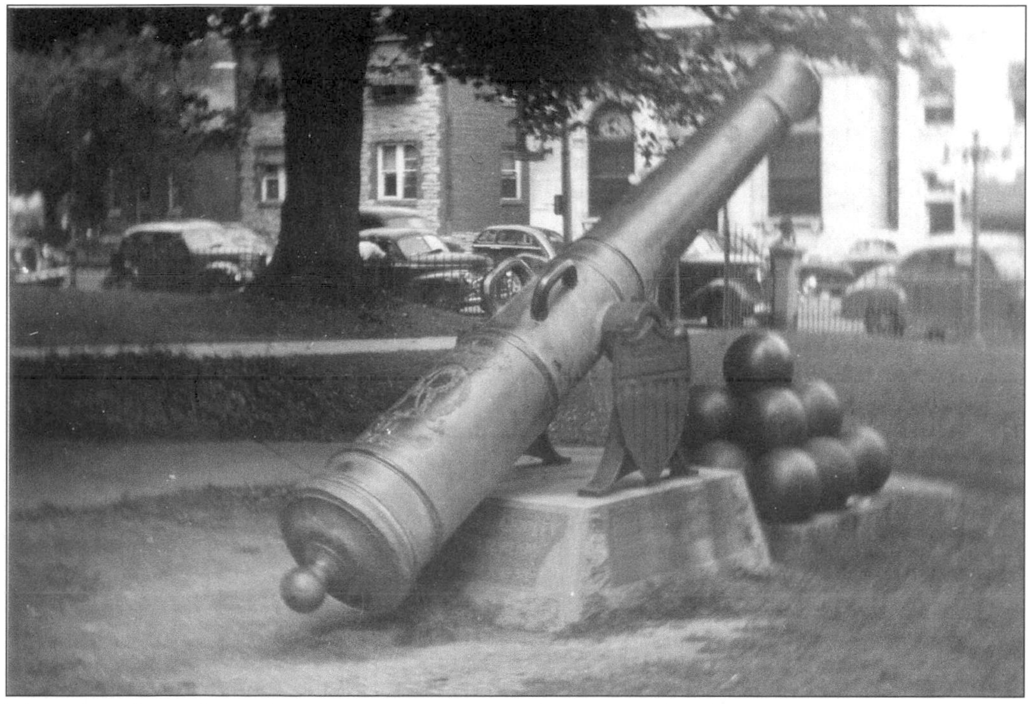

This 1946 photo shows the 5-ton canon captured in Manila Bay during the Spanish-American War on May 1, 1889, by Admiral Dewey. Were it to be fired from its position on the courthouse lawn, the cannonball would burst into the bank across the street. (Courtesy John W. McGrain.)

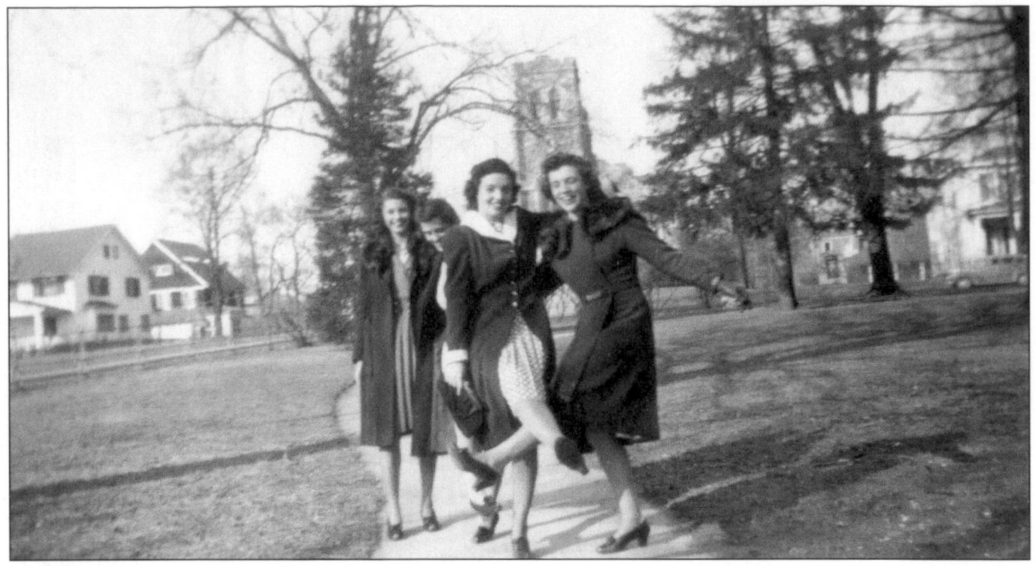

Joan Kaltenbach (née Anderson) and friends kick up their heels in the Courthouse Square. In the background is Calvary Baptist Church. (Courtesy Mrs. Joan Kaltenbach.)

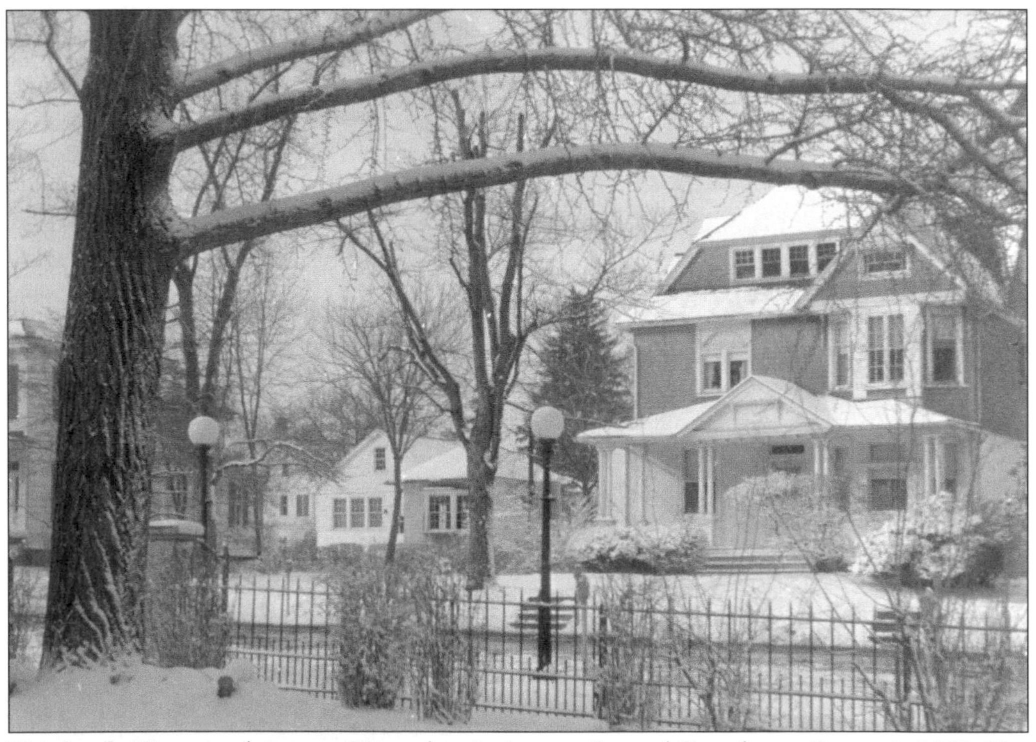

This lovely Victorian house on Pennsylvania Avenue fronted Courthouse Square in 1958. The block was razed in 1963. The lampposts stood at the entry into the square. (Courtesy John W. McGrain.)

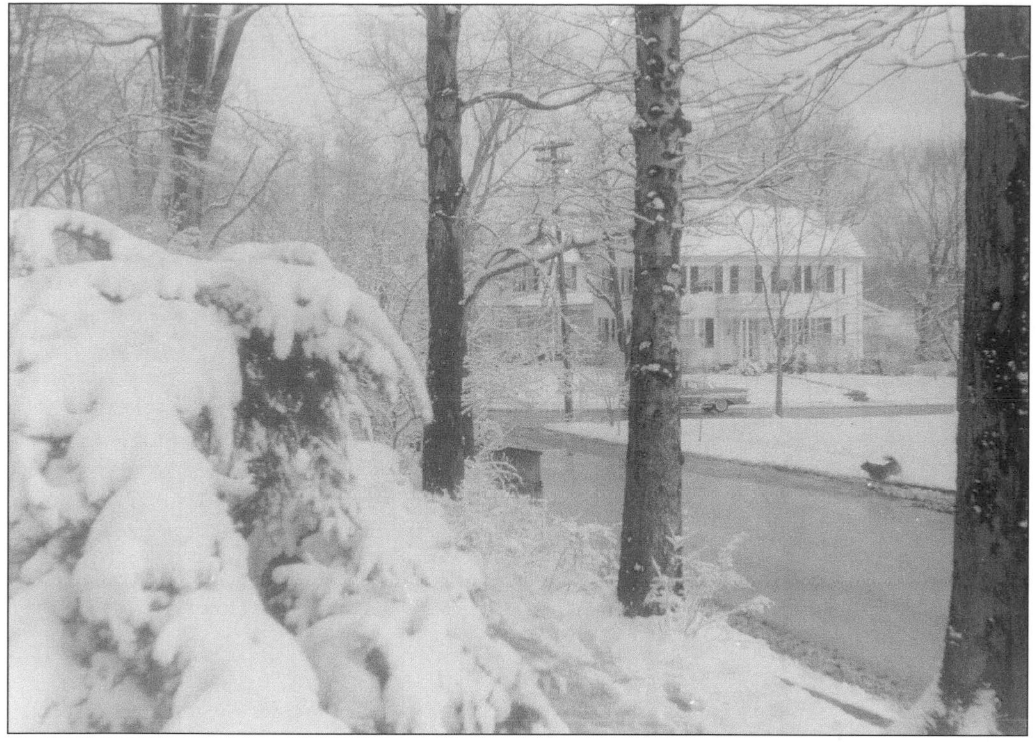

The gracious colonial, belonging to a member of the Lee family, was located on the southeast corner of Washington and Pennsylvania Avenues in February 1958. The site is now a parking lot. (Courtesy John W. McGrain.)

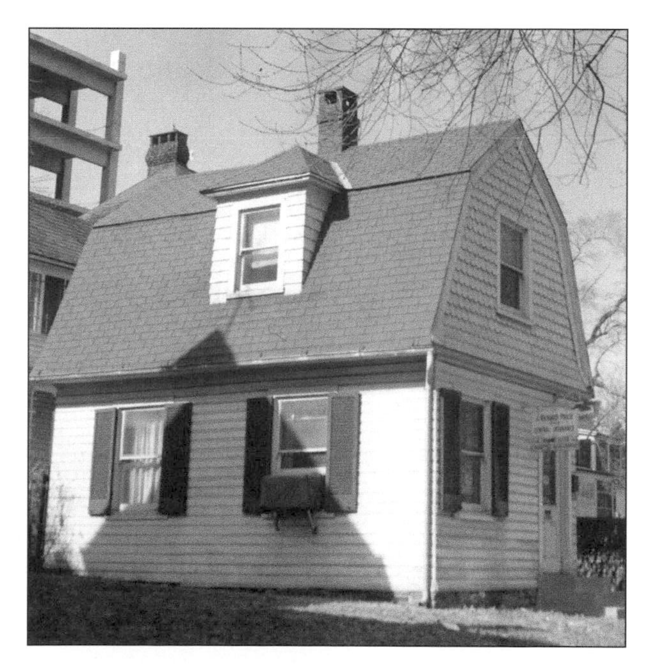

This small building was a doctor's office located behind houses on Washington Avenue. When they were destroyed, the structure was moved to its present location on Joppa Road. (Courtesy Baltimore County Historical Society.)

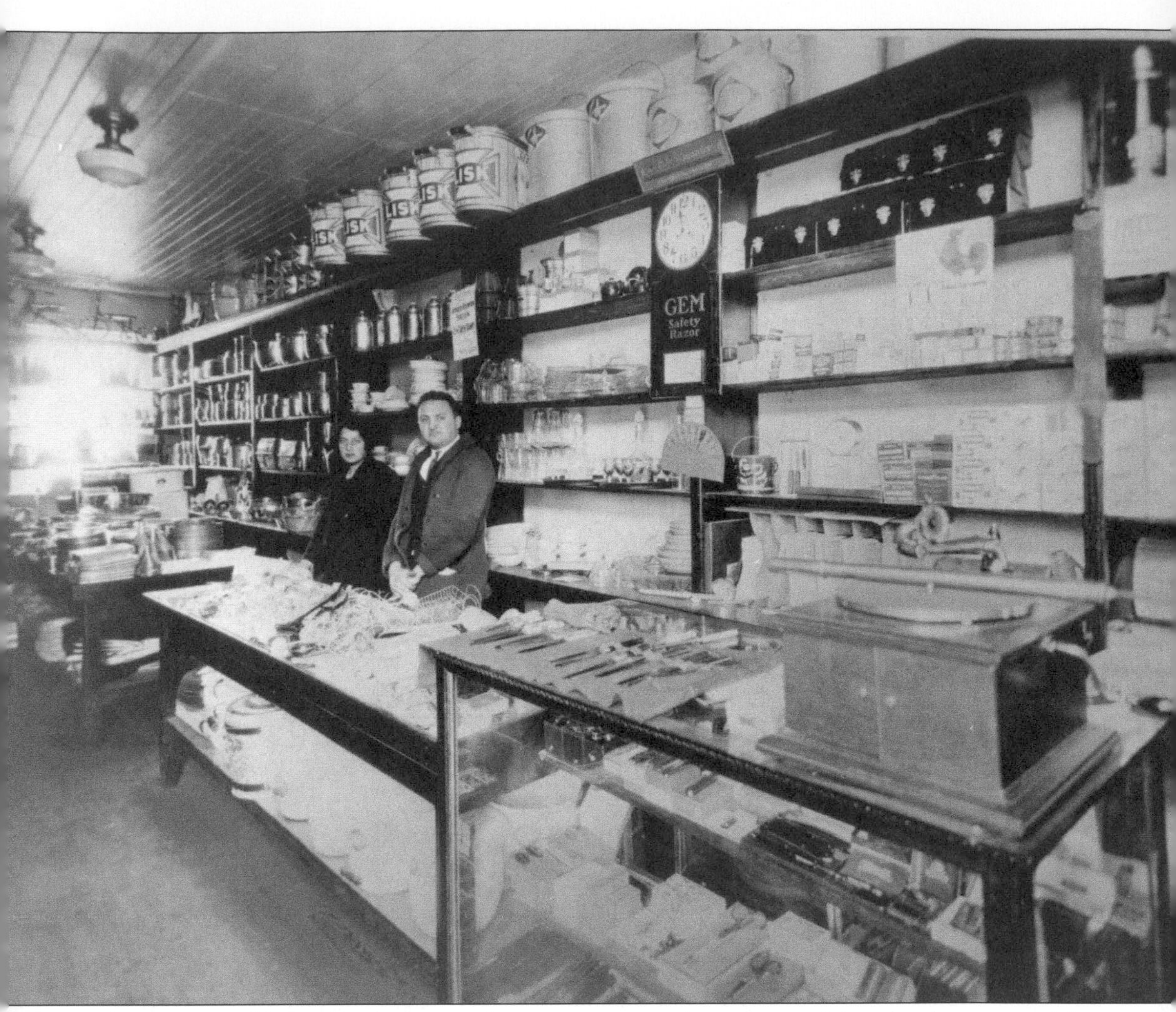

Benjamin and Edna Gorfine await their customers at the counter of their hardware store. Note the gramophone in the right foreground. (Courtesy Baltimore County Historical Society.)

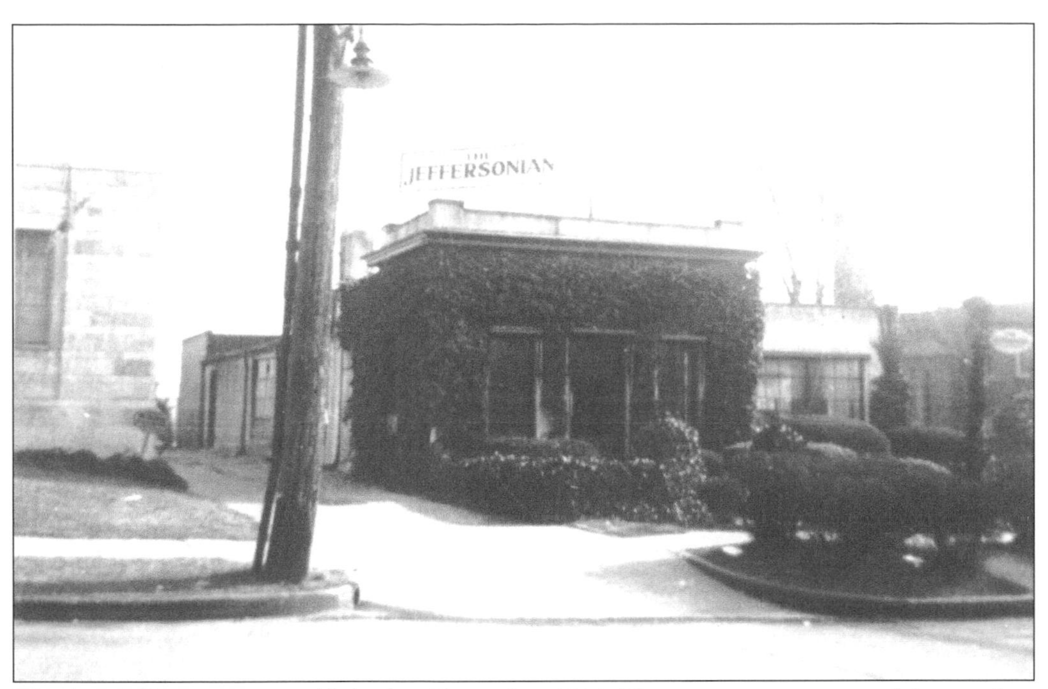

The first *Jeffersonian* was published in December 1911. The paper was so successful in its first year of circulation that it began to buy the other newspapers in Baltimore County. The paper was produced in the sandstone building on Washington Avenue next to the National Guard Armory. The *Jeffersonian* continues to boast a wide readership in both Baltimore County and Baltimore City. (Courtesy Baltimore County Historical Society.)

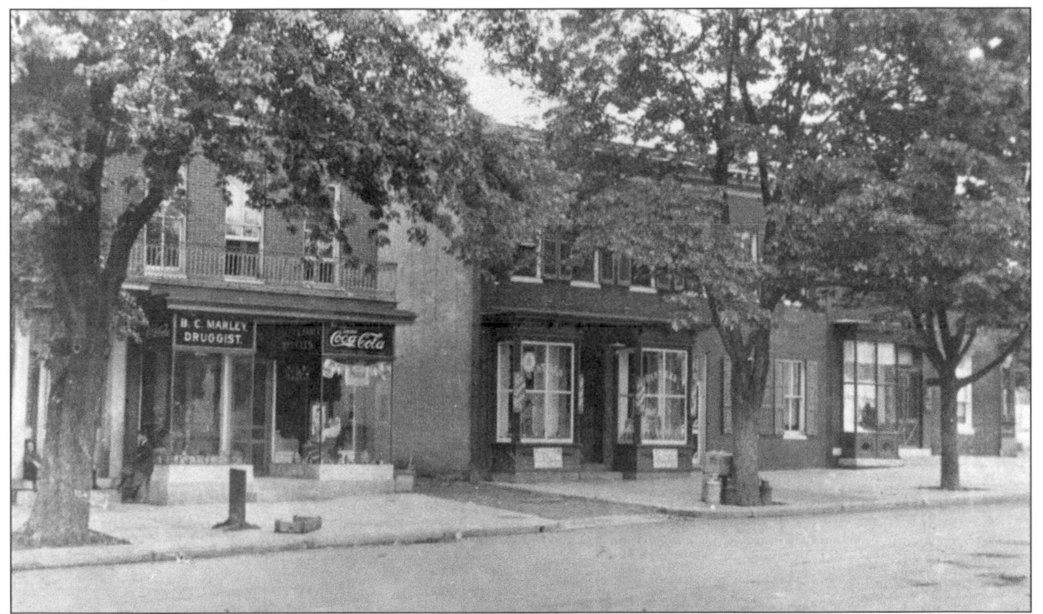

Pictured on York Road in 1910, Marley's Drug Store and the barbershop next door were popular. While the tree-lined street might be unfamiliar, not all things change (as demonstrated by the Coca-Cola sign in the store window). (Courtesy Baltimore County Historical Society.)

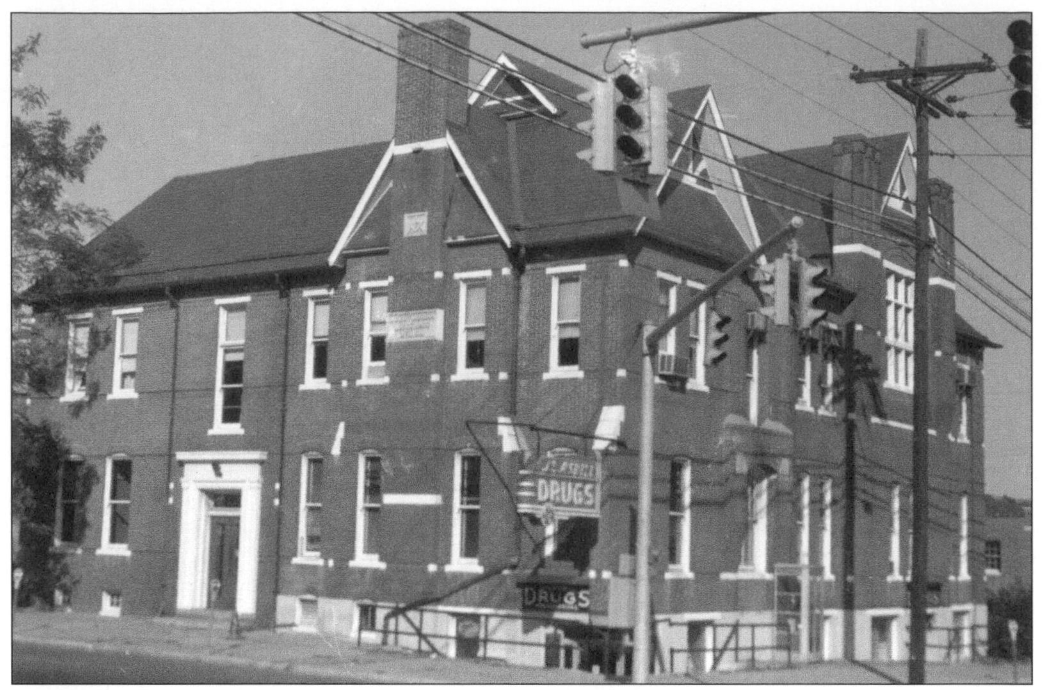

Asbill's Pharmacy occupied the lower level of the Mt. Moriah Lodge. The Lodge was an important part of the lives of many Towson men. Located on the northeast corner of Washington and Chesapeake Avenues, the Lodge was torn down and replaced by an office building. A new lodge was built in West Towson on Chesapeake Avenue. (Courtesy Baltimore County Historical Society.)

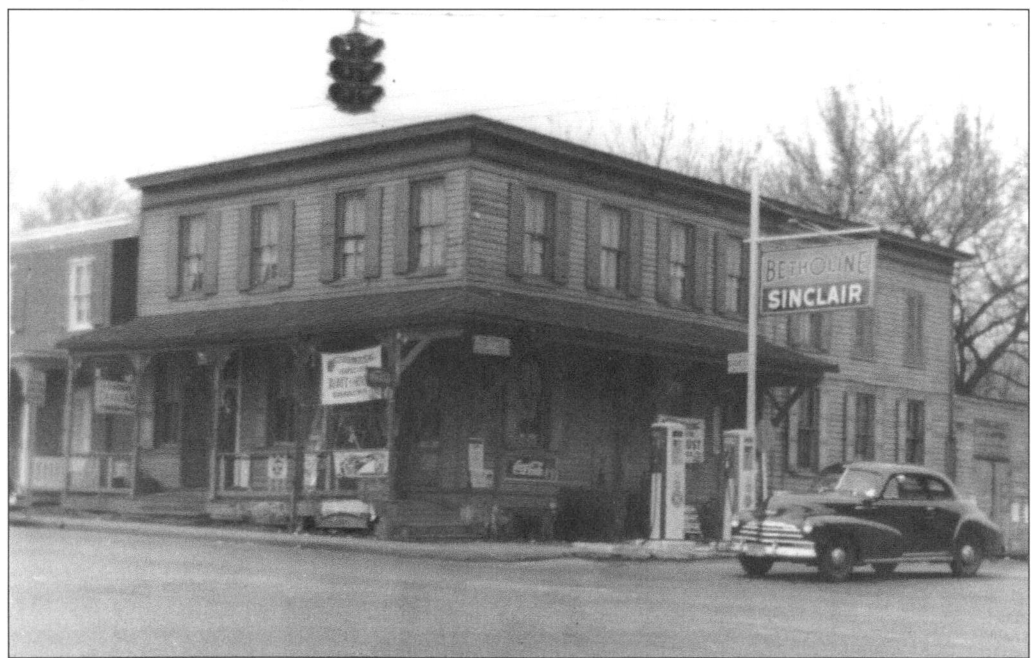

The Corbin Store stood at the corner of Joppa Road and York Road. An ophthalmologist's office currently occupies the site. (Courtesy Baltimore County Historical Society.)

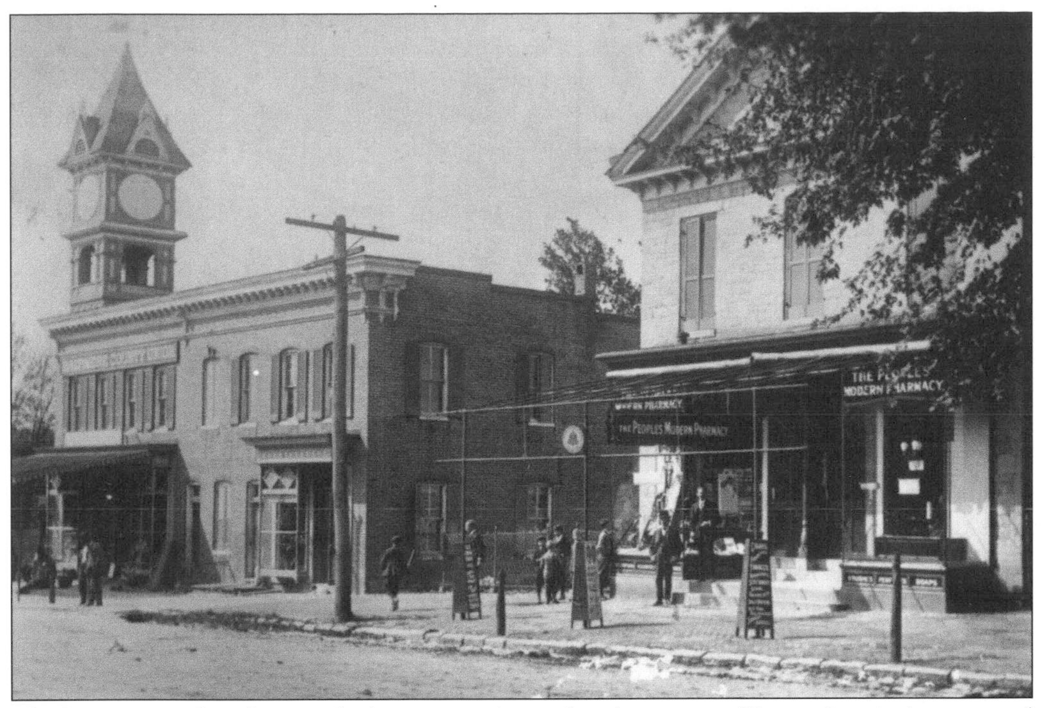

The Lee store and its famous clock tower are located at the corner of Pennsylvania Avenue and York Road. Next door is the People's Modern Pharmacy. (Courtesy Baltimore County Historical Society.)

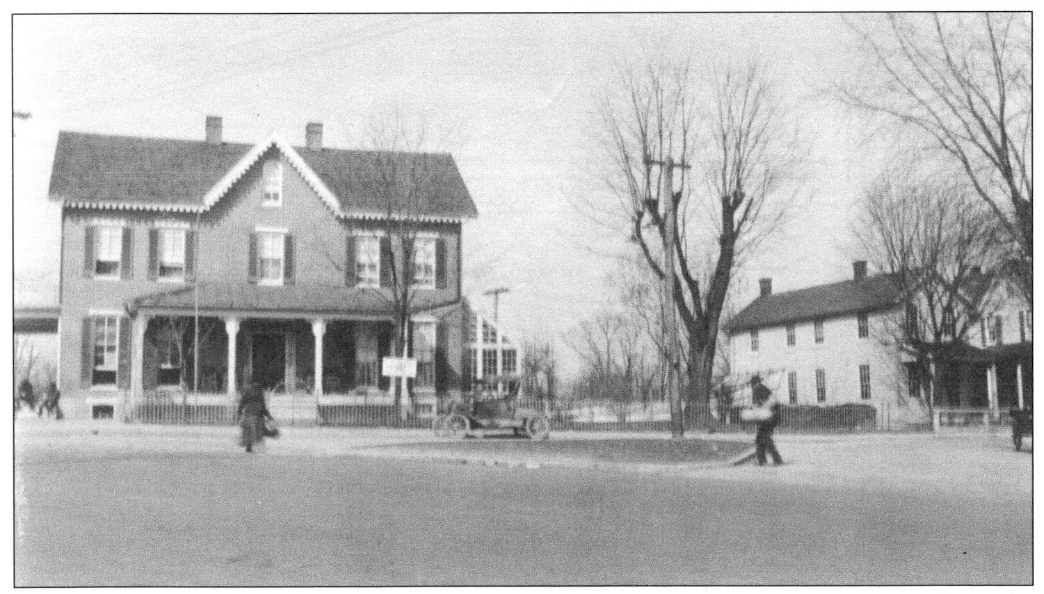

The Bosley Hotel was built in the 1820s and named for its proprietor, Charles Bosley. The building was torn down in 1950 and replaced by Hutzler's. (Courtesy Baltimore County Historical Society.)

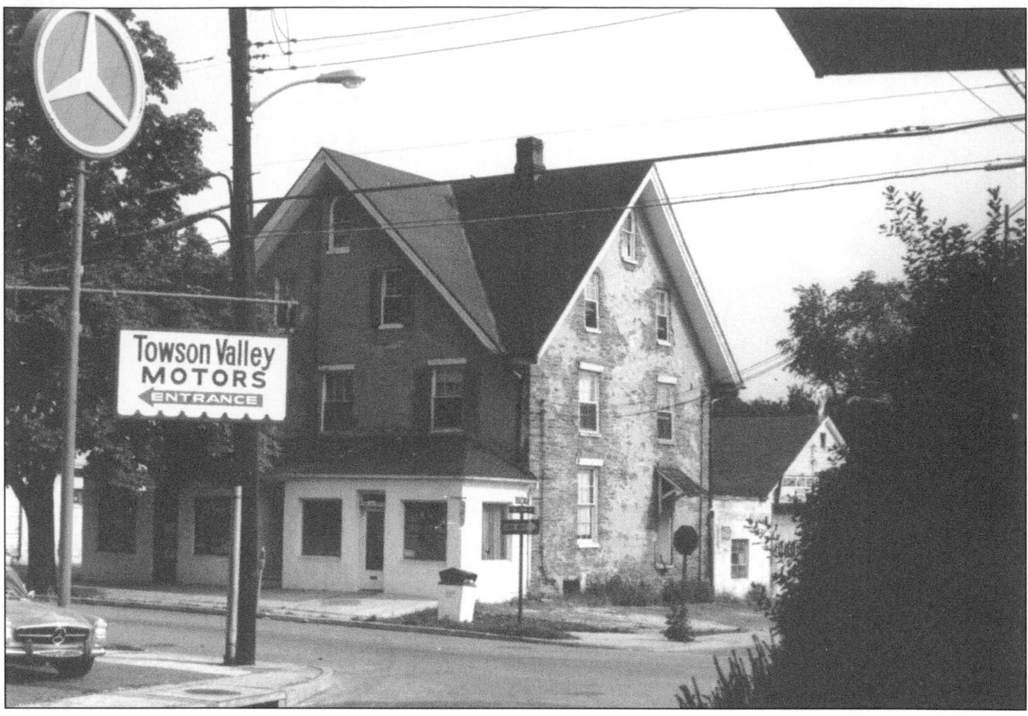

Before the dealership moved out to Cockeysville, Valley Motors was located on York Road in Towson. A Honda dealership currently owns the property. (Courtesy Baltimore County Historical Society.)

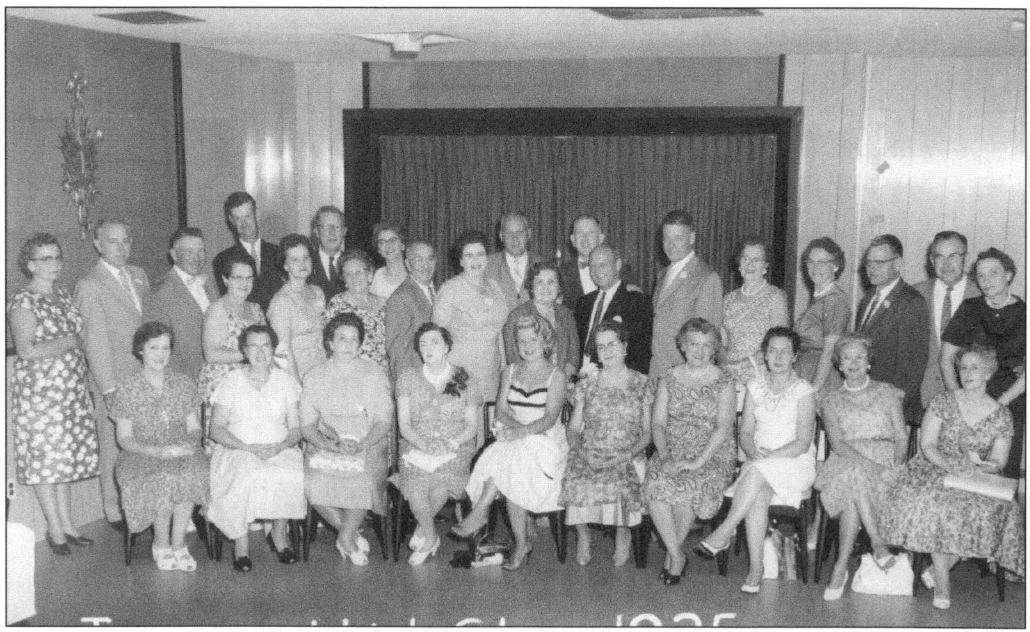

The Penn Hotel, located on Pennsylvania Avenue, was a private home until 1922, when it became a popular gathering spot for Towsonians. Here, the members of the Towson High School Class of 1925 enjoy their 35th reunion. (Courtesy Baltimore County Historical Society.)

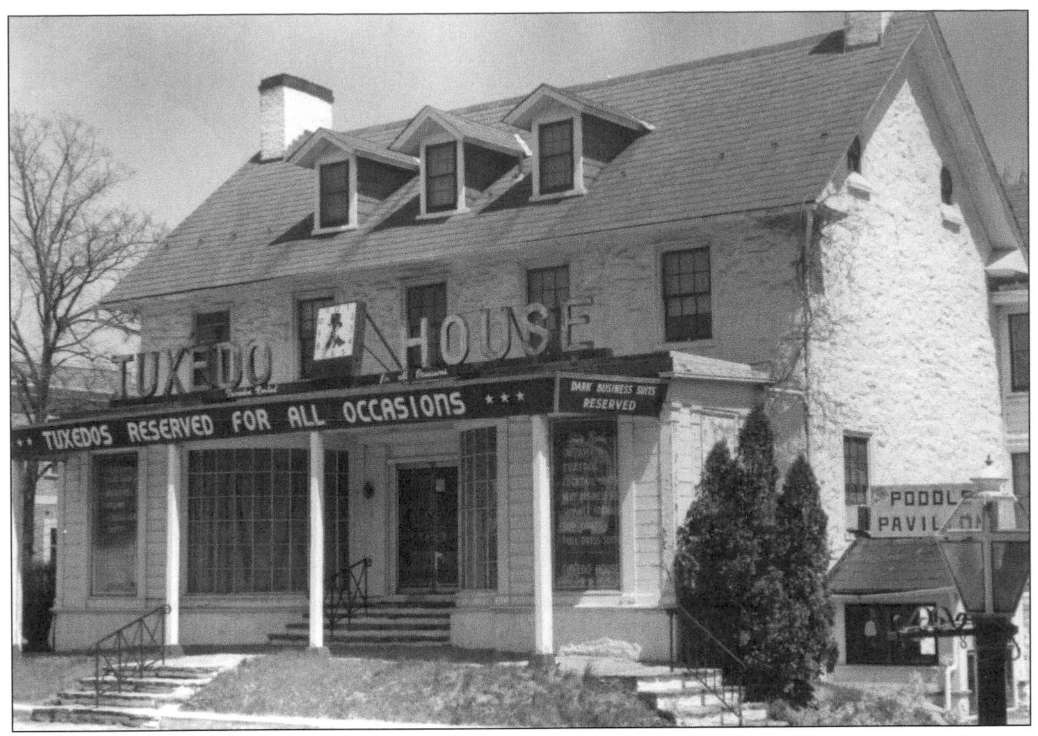

Originally a home built by a member of the Bowen family, the Tuxedo House was the place in town where men prepared for the formal events in their lives. (Courtesy Baltimore County Historical Society.)

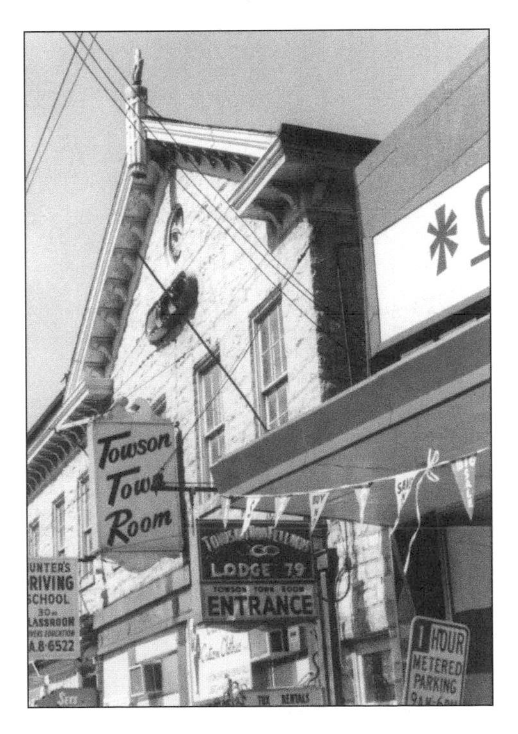

Towson's Odd Fellows Hall stood shoulder to shoulder with taverns and shops in the late 1950s. (Courtesy Baltimore County Historical Society.)

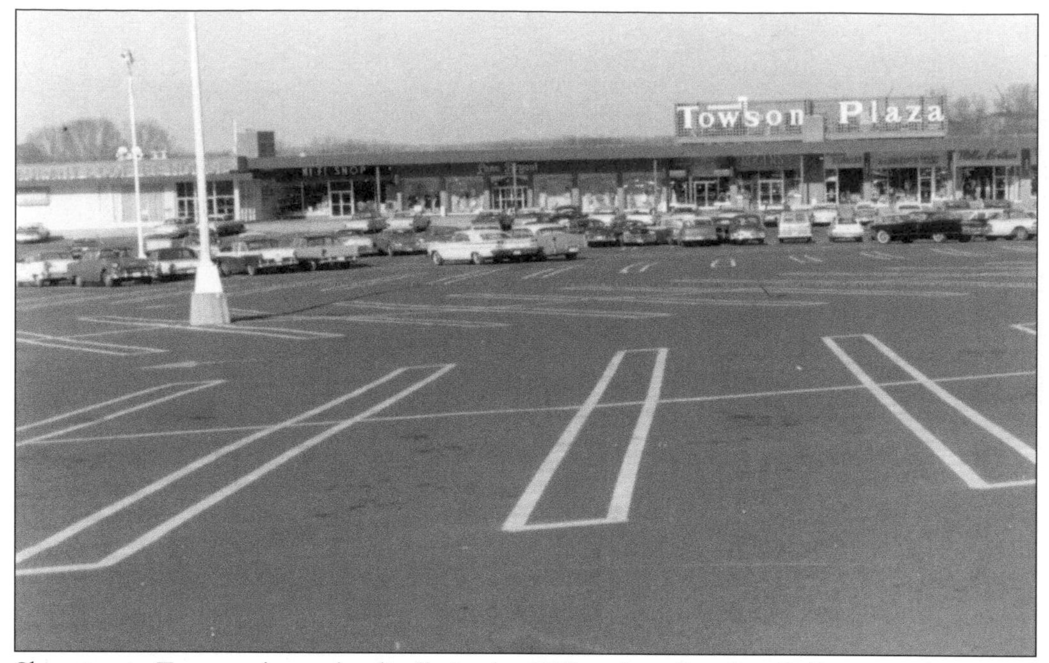

Shopping in Towson changed radically in the 1950s, when Goucher College issued a ground lease and then finally sold several acres to accommodate the new Towson Plaza. Hutzler's, a high-end department store, was built on the parcel once occupied by the Bosley Hotel. Many locals fondly recall enjoying lunch and a spectacular view from the Hutzler's lunchroom. Of course, more recent residents could hardly imagine the complex pictured here as the forerunner to the glittering TowsonTown Center! (Courtesy Baltimore County Historical Society.)

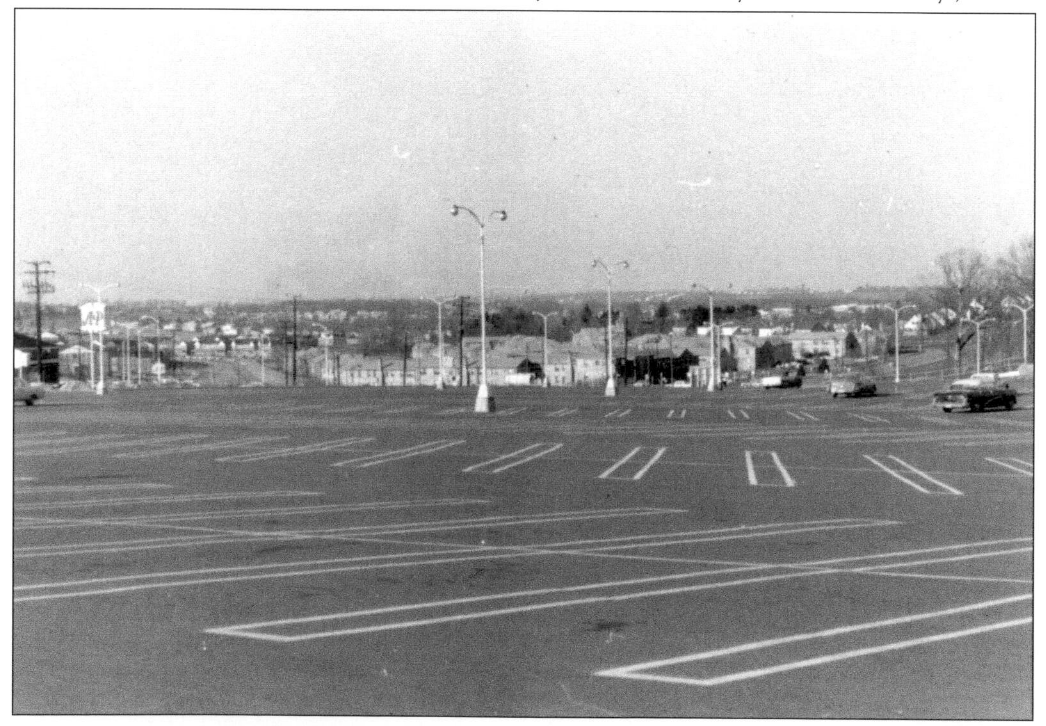

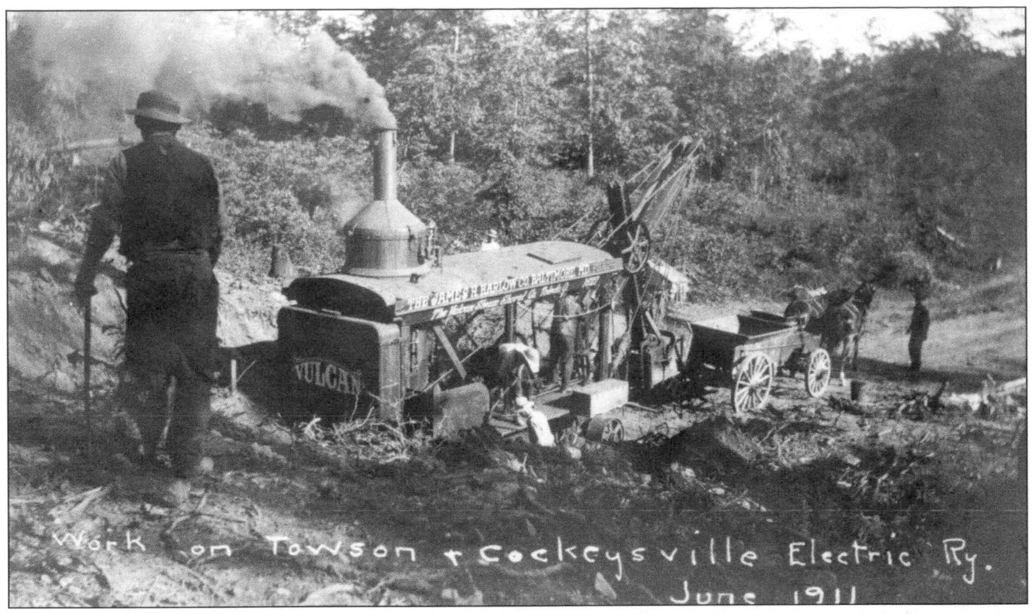

The Towson–Cockeysville electric railroad, or "Toonerville Trolley," connected the growing communities of Towson, Lutherville, and Timonium, allowing for an increase in commerce and residential opportunities. Construction on the line began in 1911, with the intent of extending service to Cockeysville; however, failure to gain a right of way over the Northern Central Line prevented it. (Courtesy Baltimore County Historical Society.)

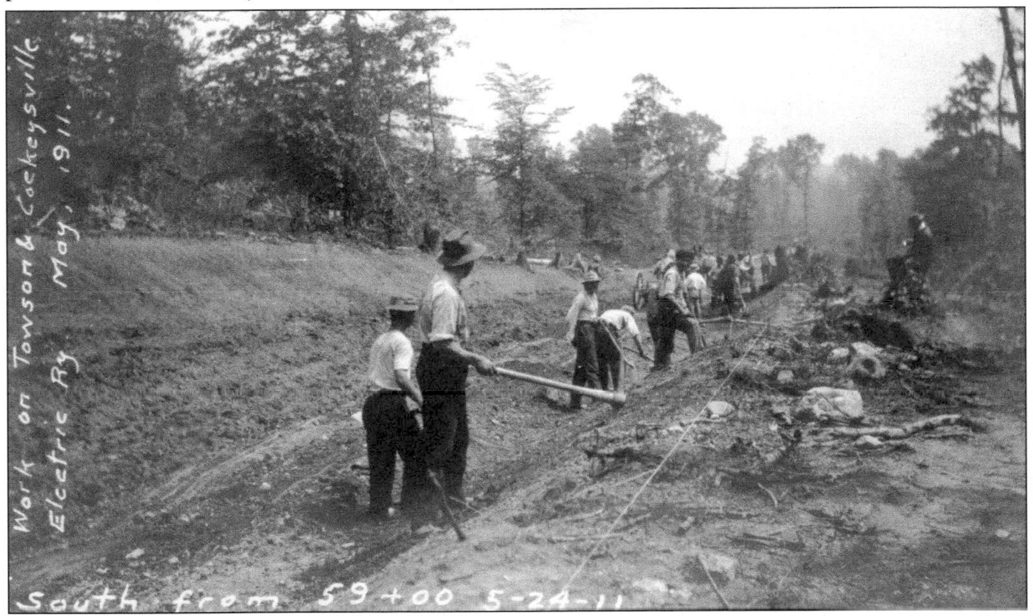

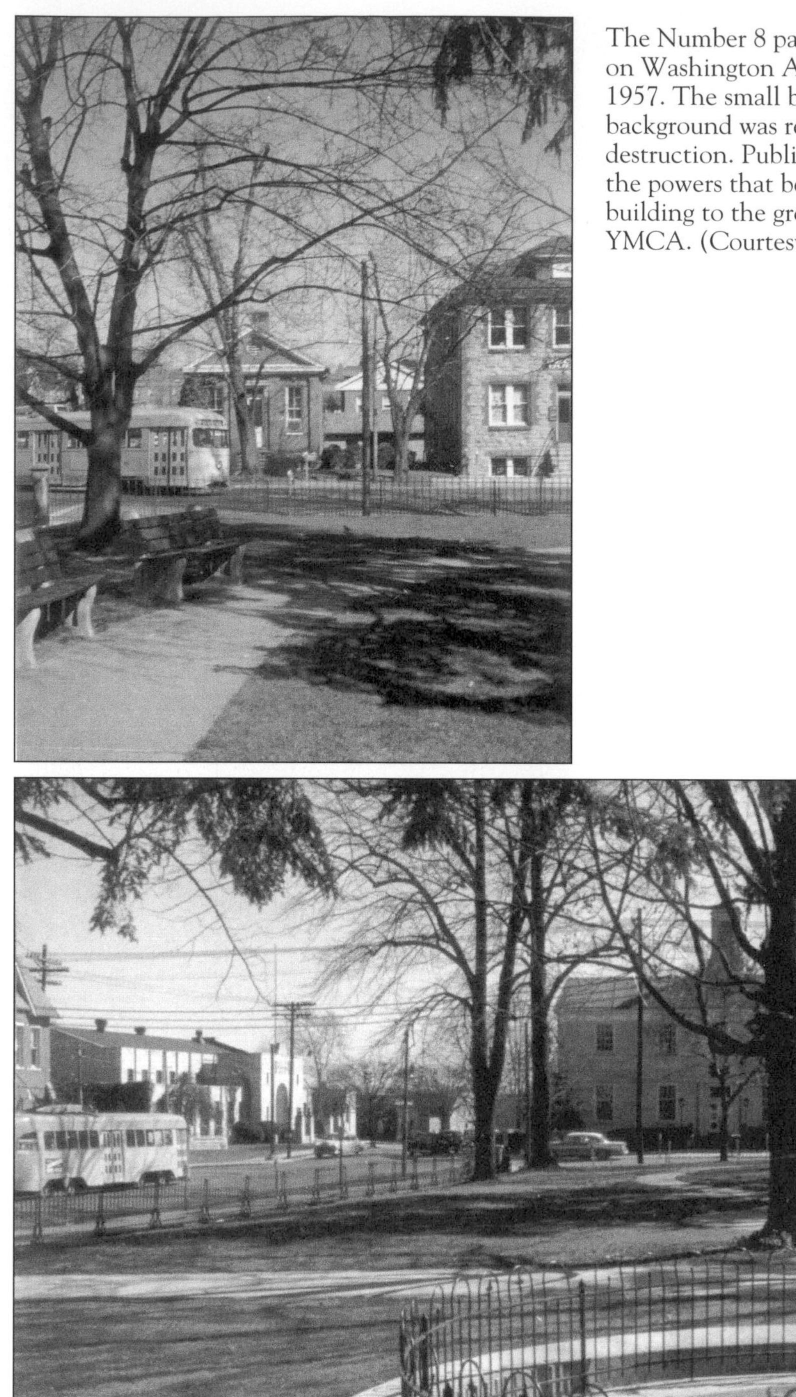

The Number 8 passes the courthouse on Washington Avenue in March of 1957. The small brick building in the background was rescued from destruction. Public outcry persuaded the powers that be to move the building to the grounds of the Towson YMCA. (Courtesy John W. McGrain.)

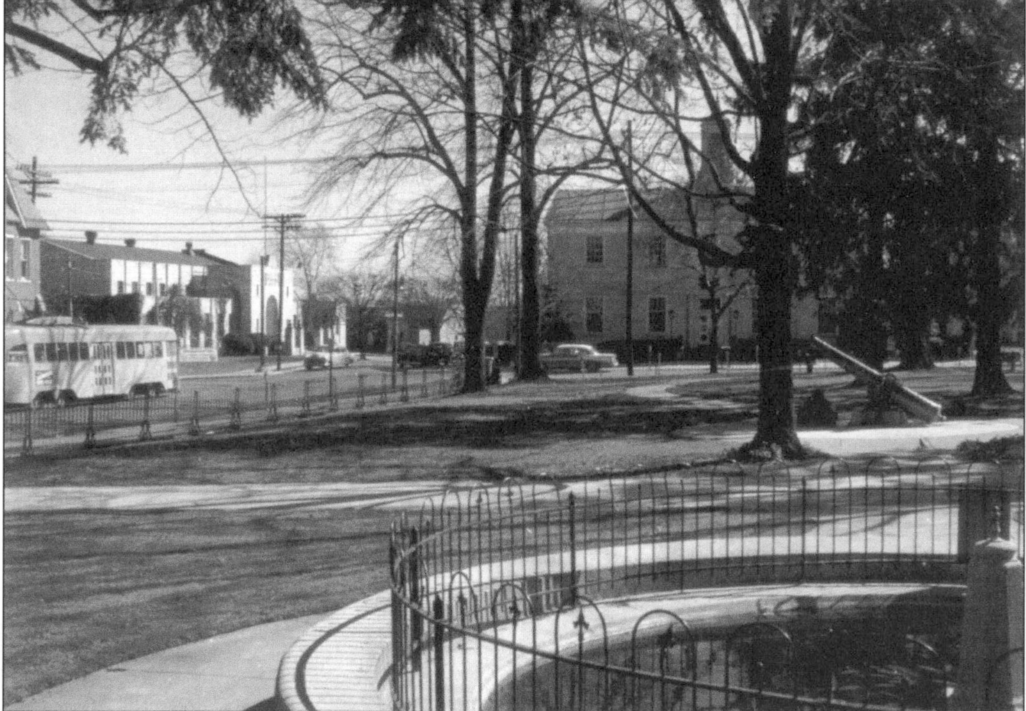

The Number 8 approaches the post office. Buses replaced the streetcars in 1963. (Courtesy John W. McGrain.)

The Towson Fire Station moved to this building in the center of the intersections of York and Dulaney Valley Roads in 1893. Prior to that, the station had been on East Chesapeake Avenue. The Towson Volunteer Fire Department was formed a year later. This photo was taken in the 1940s, about 15 years before the building was razed. (Courtesy Baltimore County Historical Society.)

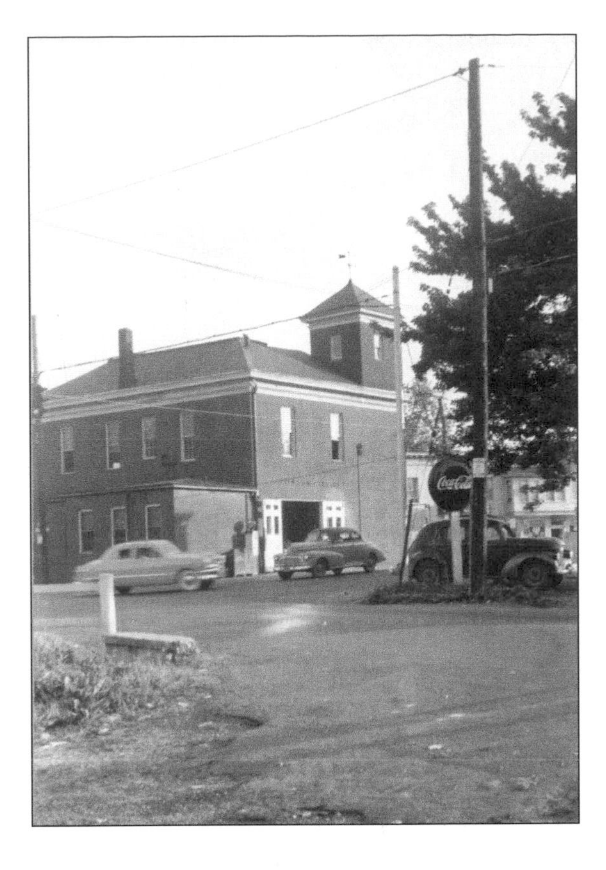

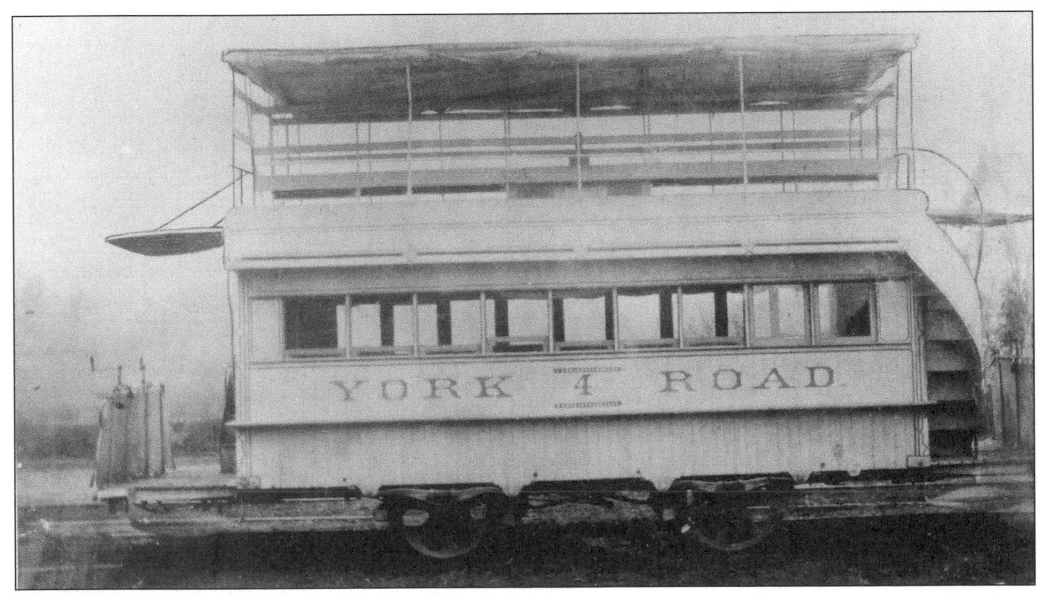

Horse-drawn, double-decker streetcars were the first to serve Towson. For an especially steep hill, a second horse, or "hill horse," would be added. (Courtesy Baltimore County Public Library.)

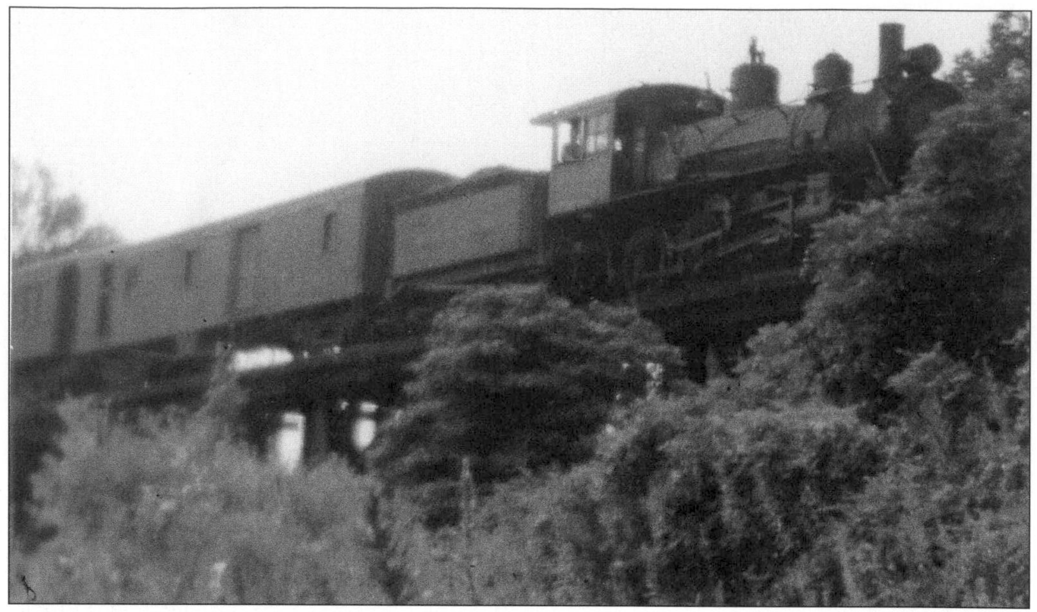

The northbound Number 6 thunders over the jail trestle at about 20 miles per hour. The trestle was located near the current intersection of Bosley Avenue and Towsontown Boulevard. (Courtesy John W. McGrain.)

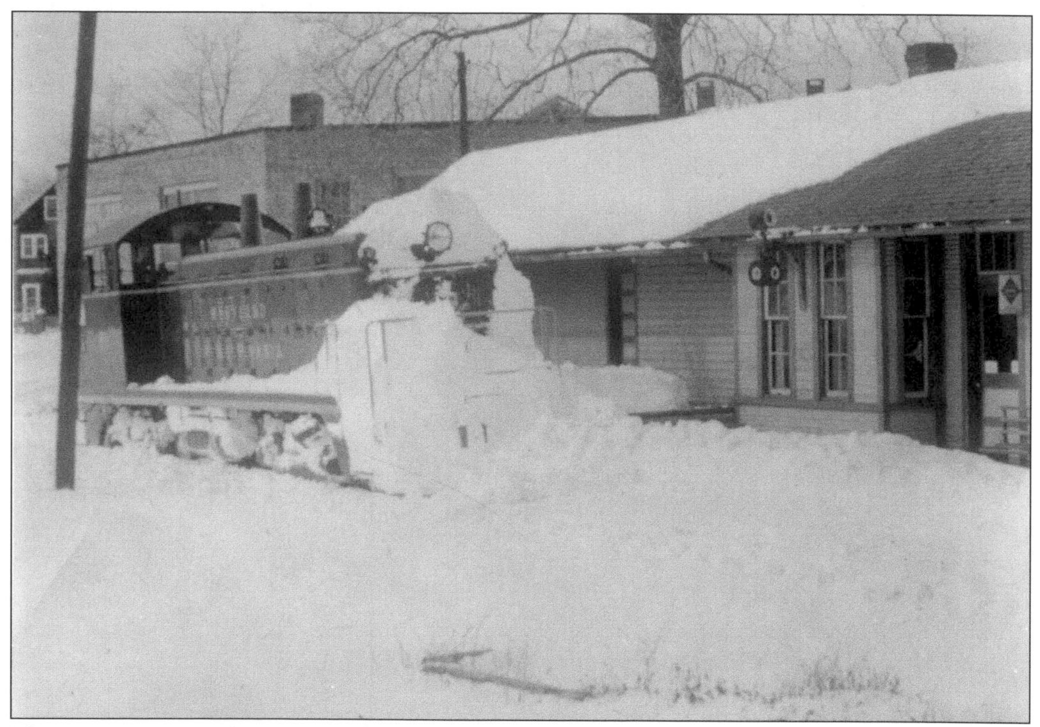

The Towson Train Station stood on the south side of Susquehanna Avenue. Service between Towson and Baltimore began on April 17, 1882, with eight trips daily. In 1889, service to York, Pennsylvania, was added, thus the line gained its nickname, the Ma & Pa. (Courtesy Baltimore County Historical Society.)

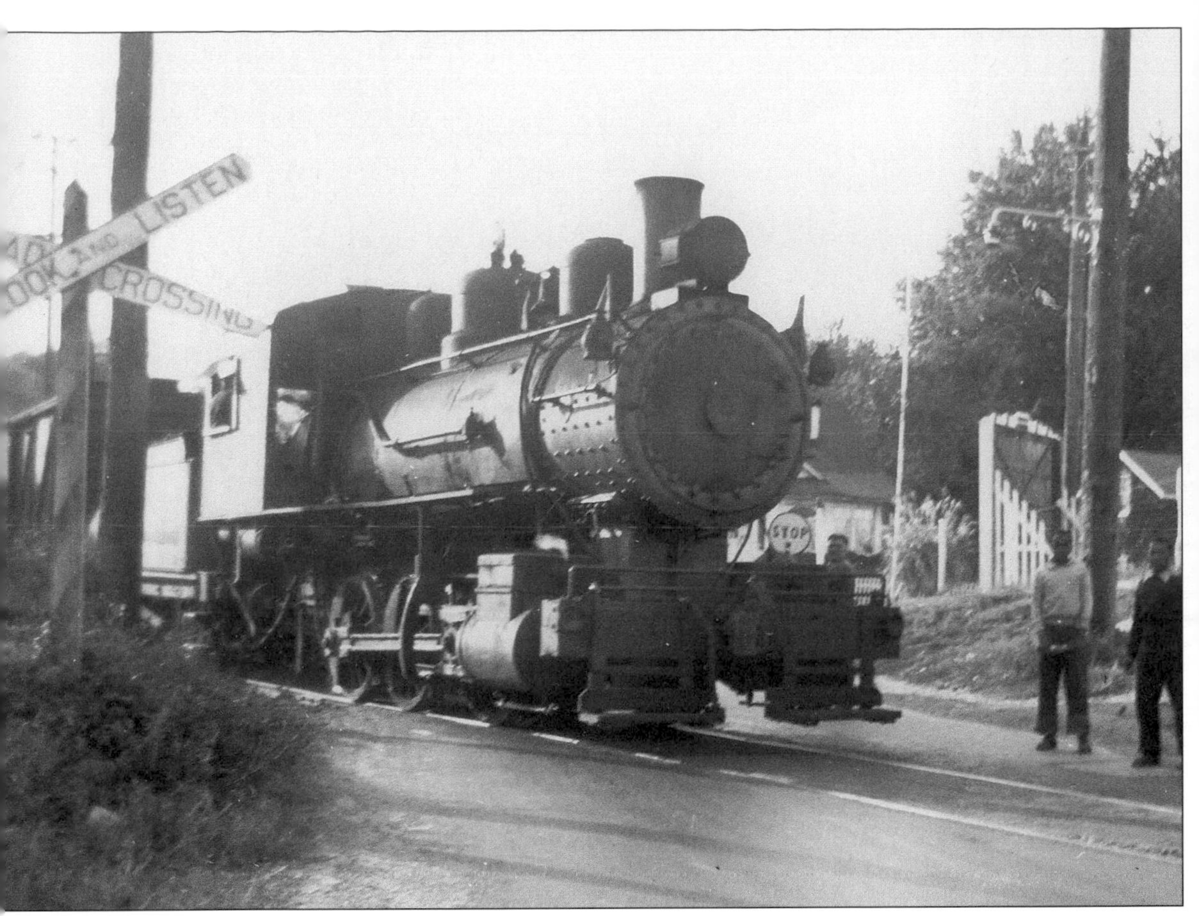

The Number 29 crosses Jefferson Avenue in 1947. Note the sign urging pedestrians to "Stop, Look, and Listen" before crossing the tracks. (Courtesy John W. McGrain.)

Today, this view of Towson University's Stephen's Hall from the Towson train station would be dominated by the Berkshire Apartments. (Courtesy John W. McGrain.)

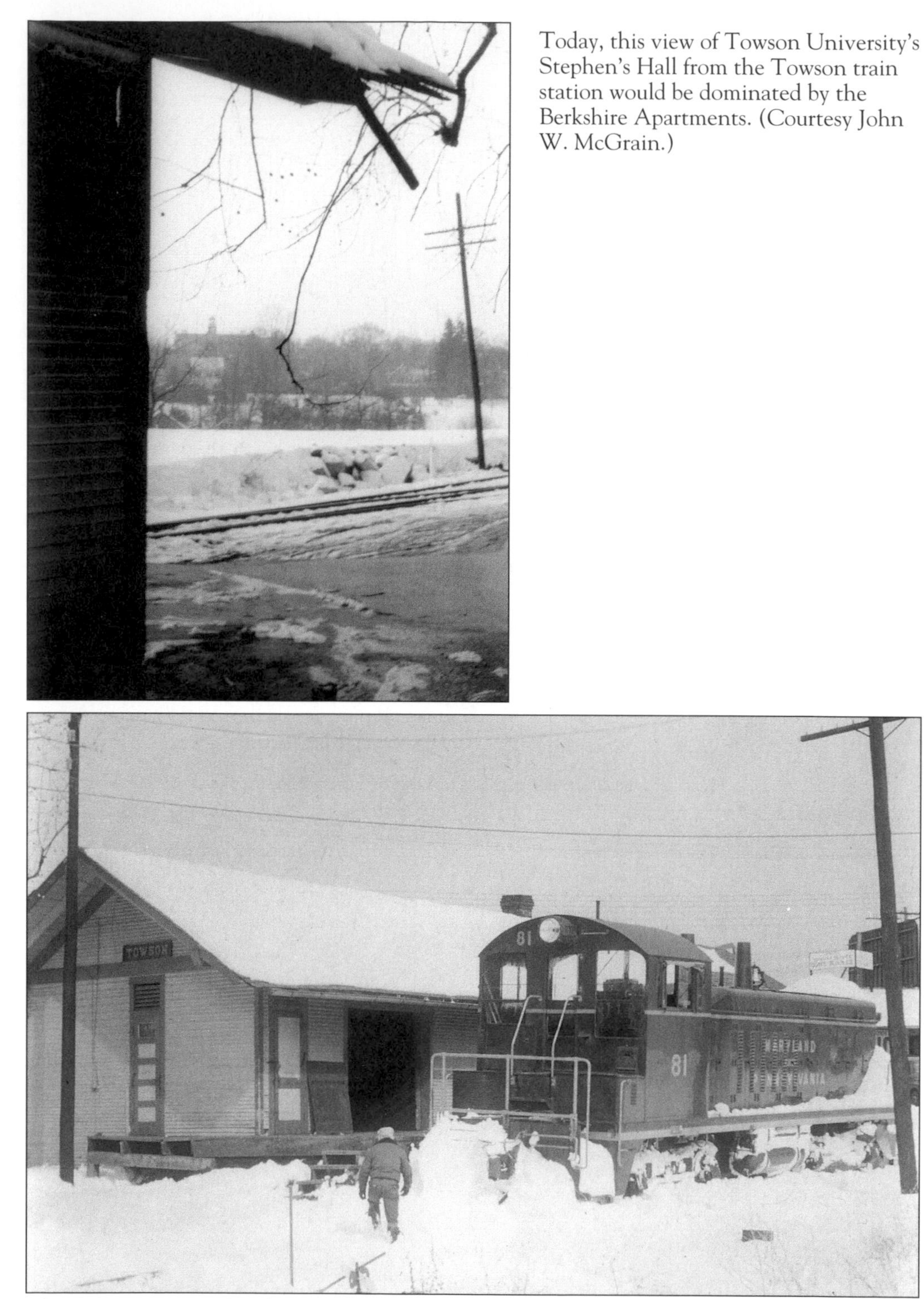

The narrow gauge railroad, or Ma & Pa, enjoyed a great deal of popularity with the residents of Baltimore County, who used it to commute, as well as to travel, between the many towns along the line. (Courtesy John W. McGrain.)

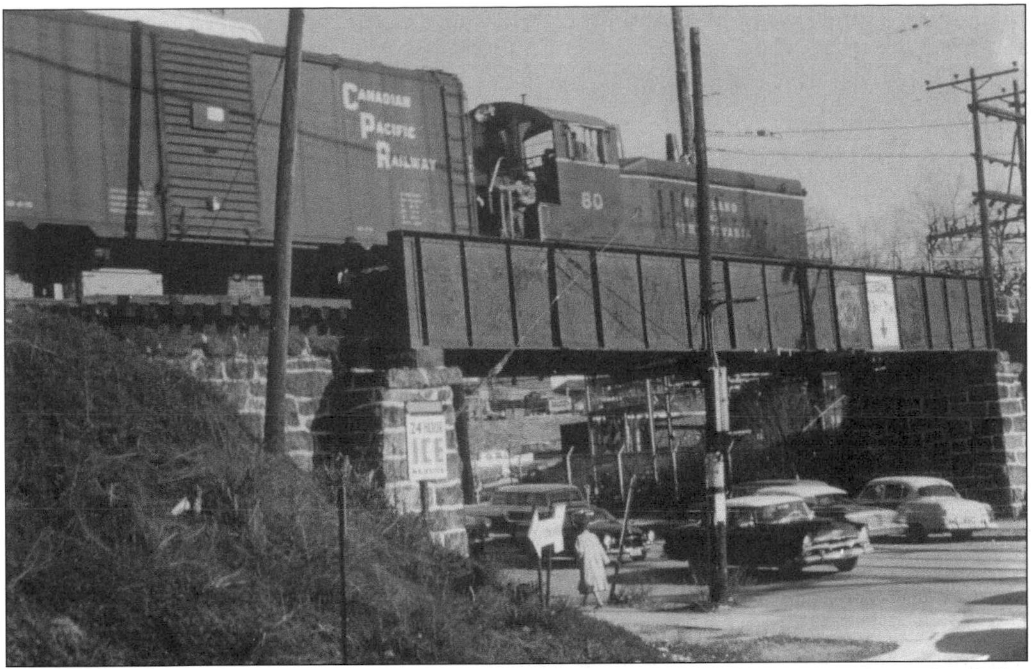

The trestle over York Road is pictured here with the Number 6 heading east in the early 1950s. (Courtesy Baltimore County Historical Society.)

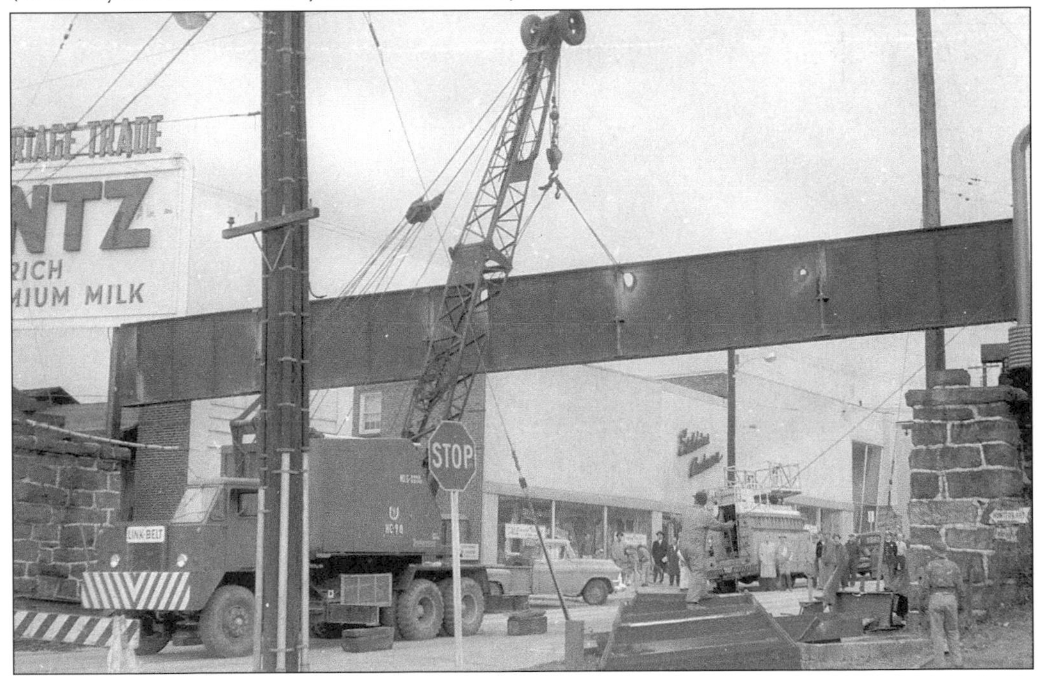

Signifying the end of an era, the York Road trestle is dismantled in 1959, and the Ma & Pa becomes only a memory. In 1958, the narrow gauge fell victim to operating expenses and declining revenue. The stone abutments remain and serve not only as a handsome gateway to Towson, but also as a reminder of a once beloved railroad. (Courtesy Baltimore County Historical Society.)

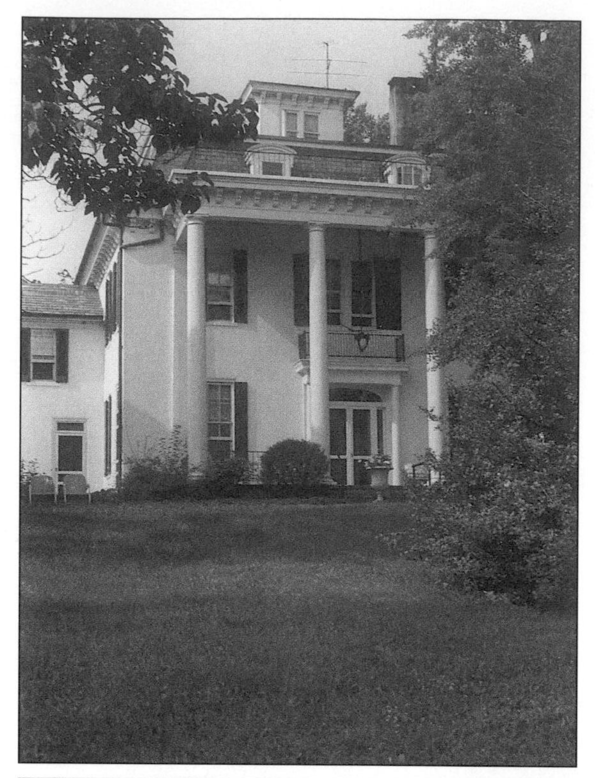

Grafton Bosley built this elegant mansion in 1860, just west of Towson, on what is now Georgia Court. The Offutt family was the last private owner, before the house became the Presbyterian Home of Maryland. (Courtesy John W. McGrain.)

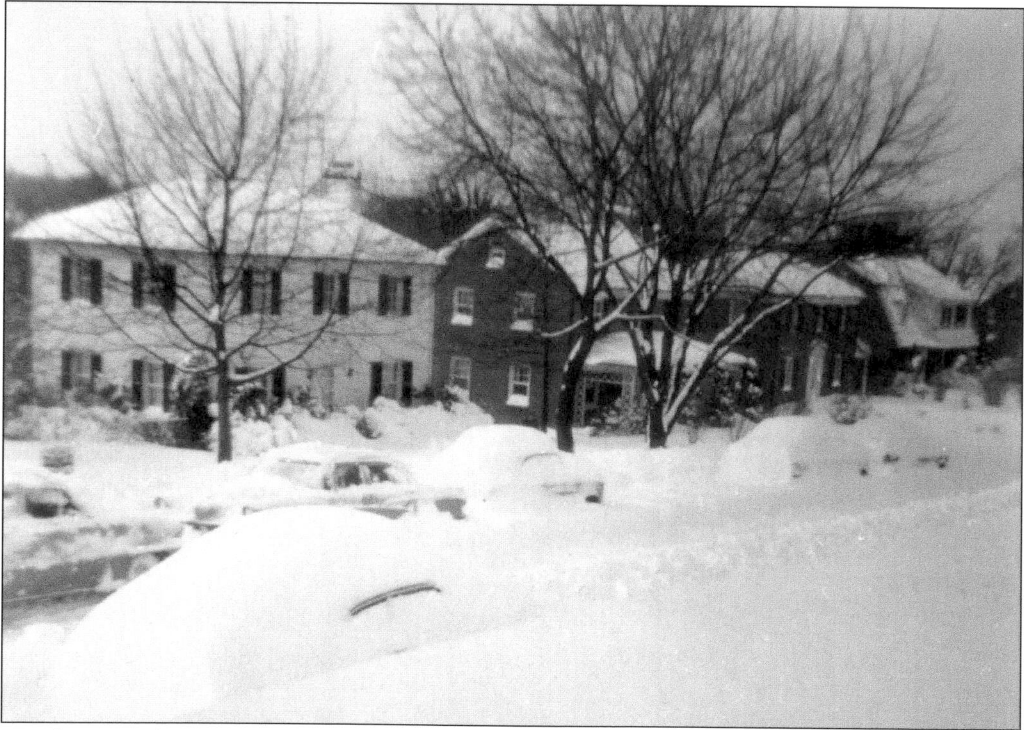

Carolina Road in West Towson is seen here after a snow storm in 1958. The neighborhood, Southland Hills, still retains its charm today. (Courtesy Mrs. Joan Kaltenbach.)

Charlotte Emerson and Wanda McFarlane are enjoying the snowy hills of West Towson in the 1930s. The girls are in front of 537 Allegheny Avenue. (Courtesy Baltimore County Public Library.)

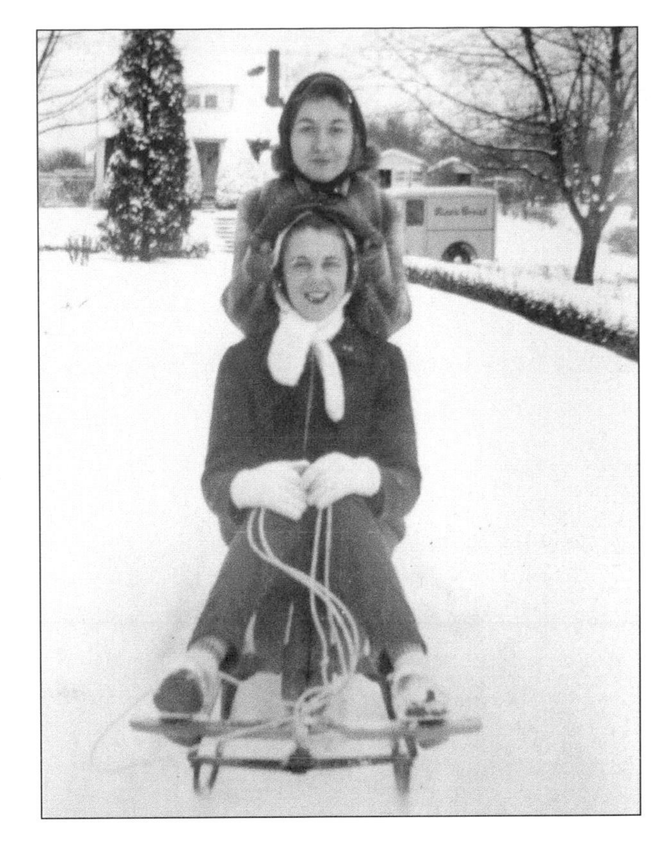

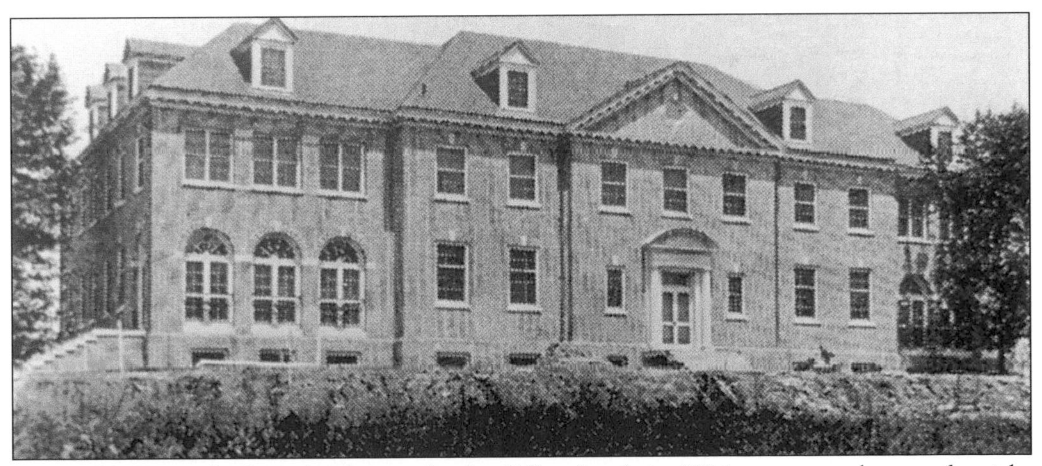

The Kelso Home, built on land given by the Offutt family in 1924, was an orphanage for girls. The Towson YMCA occupies the building located between Chesapeake and Allegheny Avenues. (Courtesy Baltimore County Public Library.)

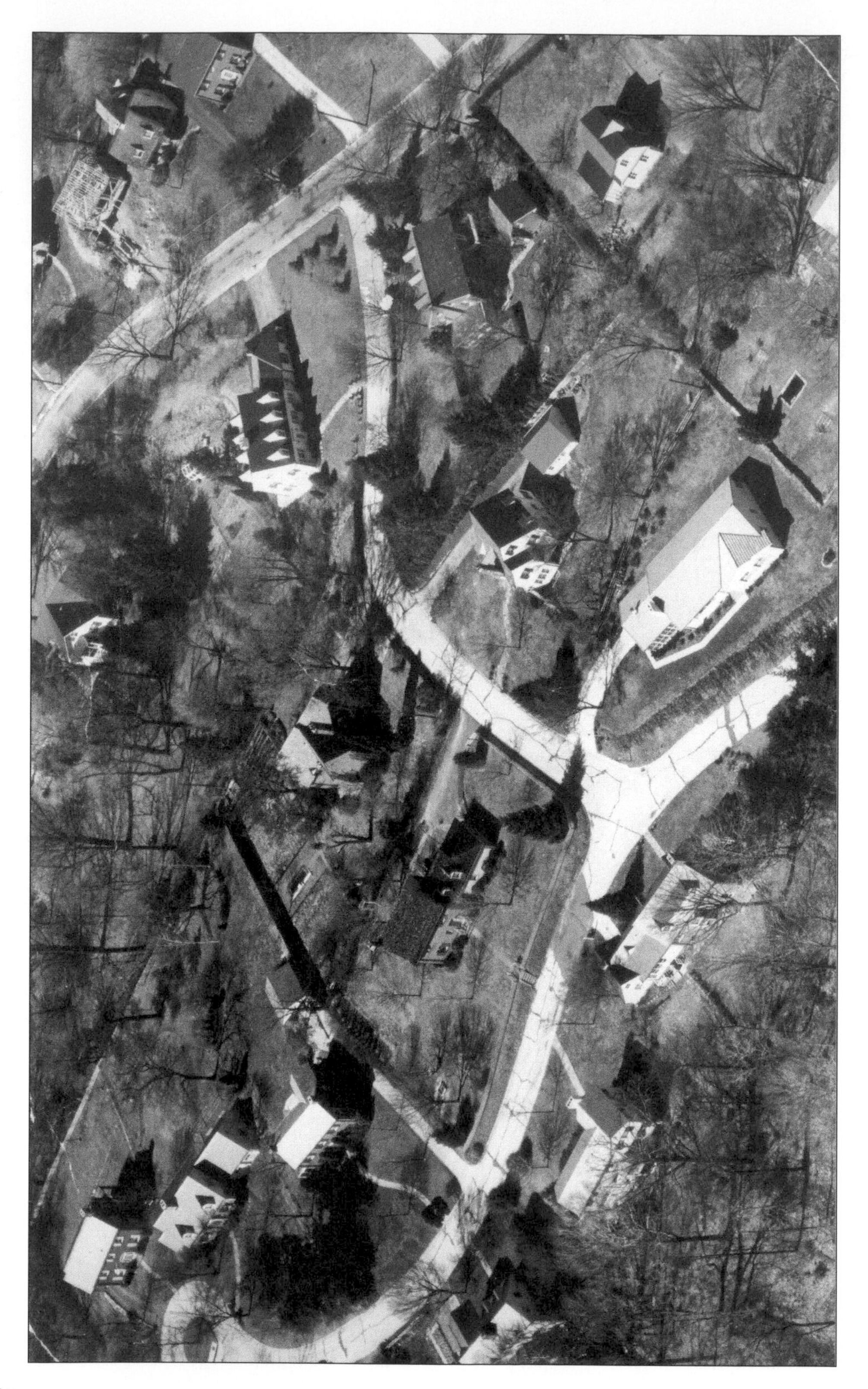

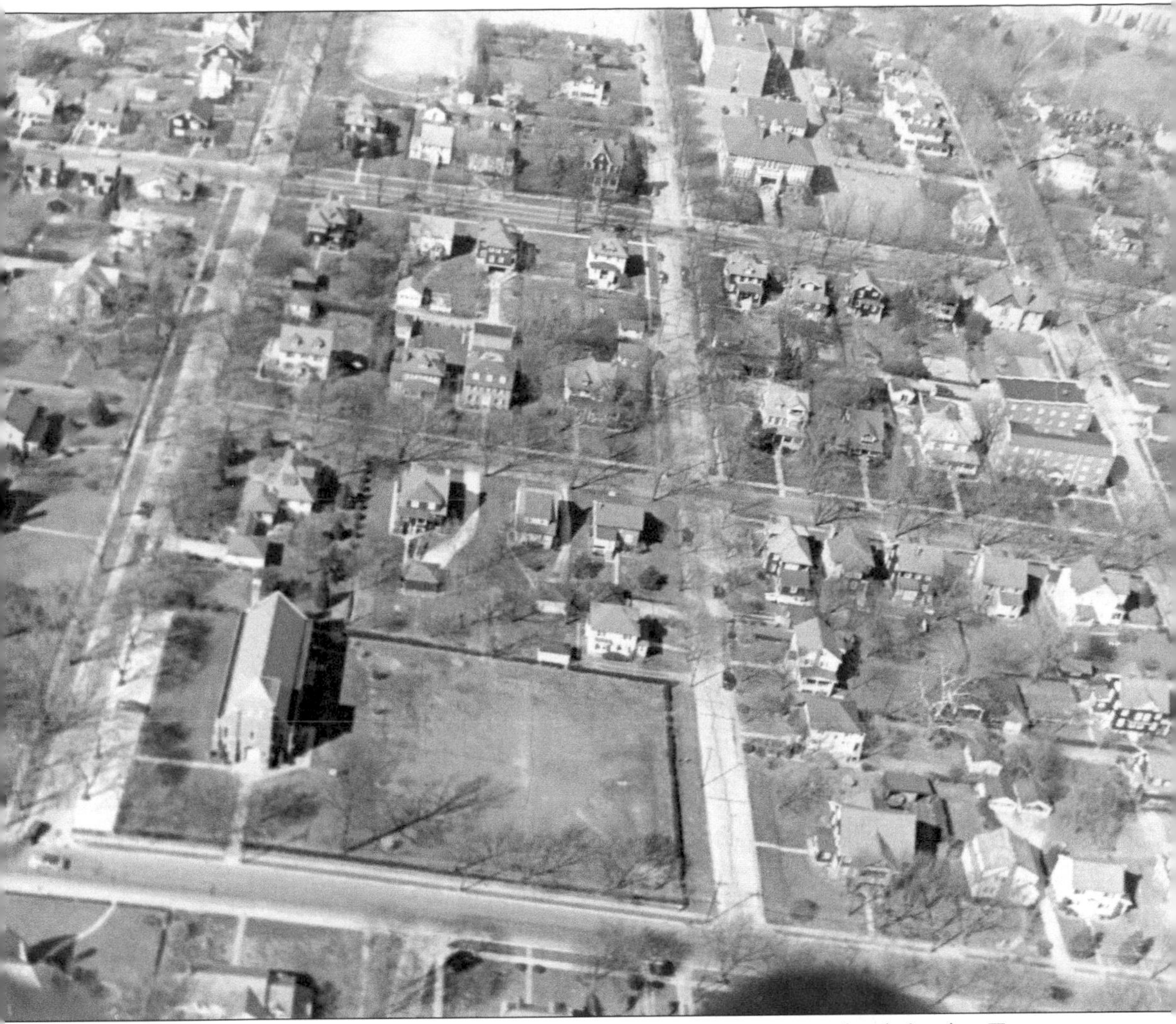

In this aerial shot of West Towson, Highland Avenue is seen on the left, the Towson Presbyterian Church is in the lower left corner, and Bosley Avenue is the road in the upper right. At the time this photograph was taken in the 1950s, this area was almost entirely residential, but now the houses east of Highland Avenue are offices. (Courtesy Mrs. Sarah Cunningham Larrabee.)

Page 54: This is an aerial view of Burnbrae Road and Bonnie Hill Road in the 1950s. The houses pictured were built on lots developed in the 1940s by Alfred S. Loizeaux, the landowner, with the help of the Roland Park Company. (Courtesy E. Dodson Poe IV.)

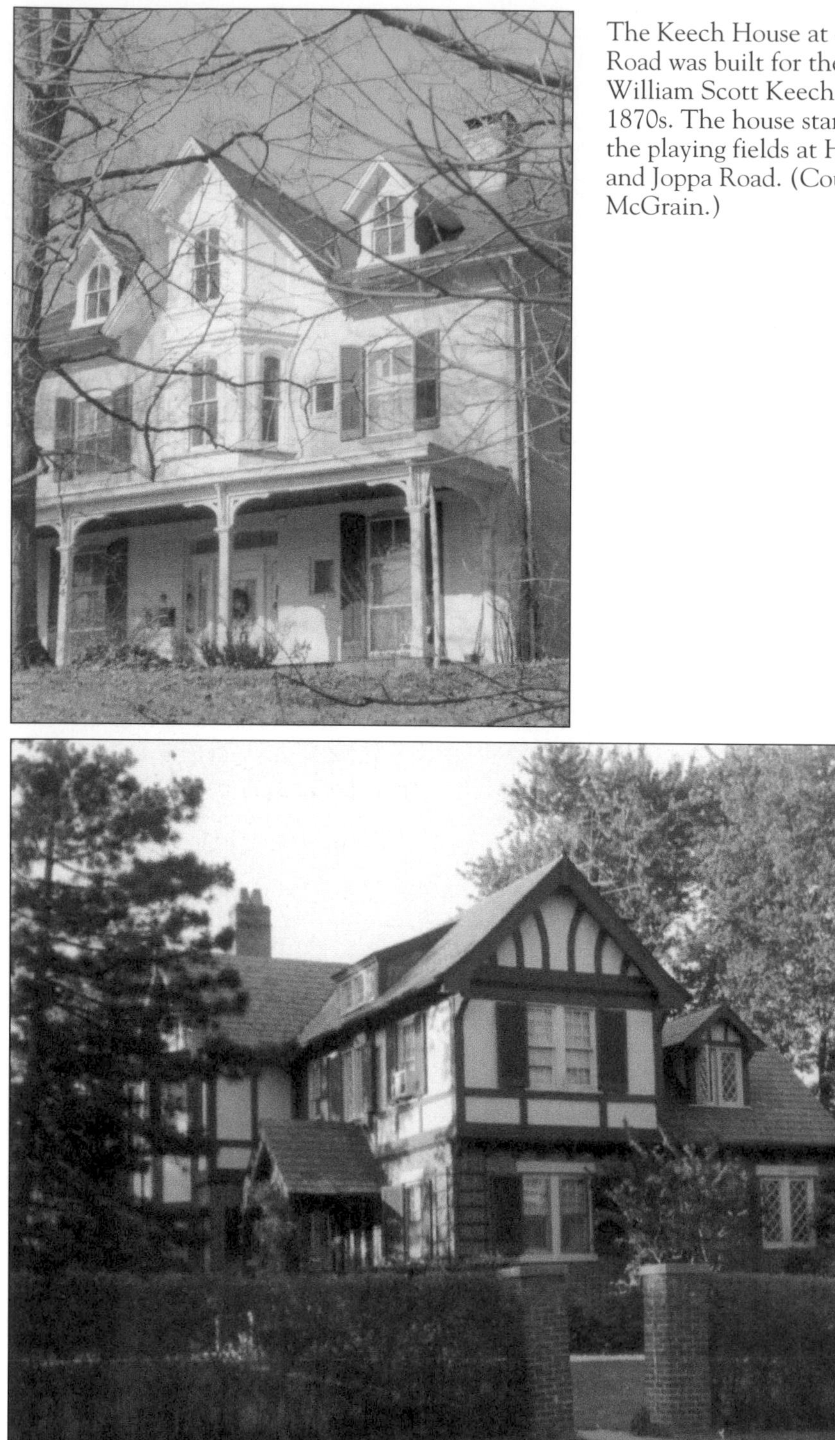

The Keech House at 404 W. Joppa Road was built for the Towson attorney William Scott Keech in the early 1870s. The house stands sentinel over the playing fields at Highland Avenue and Joppa Road. (Courtesy John W. McGrain.)

This attractive Tudor home, once owned by the Faulkner family, stood on the corner of Allegheny Avenue and Bosley Avenue. The house was razed when Bosley Avenue was widened. (Courtesy John W. McGrain.)

This beautiful home called Burnbrae, which means "hill on a brook," was built in 1917 on 20 acres of land on Woodbine Avenue by Alfred S. Loizeaux. (Courtesy A. Milton Loizeaux.)

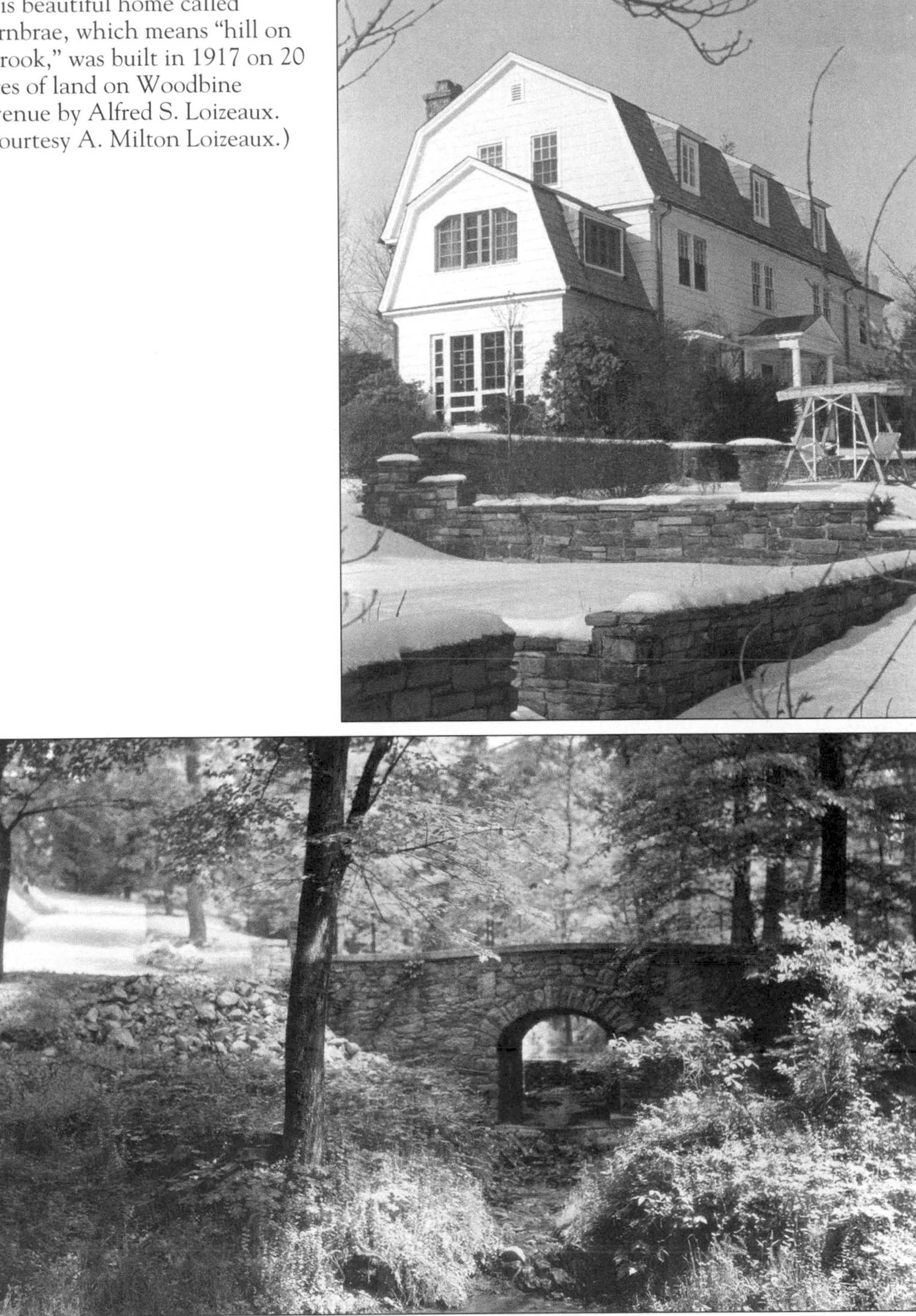

Before extensive residential construction, the intersection of Chesapeake Avenue and Burnbrae Road resembled a country lane. This picturesque bridge was built from stone excavated from Mr. Loizeaux's property when his house was built, and the bridge remains in use today. (Courtesy A. Milton Loizeaux.)

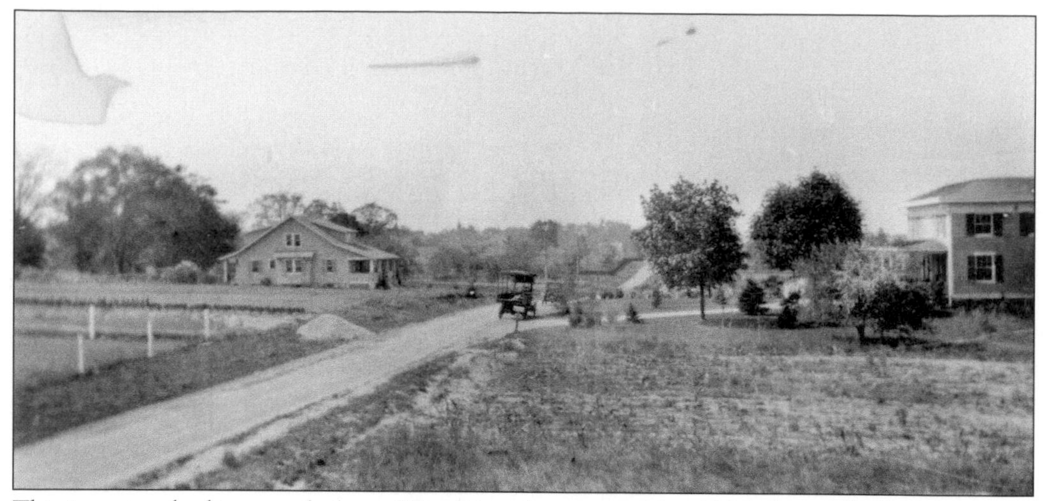

This is a view looking south down Woodbine Avenue in May 1926, from Allegheny Avenue. The houses in the distance are, at left, Groom's Dairy and, at right, Klein's Florist. Both buildings eventually became private homes. (Courtesy Baltimore County Public Library.)

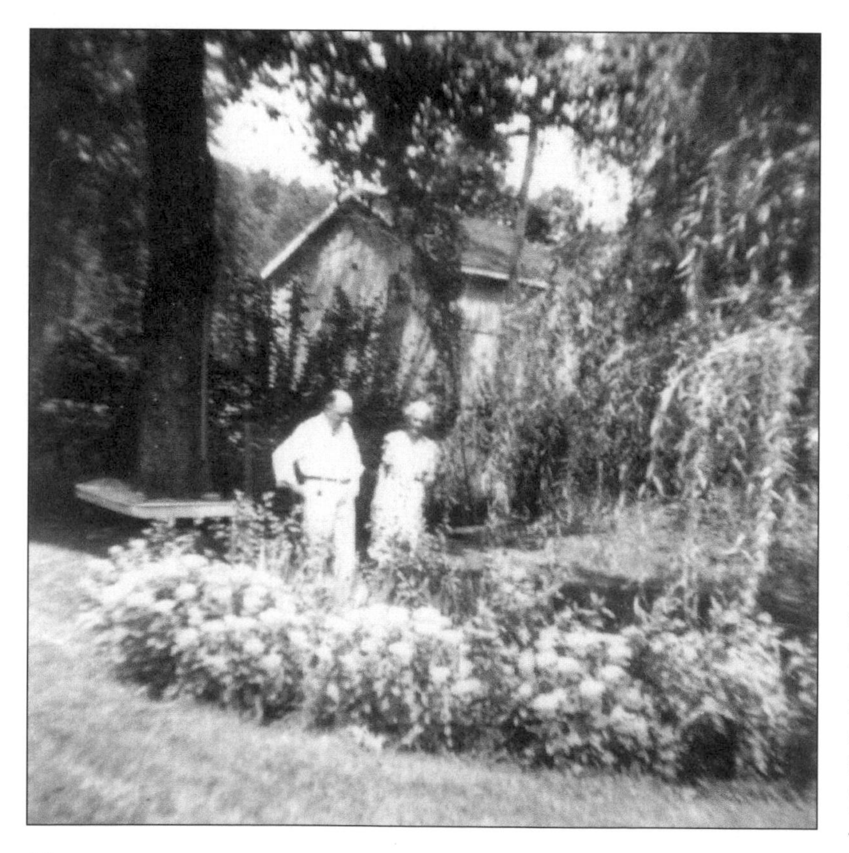

Mr. and Mrs. J.L. Anderson pose by the fishpond in their garden on Bosley Avenue. The house was razed to accommodate the expansion of the Towson Jail. This idyllic setting was a mere half block from the jail. (Courtesy Mrs. Joan Kaltenbach.)

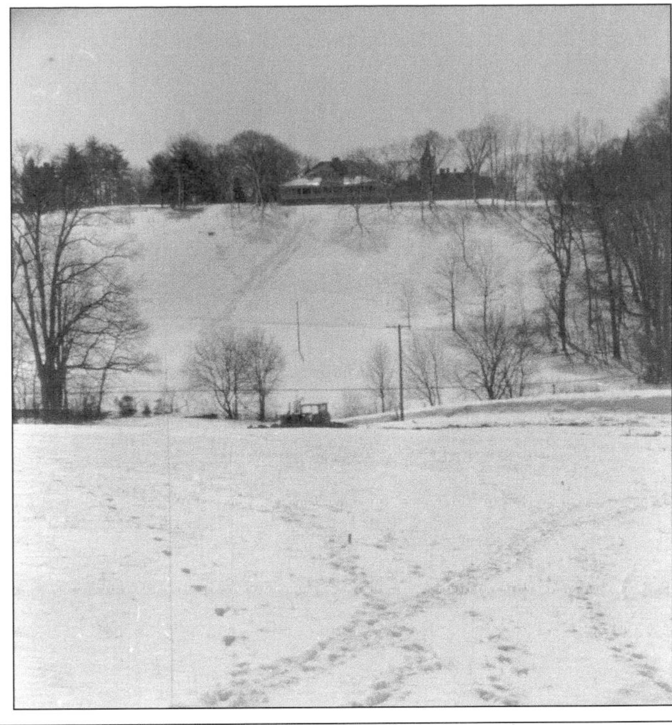

In the 1950s, one could see Sheppard Pratt's beautiful Casino from Dixie Drive in West Towson. The hillside had evidently been used for sledding, and revelers did not have to fear the high-speed motorists who use Towsontown Boulevard today. (Courtesy John W. McGrain.)

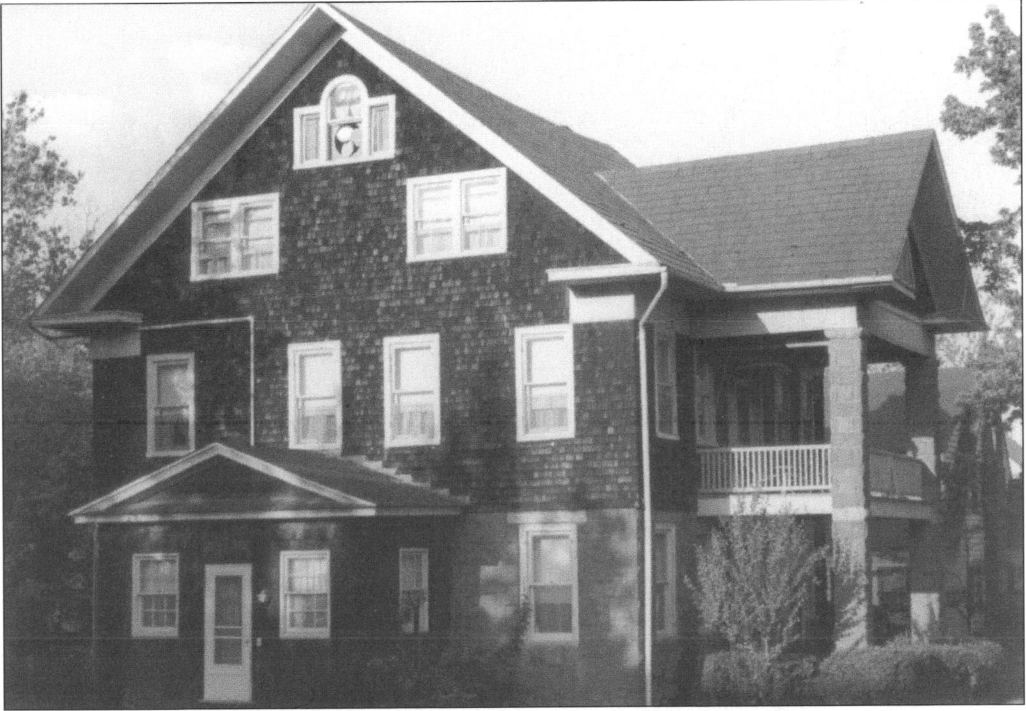

This house on Pennsylvania Avenue was still a private residence in the late 1950s, but like most of the houses in the first two blocks west of Bosley Avenue, it was converted to offices in the 1960s. Because of the proximity to the courthouse, most of the nearby buildings are law offices. (Courtesy John W. McGrain.)

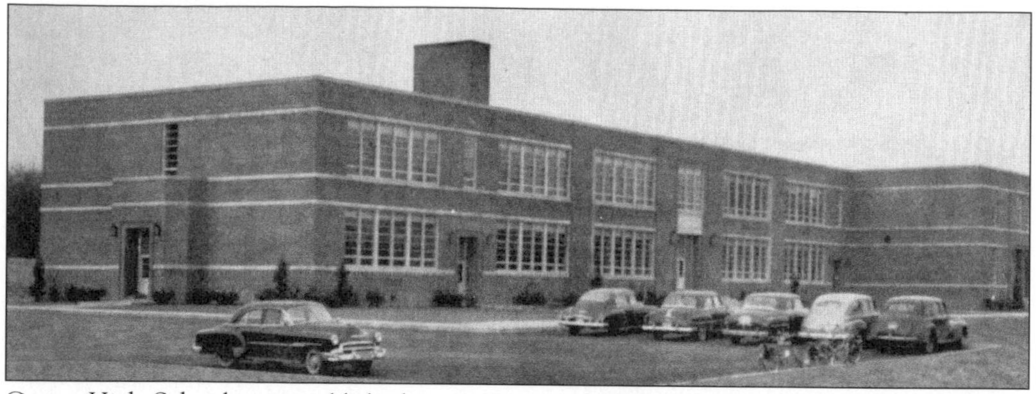

Carver High School was established in 1867 to provide an education for Towson's African-American community. The intense desire on the part of East Towson residents to educate their children was demonstrated by their resourcefulness in the face of prejudice. The first classes were held in an unused army barracks that had been transported to the site on Hillen Road. Money to support the school had to be privately raised, as Baltimore County would not appropriate money for the construction of African-American schools until 1897. The Carver School on Jefferson Avenue was built in 1939, and in 1949, the facility pictured above was constructed. (Courtesy Louis S. Diggs Photographic Collection of African American Life in Baltimore County, MD.)

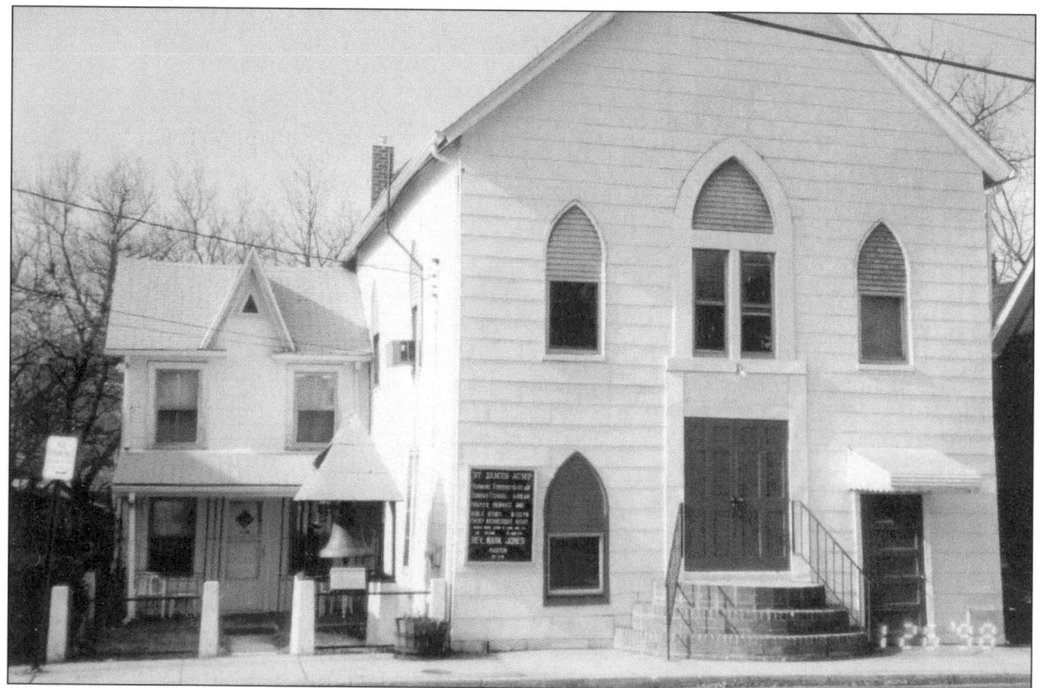

The St. James AUMP Church first held services in the Carver School. The Reverend J.H. Manley, determined to raise funds for a proper sanctuary, thought of several fun and creative fundraising events, one of which was a "Pigeon Toss." A live pigeon was gently tossed in the air, and the first person to catch it would win a prize. With resolve like this, it was not long before the St. James congregation had their own church, which was completed in 1881. The church on Jefferson Avenue is still very active in the East Towson community. (Courtesy Louis S. Diggs Photographic Collection of African American Life in Baltimore County, MD.)

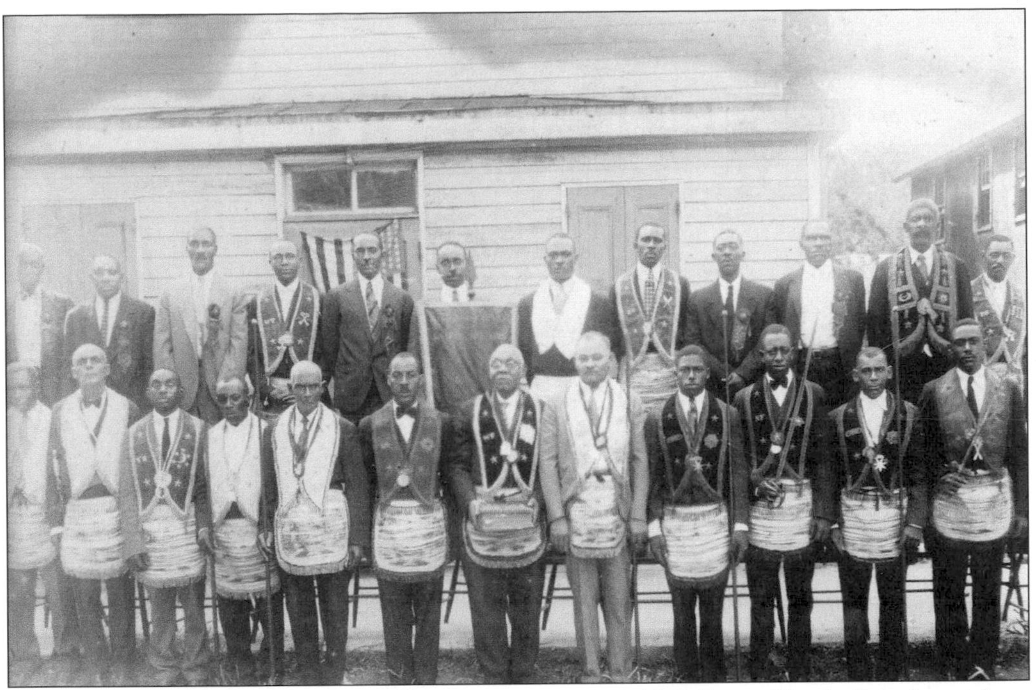

An early 1900s photograph shows the East Towson Odd Fellows. The hall is located on Jefferson Avenue, next door to the St. James Church. (Courtesy Louis S. Diggs Photographic Collection of African American Life in Baltimore County, MD.)

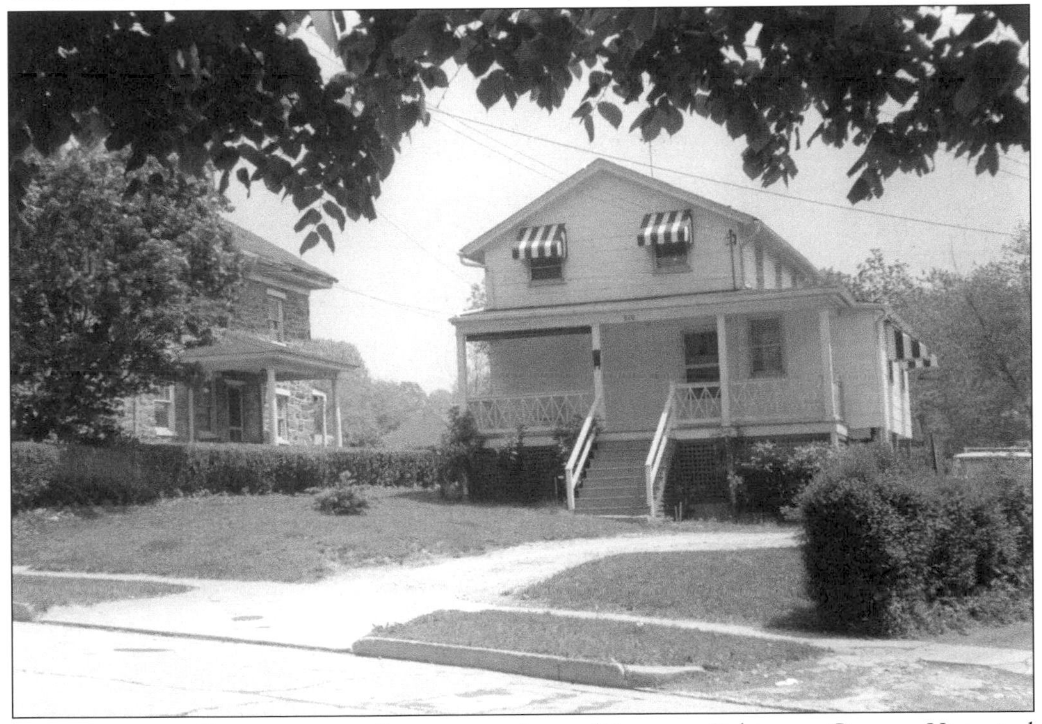

East Towson still retains its village atmosphere. (Courtesy Baltimore County Historical Society.)

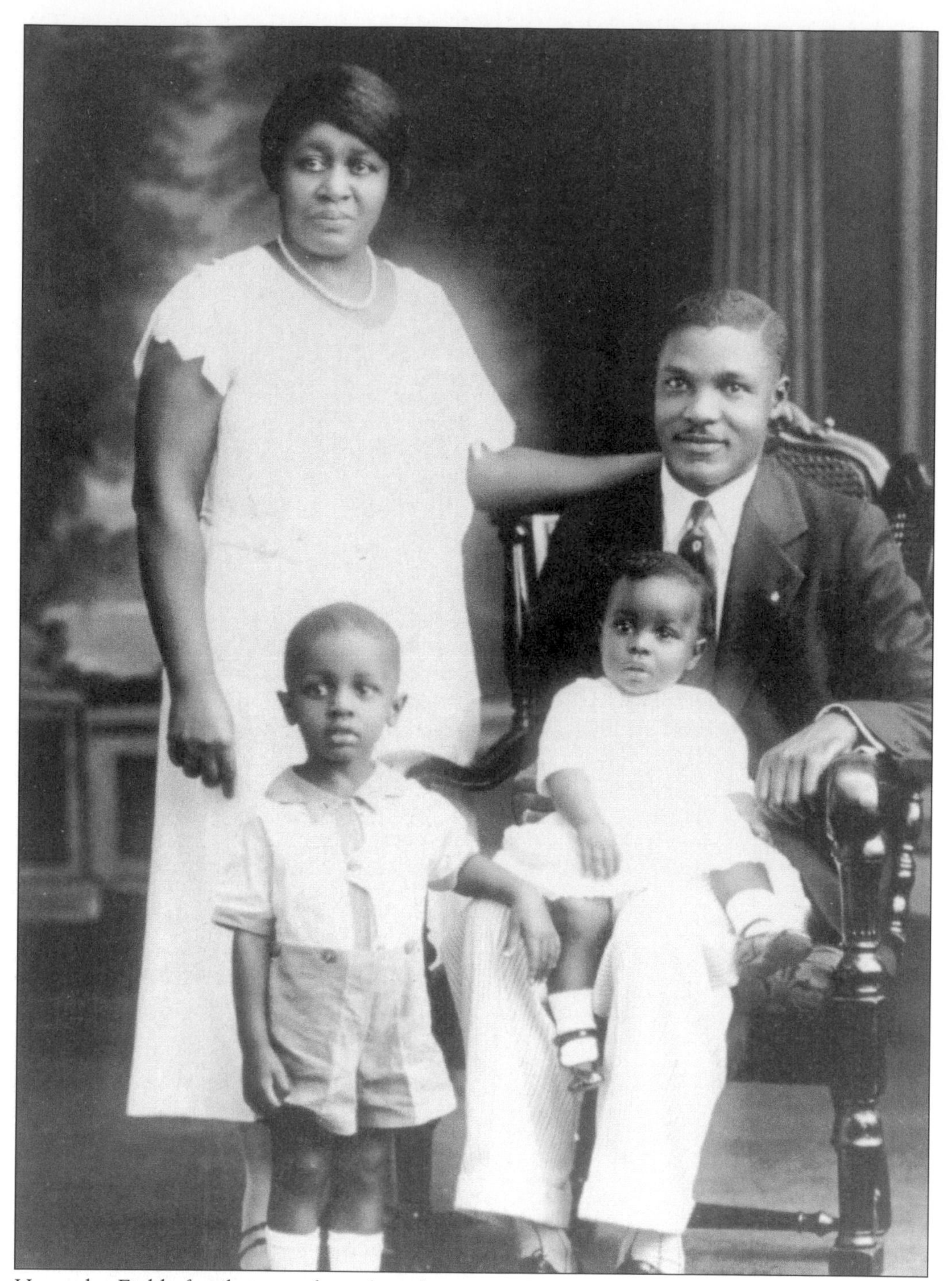

Here, the Fields family poses for a formal portrait. East Towson residents have reason to be proud. As homeowners, they have been able to unite and fend off developers who, over the decades, sought to replace the community with new buildings and parking facilities. (Courtesy Louis S. Diggs Photographic Collection of African American Life in Baltimore County, MD.)

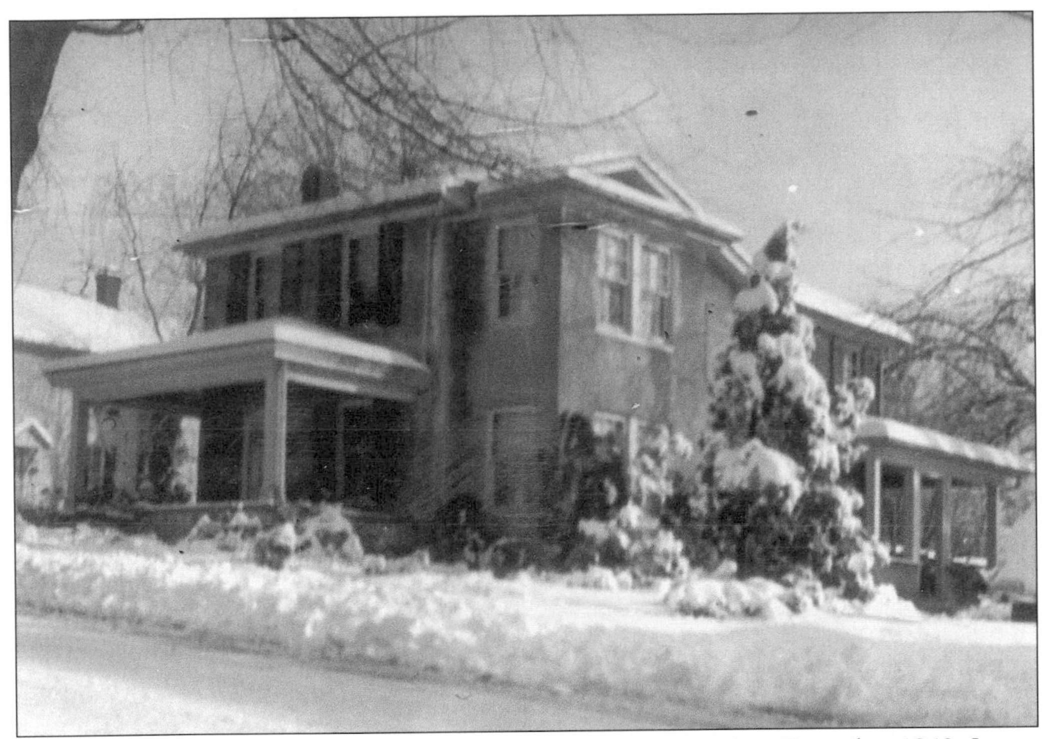

The Griffin-Goodwin House on 504 Virginia Avenue is pictured in December 1948. It was razed in October 1973. (Courtesy John W. McGrain.)

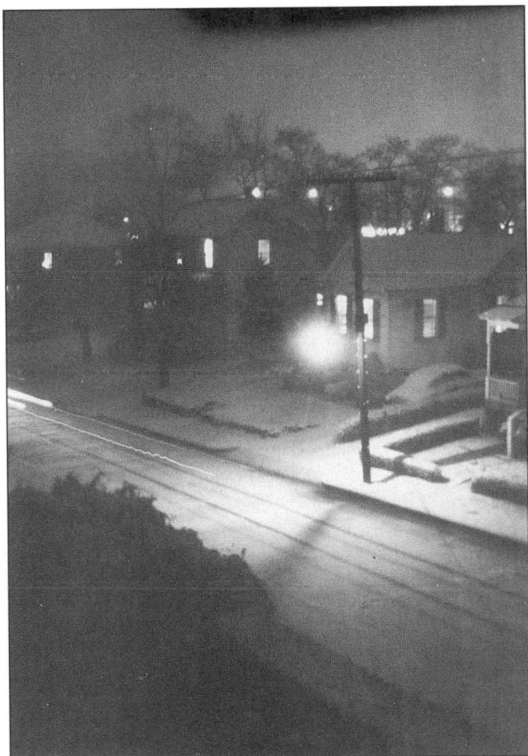

Willow Avenue in East Towson sits quietly a few nights before Christmas in 1950. (Courtesy John W. McGrain.)

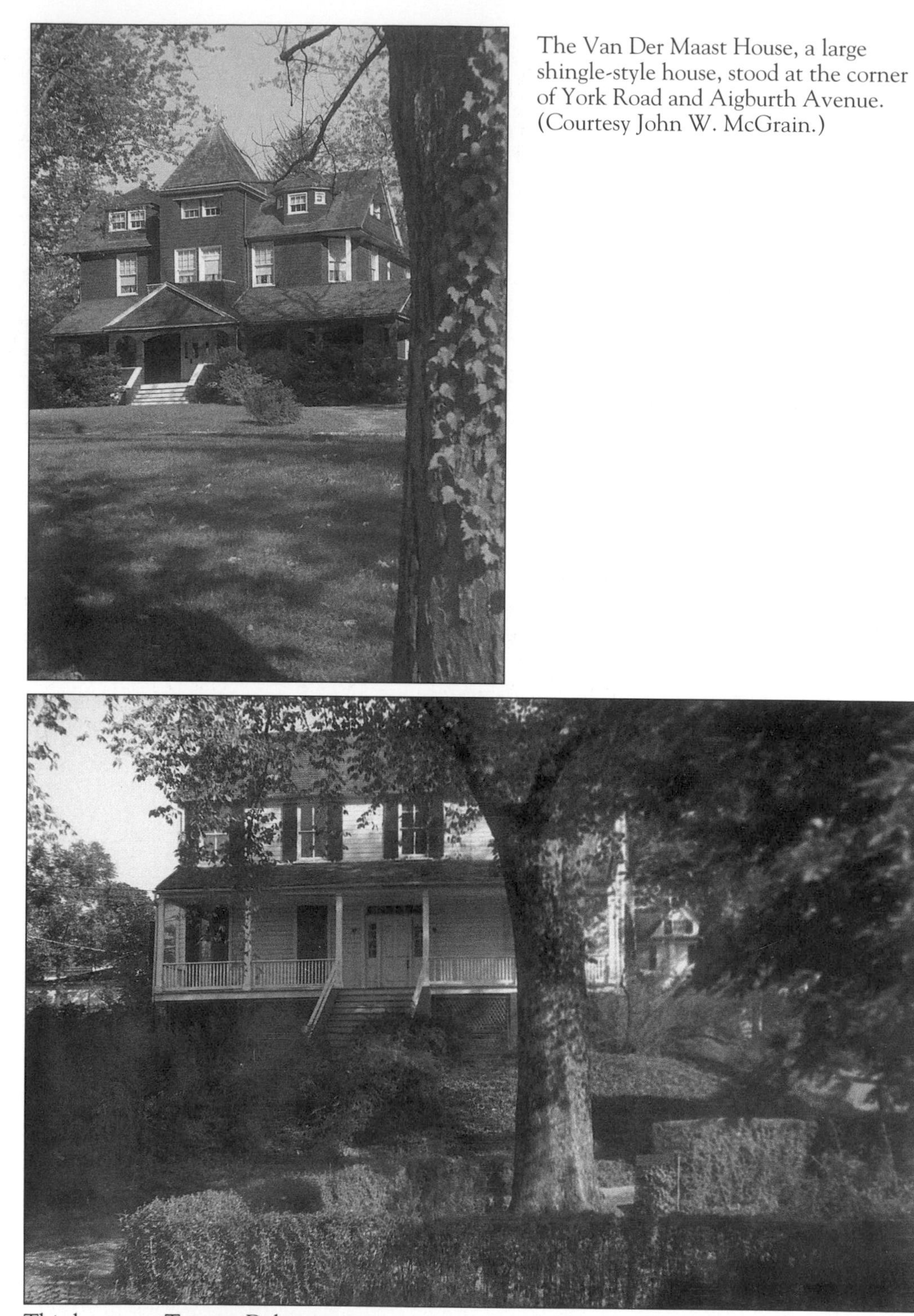

The Van Der Maast House, a large shingle-style house, stood at the corner of York Road and Aigburth Avenue. (Courtesy John W. McGrain.)

This home on Terrace Dale was on property surrounded by the nationally recognized Towson Nurseries. This frame house was built by one of the general contractors who also built many of the houses in Roland Park. (Courtesy John W. McGrain.)

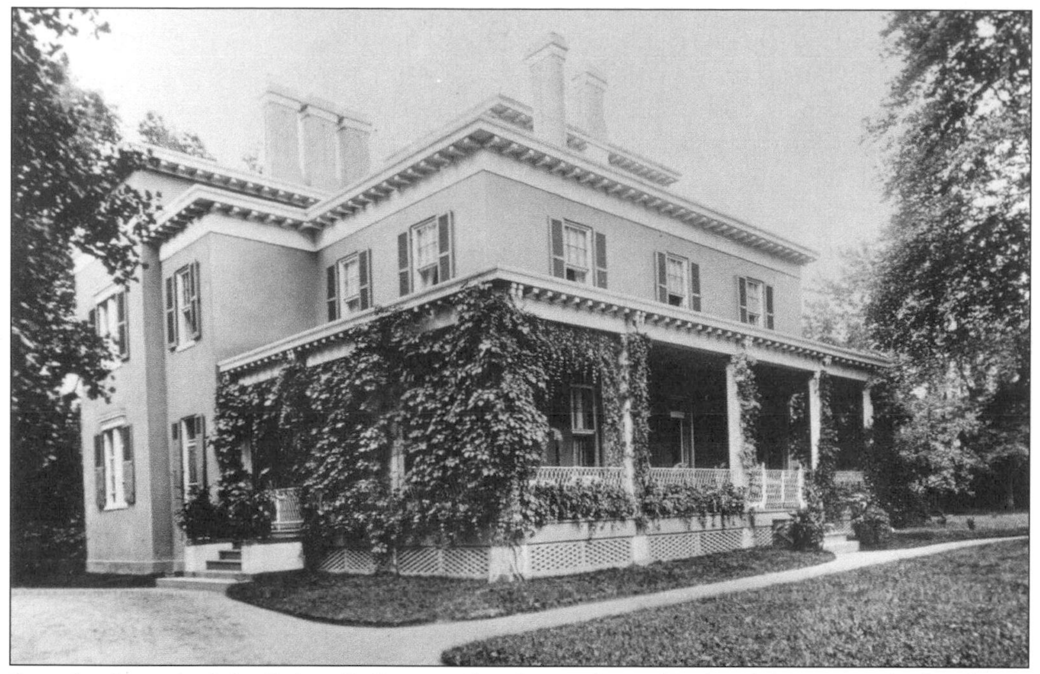

Stoneleigh was built by Robert P. Brown, a brother-in-law to Frederick Harrison who lived next door at Anneslie. In the 1920s, 123 acres were sold in lots to create the neighborhood named for the estate. The driveway into the estate became Stoneleigh Road. The house was demolished in 1955, and the remaining 7 acres were used for the building of another 77 homes. (Courtesy Baltimore County Public Library.)

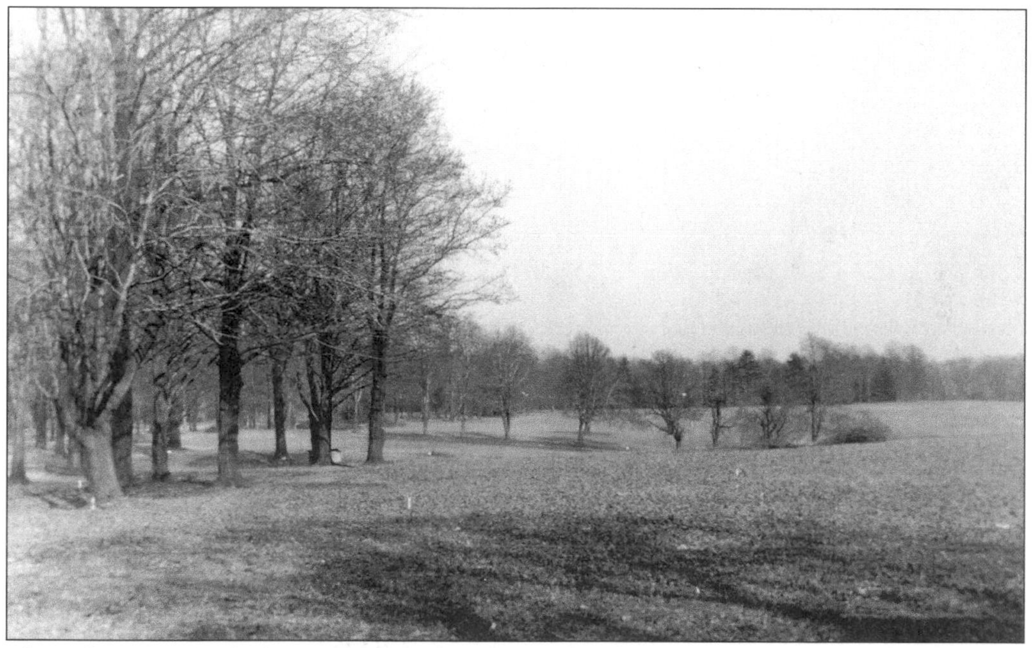

The rolling farmland of Stoneleigh is seen here before construction began in the 1920s. The pond that had once furnished ice for the Browns became the Stoneleigh community pool. (Courtesy Baltimore County Public Library.)

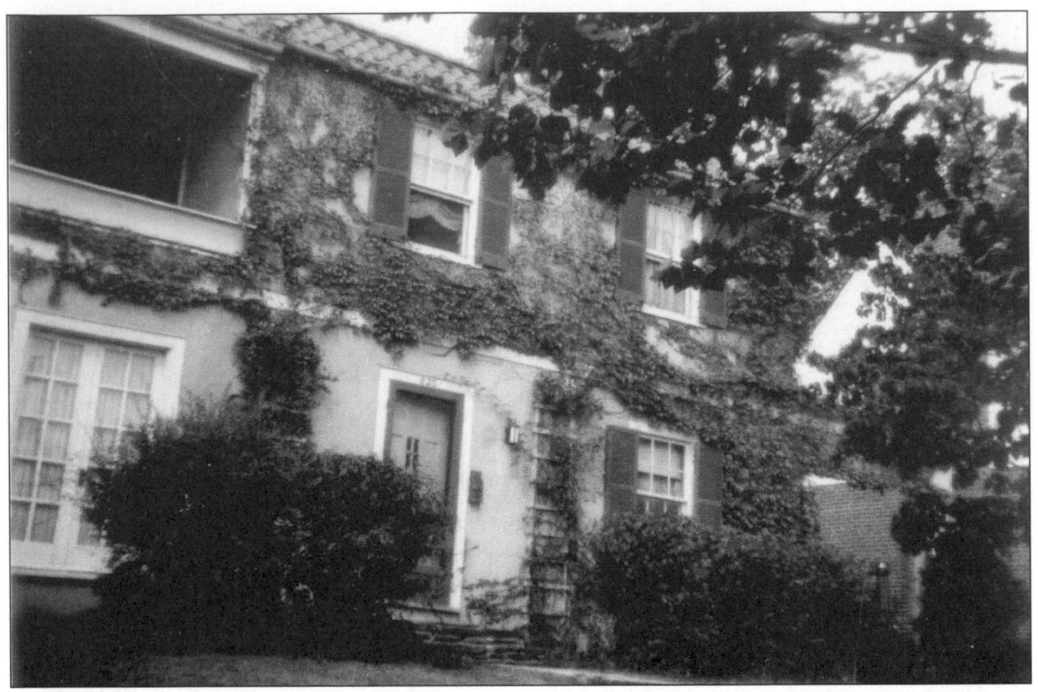

820 Kingstone Road (above) and 714 Register Avenue (below), pictured in the 1940s, are examples of the varied architectural styles that make Stoneleigh the lovely neighborhood it is. (Courtesy Katherine Reno Calvert.)

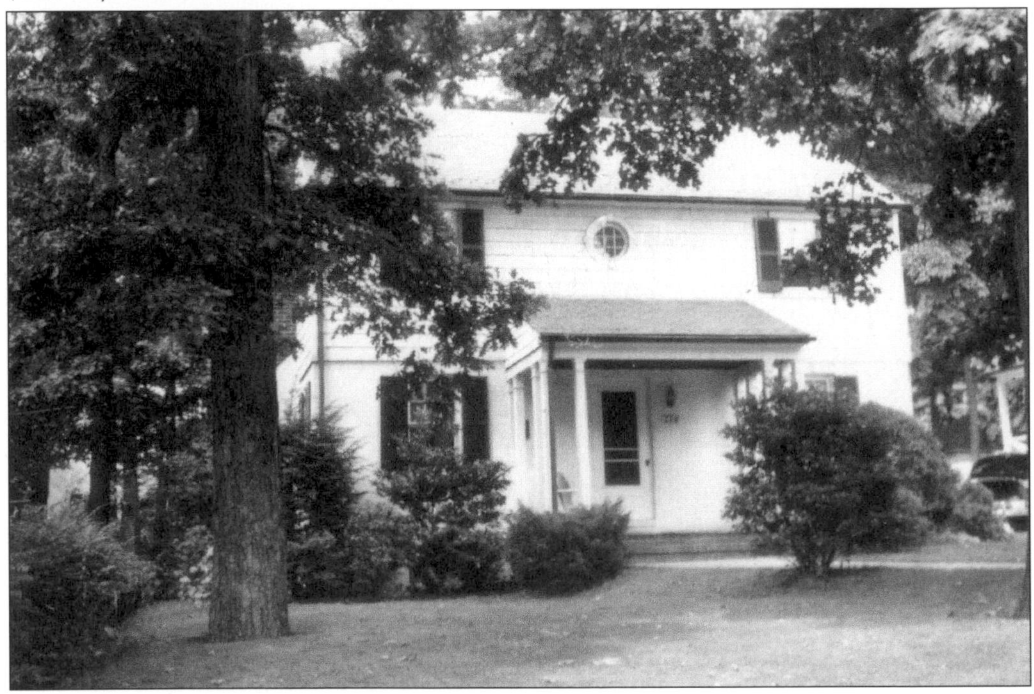

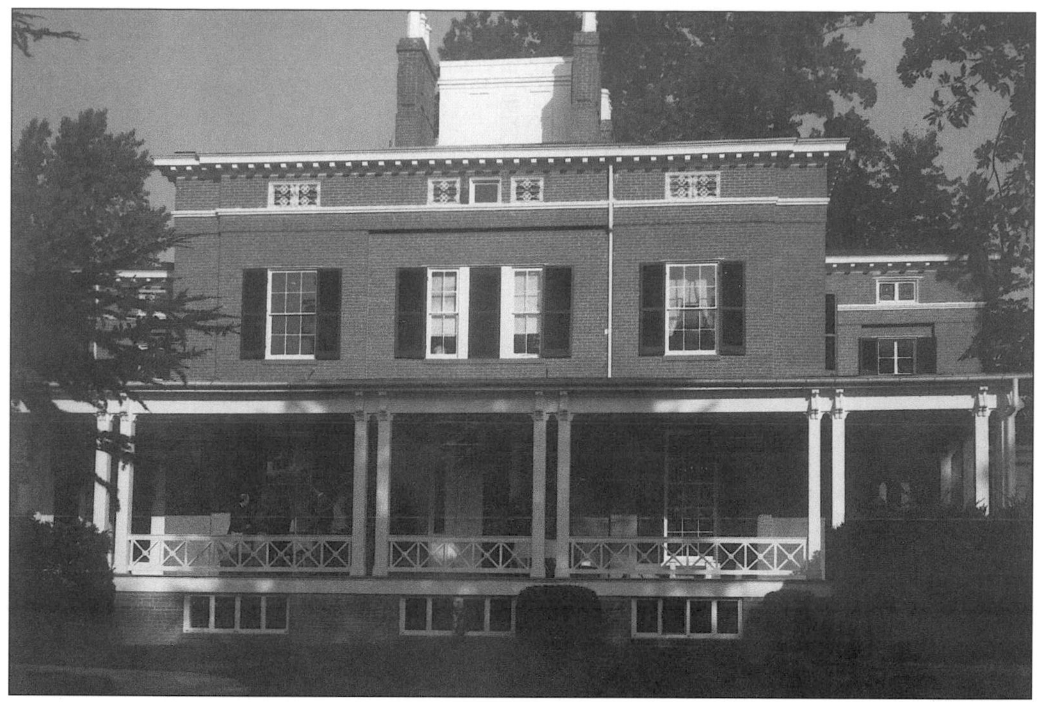

Dumbarton was built by Robert Taylor in 1854, 1.5 miles south of Towson. In 1860, Joseph Reiman purchased the farm as a summer home. In the 1920s and 1930s, the farm began to undergo a radical transformation, becoming the site for the Rodgers Forge community. Dumbarton still stands, however, serving as the Baltimore's Actor's Conservancy. (Courtesy John W. McGrain.)

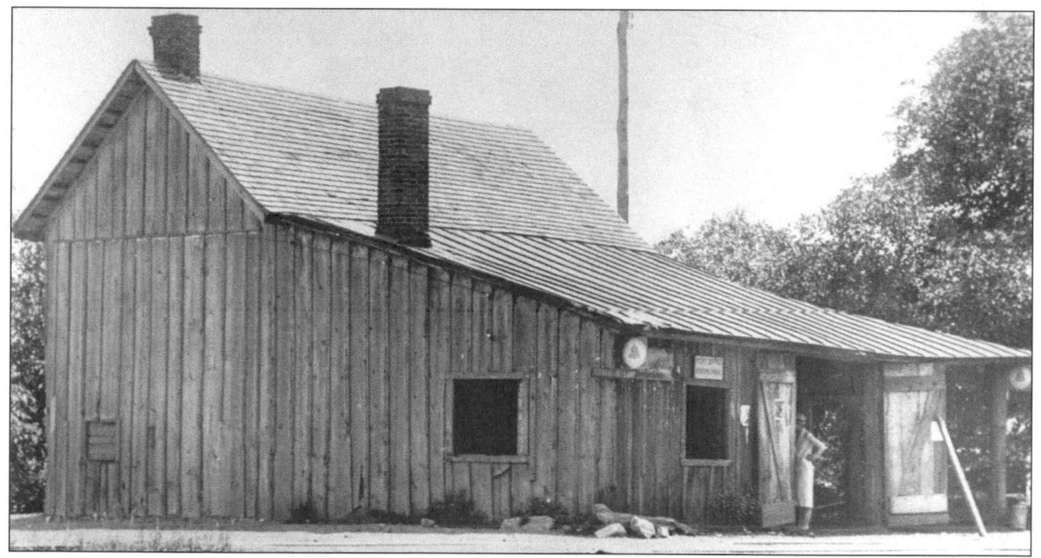

The Rodgers Forge was built in 1800 at the southeast corner of Stevenson Lane and York Road. For four generations, the Rodgers family provided blacksmith and cartwright services to the community, including the Elkridge Hunt Club. The Forge burned in 1946 but lives on in the name of the community to the west of York Road. (Courtesy Baltimore County Historical Society.)

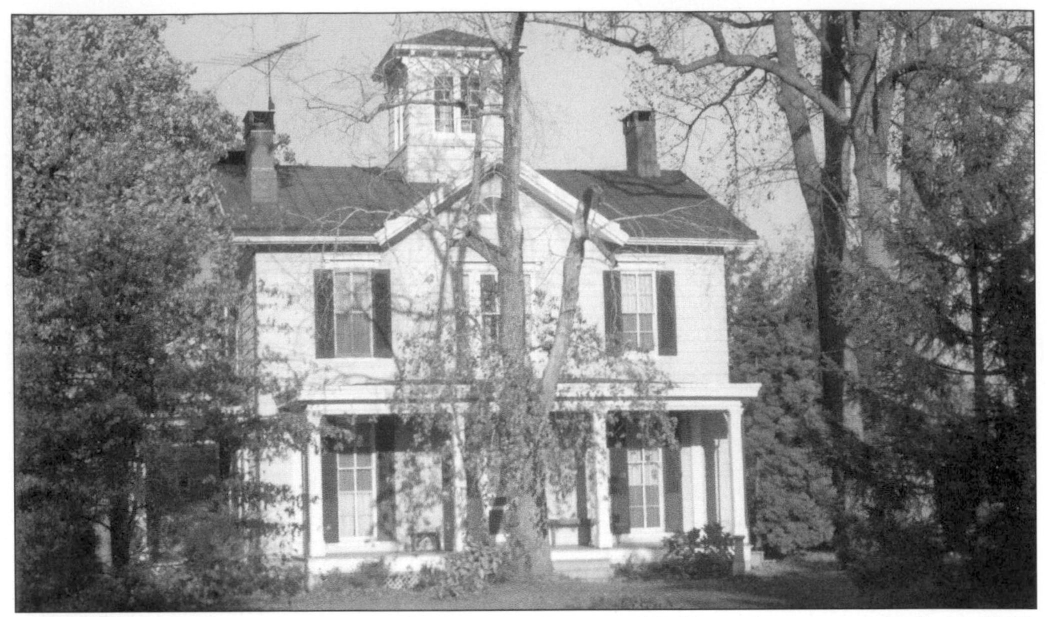

The Italianate villa at the corner of Stevenson Lane and Bellona Avenue was built in 1873. Owned by the Shepard family, the property extended northward to what is now Armagh Village, which was subdivided from the property in 1925. One of the Shepards recalled hunting for wild turkey eggs in the woods behind the house, where the Rodgers Forge Apartments now stand! (Courtesy John W. McGrain.)

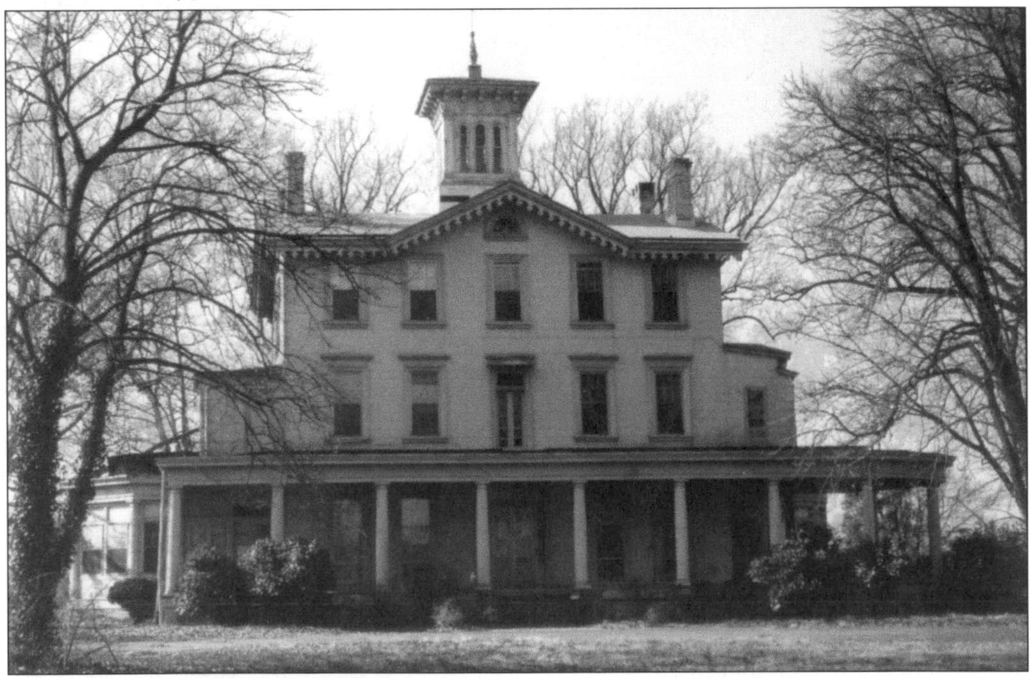

The Italianate villa known as Blenheim on Bellona Avenue was built for William Fisher. The house was bequeathed in 1920 by Mrs. William Lanahan to the Sisters of Mercy, who used it as a convalescent home and called it Mercy Villa. The house was razed in 1976 to make way for a modern facility. (Courtesy John W. McGrain.)

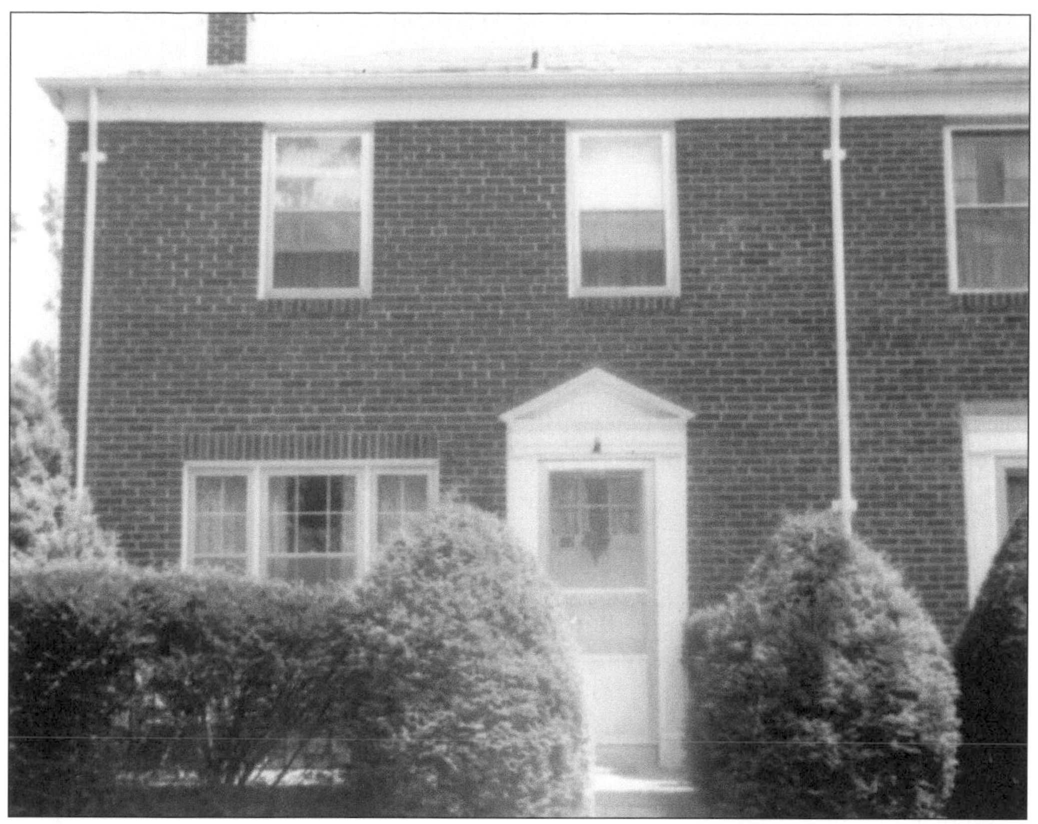

Developed in the 1930s by James Keelty & Sons, Rodgers Forge features colonial and Tudor row houses. The house at 127 Stevenson Lane appears here in the late 1950s. (Courtesy Katherine Reno Calvert.)

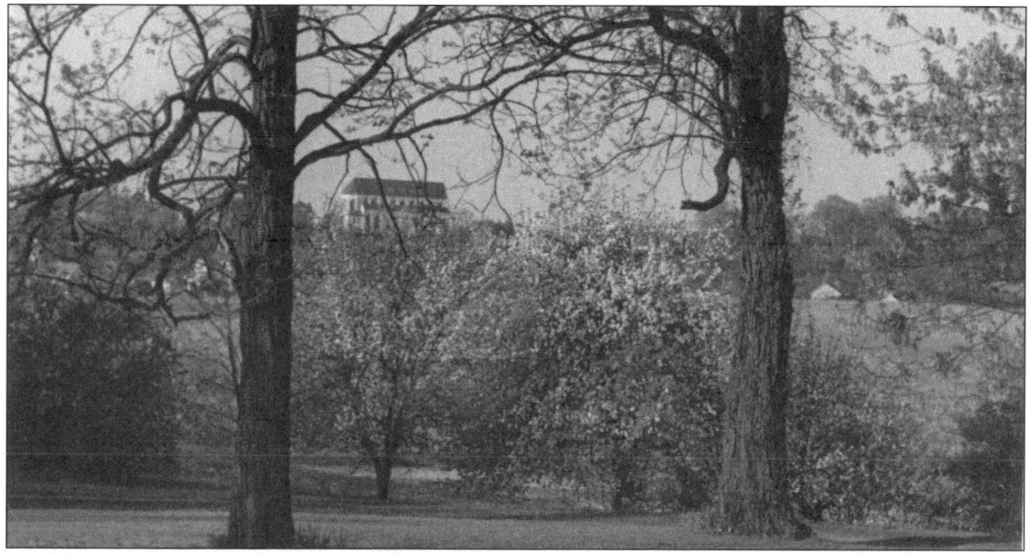

A glimpse of the Church of Immaculate Conception can be seen through an orchard located in the fields along Dulaney Valley Road. This photograph was taken in the 1930s. (Courtesy Baltimore County Historical Society.)

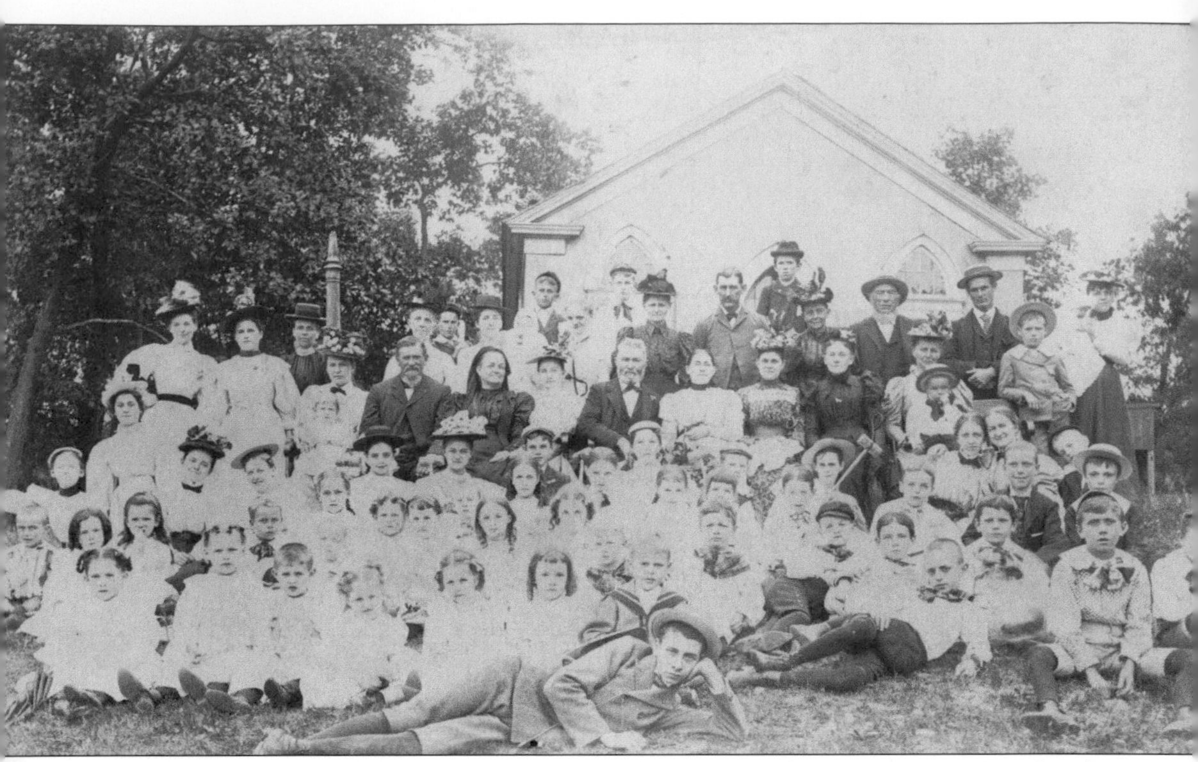

The Epsom Chapel's 1899 congregation gathered on the front lawn of Towson's first church. In 1839, Henry Chew gave 2 acres for the purpose of providing Towson with a place to hold worship services. The church welcomed any Protestant denomination. (Courtesy Baltimore County Historical Society.)

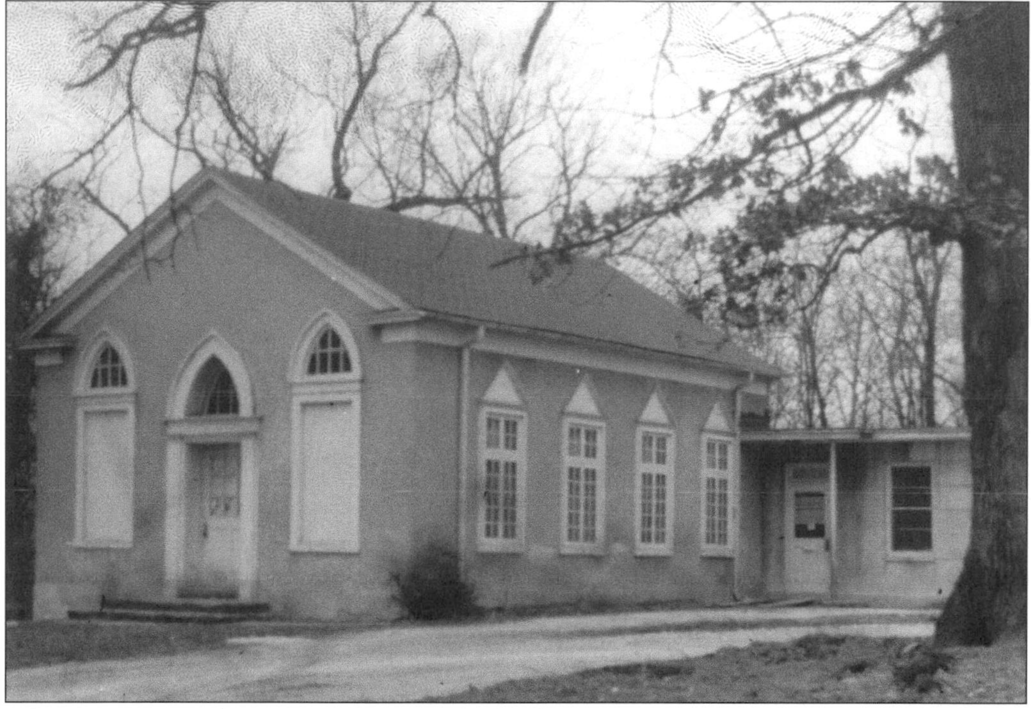

After Towson's Christian community built their own sanctuaries, Epsom Chapel was occasionally used by churches with no meeting place of their own and by the Boy Scouts. The building is beginning to show its age in this photograph. (Courtesy Baltimore County Historical Society.)

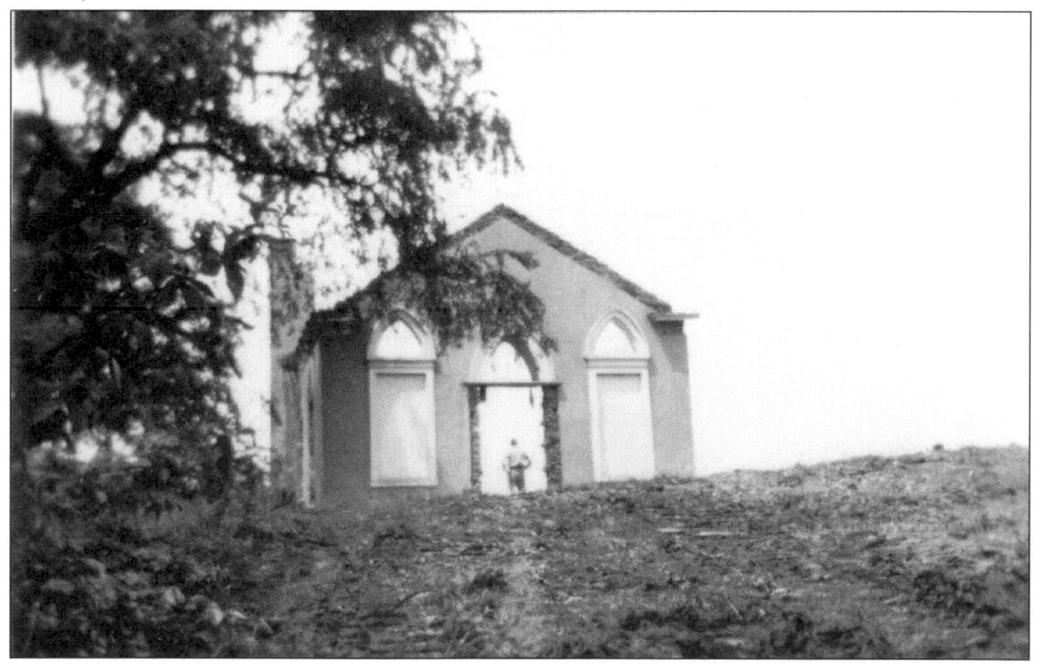

Epsom Chapel was in serious decay in April of 1950. The once important center of Towson's religious community would be razed two years later. (Courtesy John W. McGrain.)

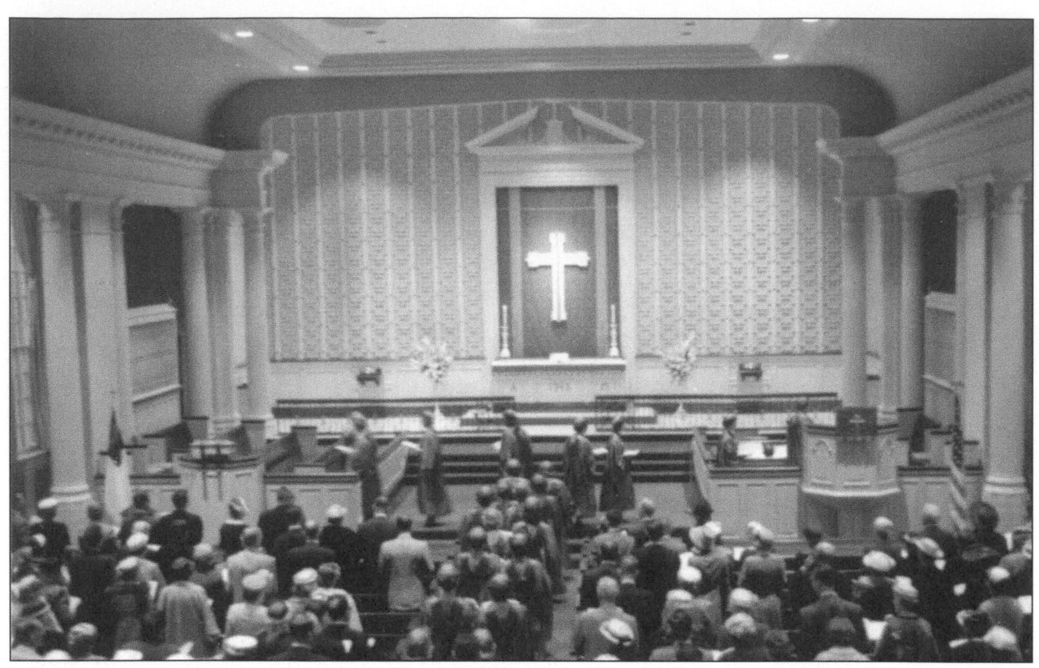

The interior of Towson United Methodist Church on Hampton Lane is pictured here in 1958, just after construction was completed. The church was built to accommodate the combined congregations of Towson Methodist Protestant Church, which previously met in the building now known as the Woman's Club of Towson, and Towson Methodist on York Road, which had been razed for new construction. The two congregations combined their resources and built the graceful sanctuary on Hampton Lane. (Courtesy Baltimore County Historical Society.)

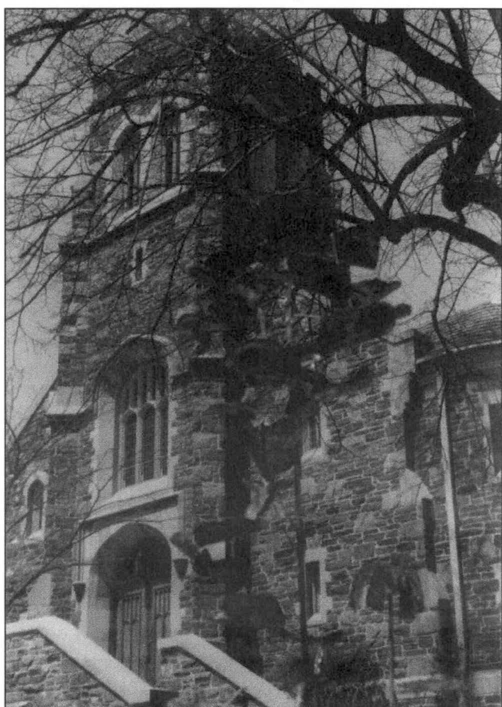

Calvary Baptist Church is seen overlooking Courthouse Square in the 1950s. Though its view has changed a bit, the church still watches over the square from the corner of Pennsylvania Avenue and Baltimore Avenue. (Courtesy John W. McGrain.)

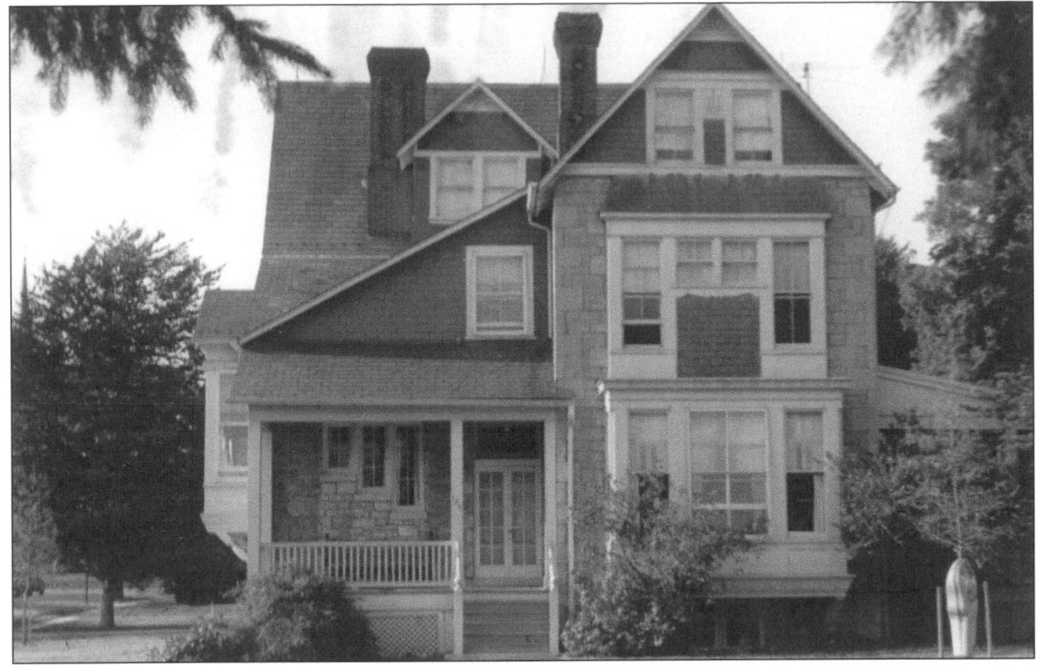

Originally the rectory for Trinity Episcopal Church, this lovely Victorian building on Allegheny Avenue now serves as the Surprise Shop. (Courtesy Baltimore County Historical Society.)

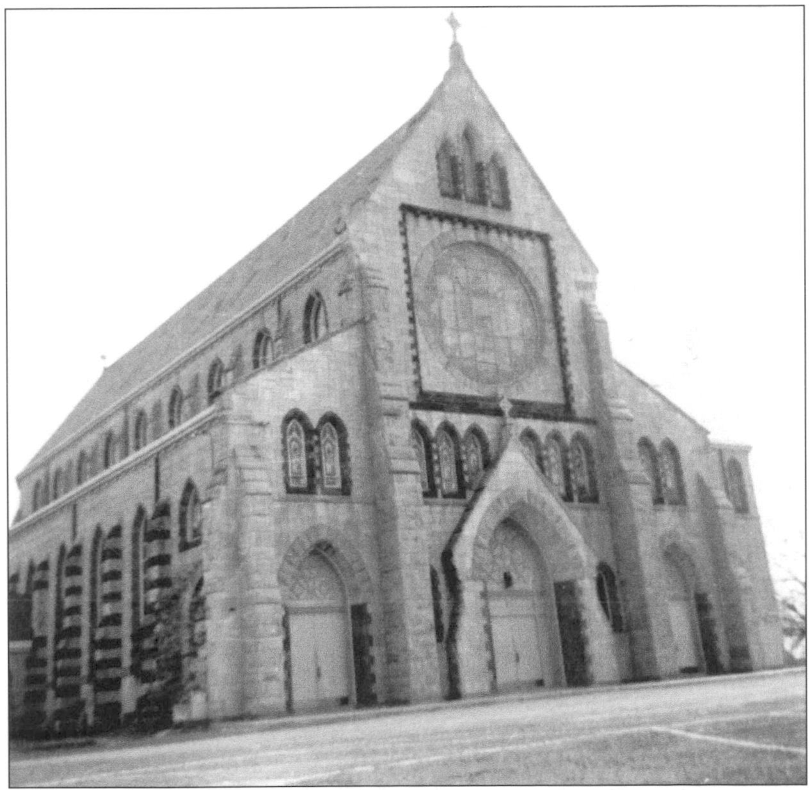

This early picture shows Immaculate Conception. (Courtesy Baltimore County Historical Society.)

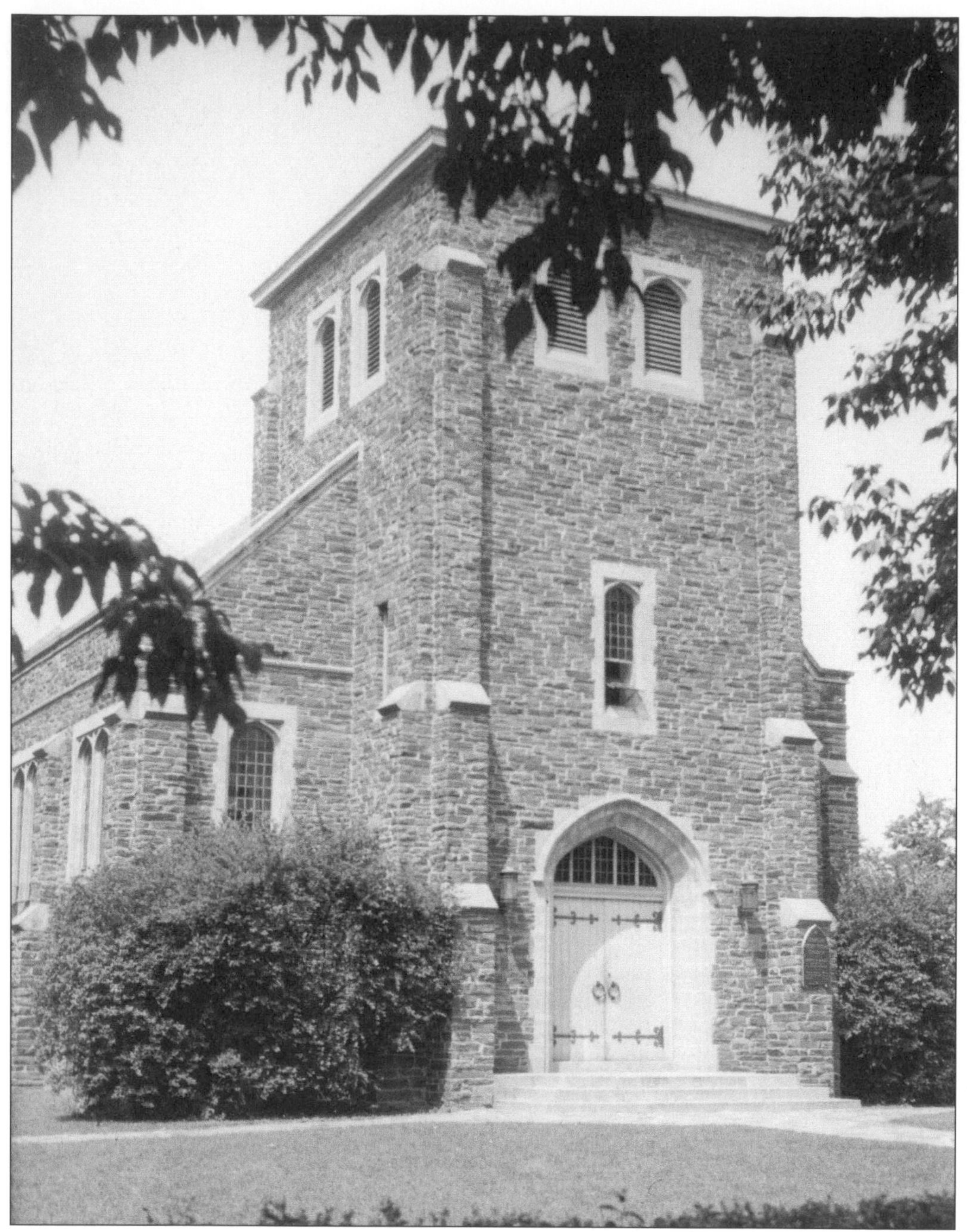

The Towson Presbyterian Church was built on West Chesapeake Avenue at Highland Avenue in 1927. In the 1950s, the church expanded and added a preschool, which has been attended by many local children. (Courtesy Mrs. Sarah Galloway Larrabee.)

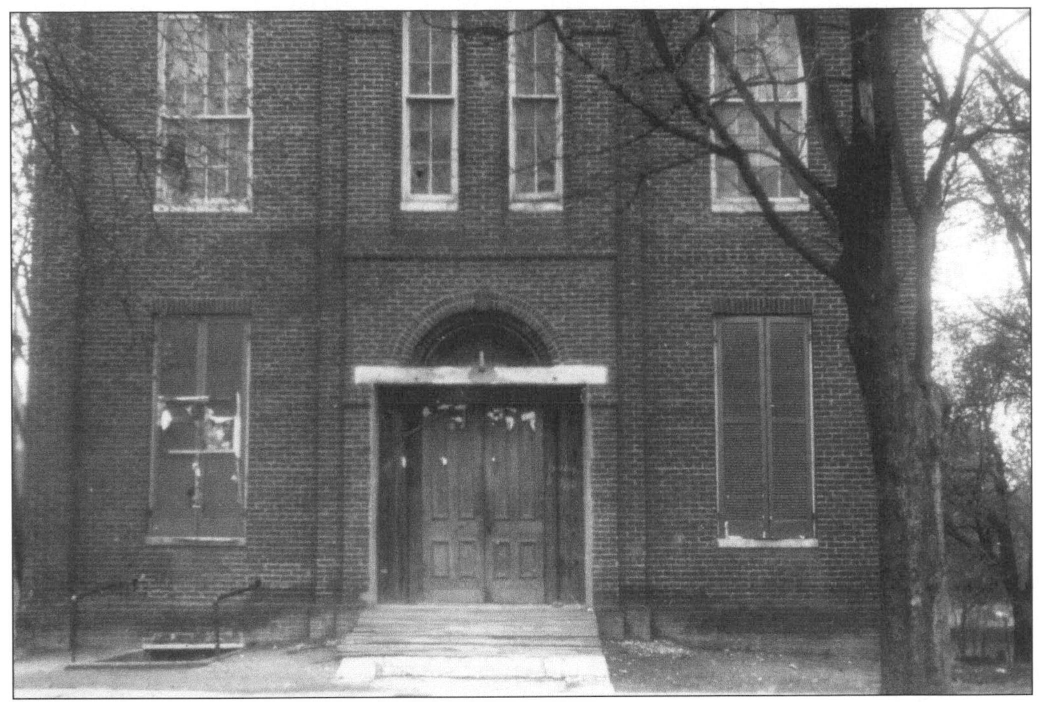

The old Towson High School on East Chesapeake Avenue was built in 1873. Fire destroyed the building in 1906. (Courtesy Carleton Seitz.)

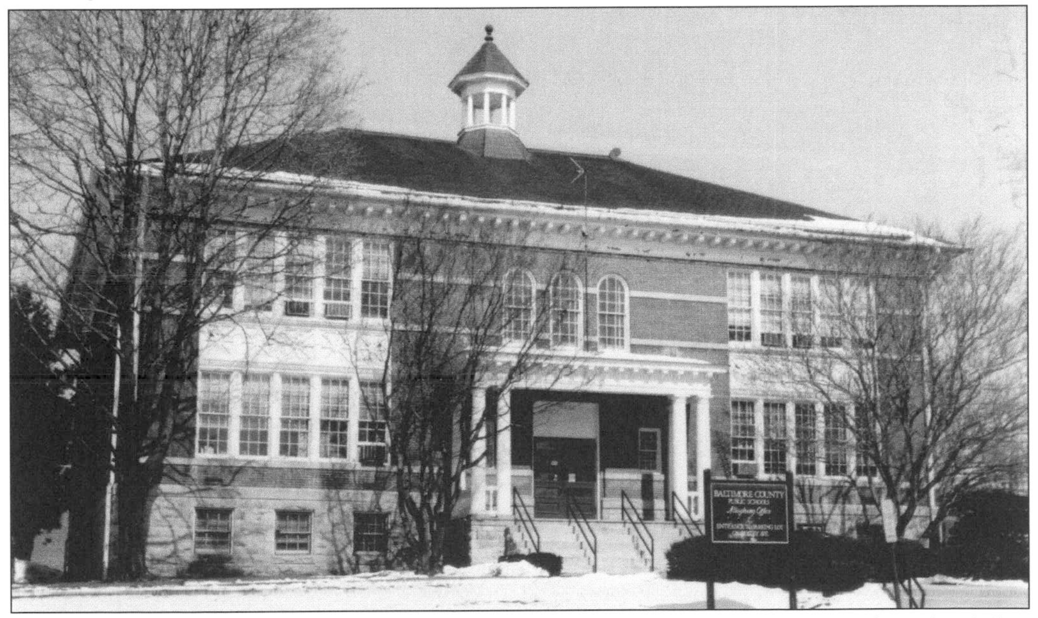

The Towson High School on Allegheny Avenue was built in 1907 to replace the school that burned the previous year. The building became the elementary school in 1926, when a larger facility was built on the corner of Joppa Road and Central Avenue. The rapid growth in the school's physical plant certainly reflects the rapid increase in Towson's population. The Chesapeake Avenue school is currently home to the Baltimore County Office of Personnel. (Courtesy John W. McGrain.)

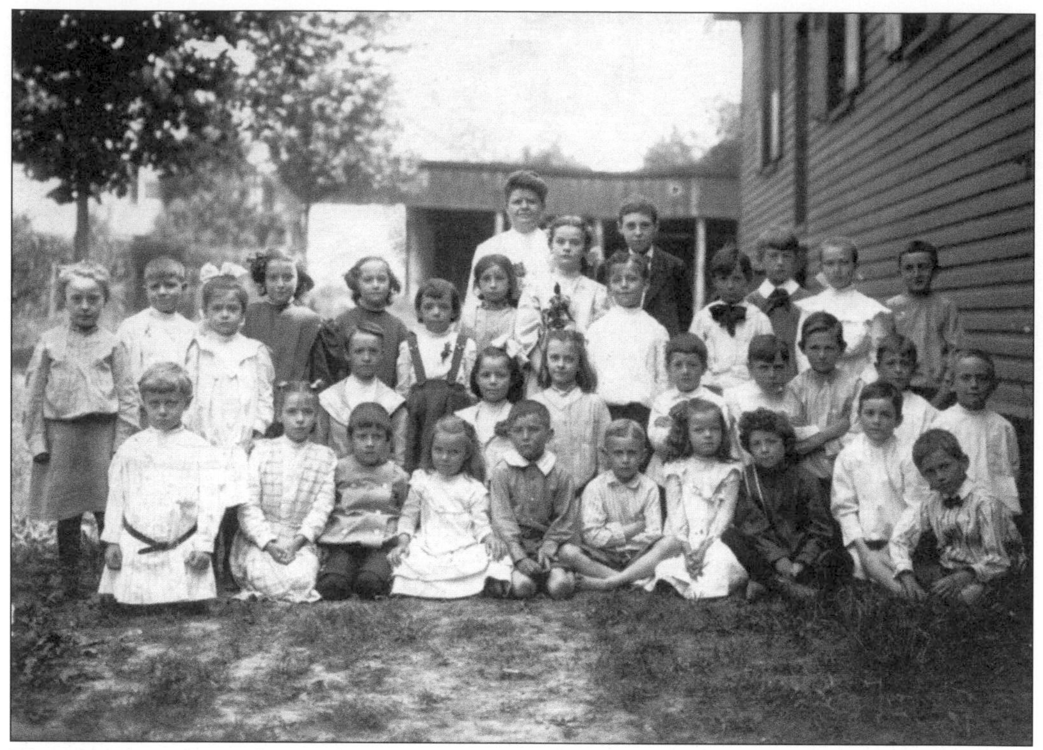

These students pose for a class picture, c. 1900. (Courtesy Baltimore County Historical Society.)

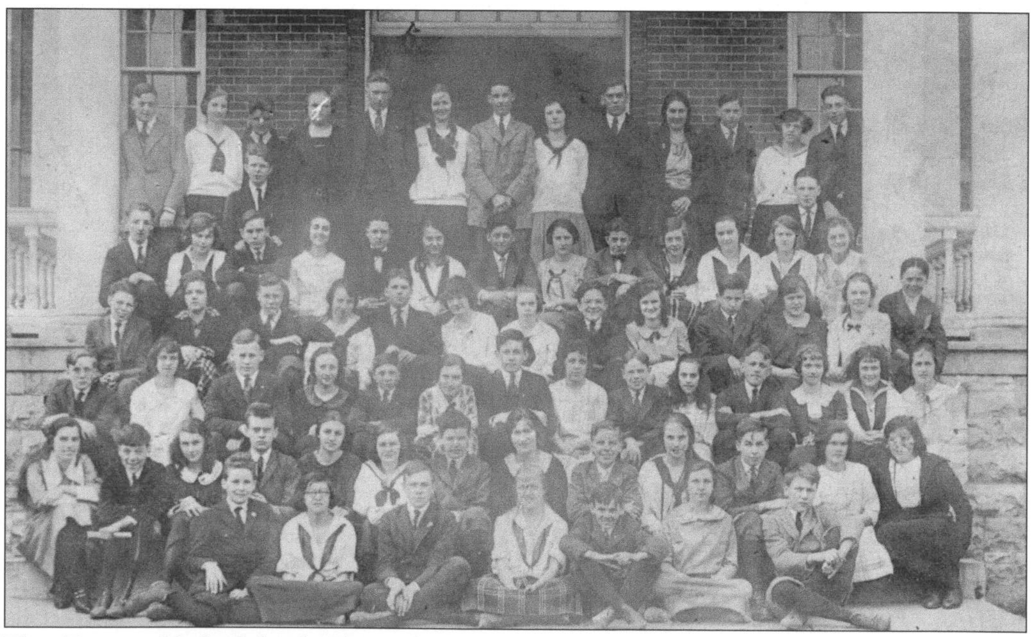

The Towson High School Class of 1924 is pictured here. (Courtesy Baltimore County Historical Society.)

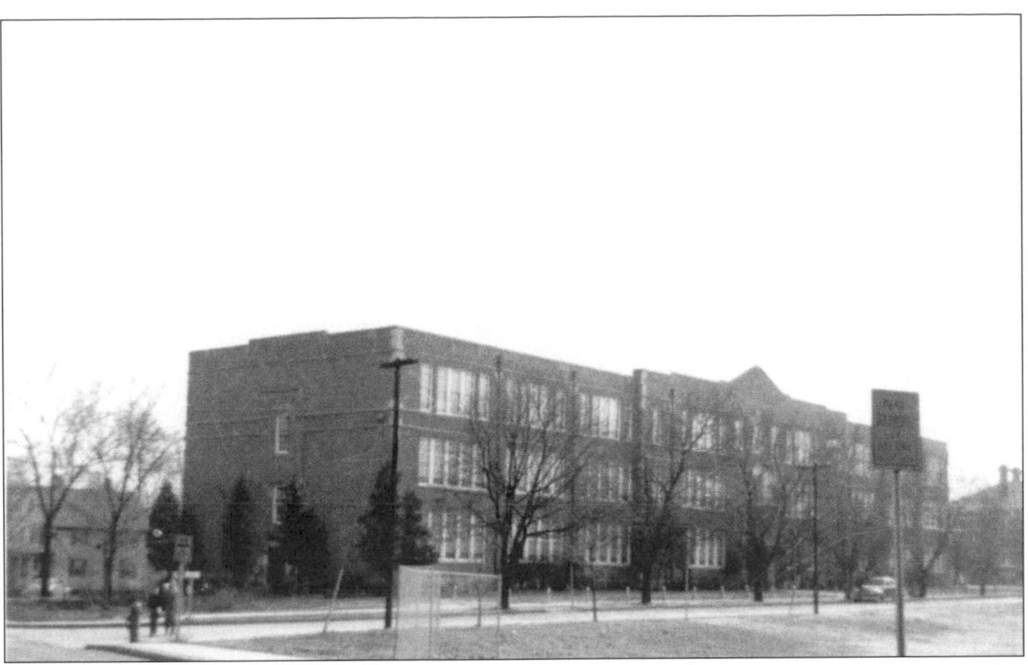

Towson's new high school is seen in 1926 from the playing fields on Joppa Road. (Courtesy Baltimore County Historical Society.)

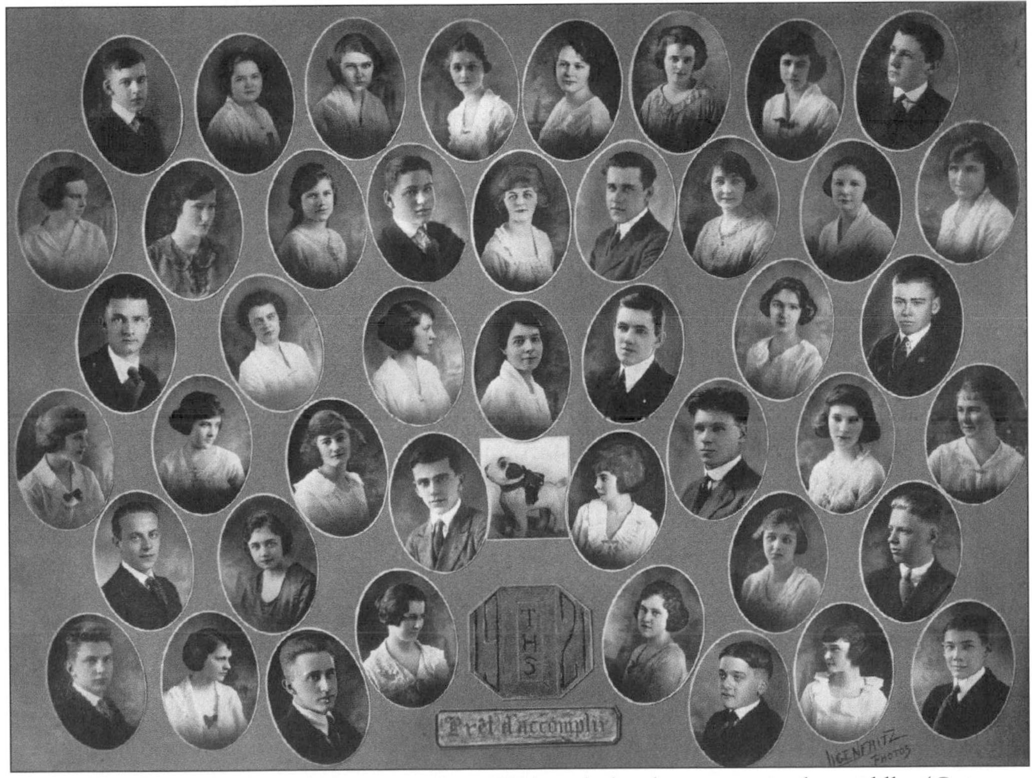

Towson High's composite class picture from 1921 includes the mascot in the middle. (Courtesy Baltimore County Historical Society.)

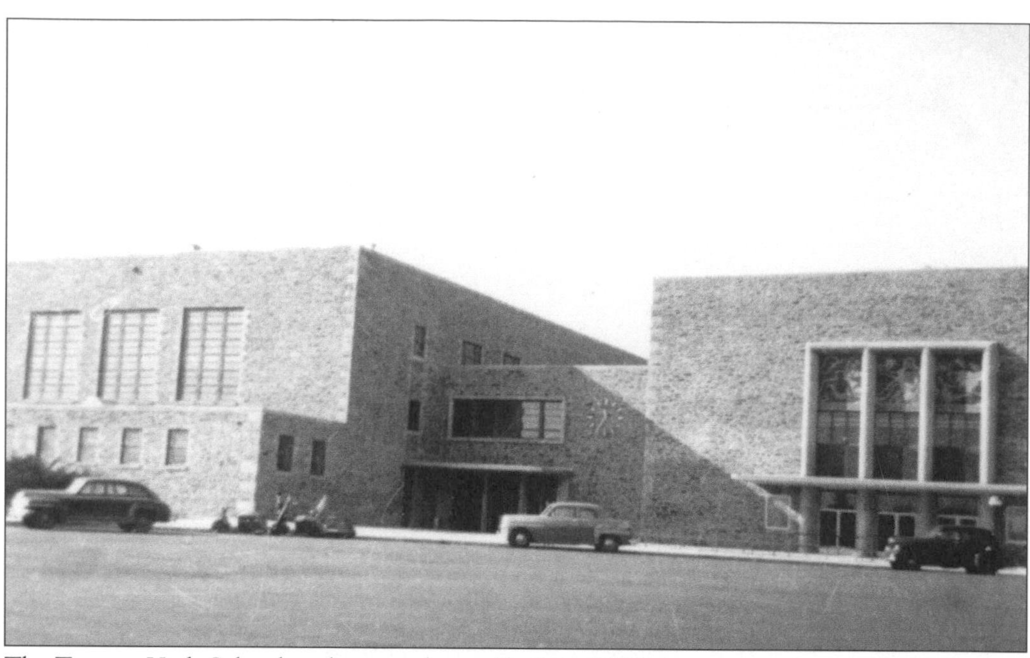

The Towson High School we know today was built in 1948 on property that once was a part of the Aigburth estate. (Courtesy Baltimore County Historical Society.)

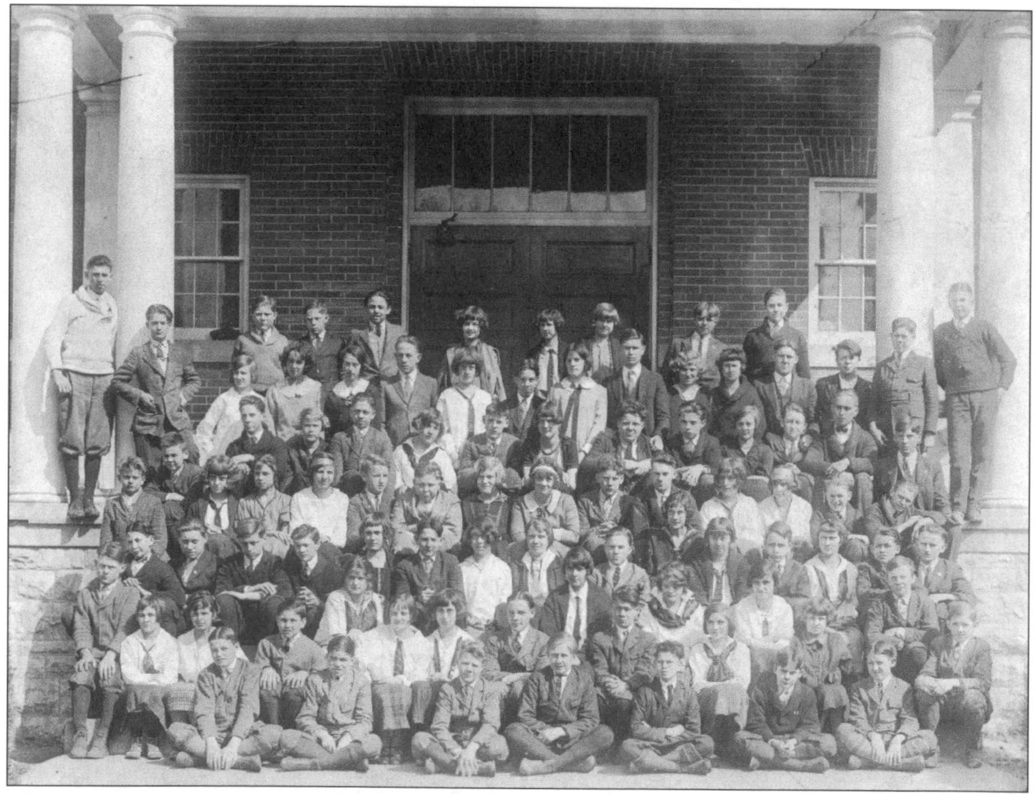

The Towson High School Class of 1928 was photographed in 1925. (Courtesy Baltimore County Historical Society.)

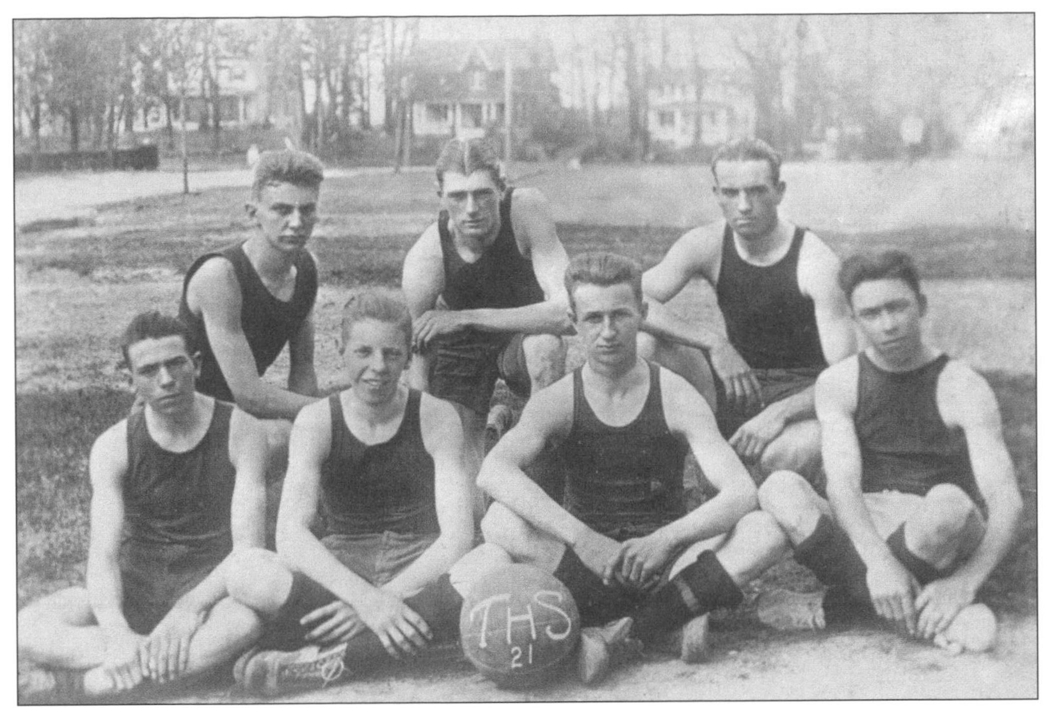

Towson High School's basketball team in 1921 is seen here. In the background are houses on Joppa Road. The field in which this picture was taken is now a public recreation area. (Courtesy Baltimore County Historical Society.)

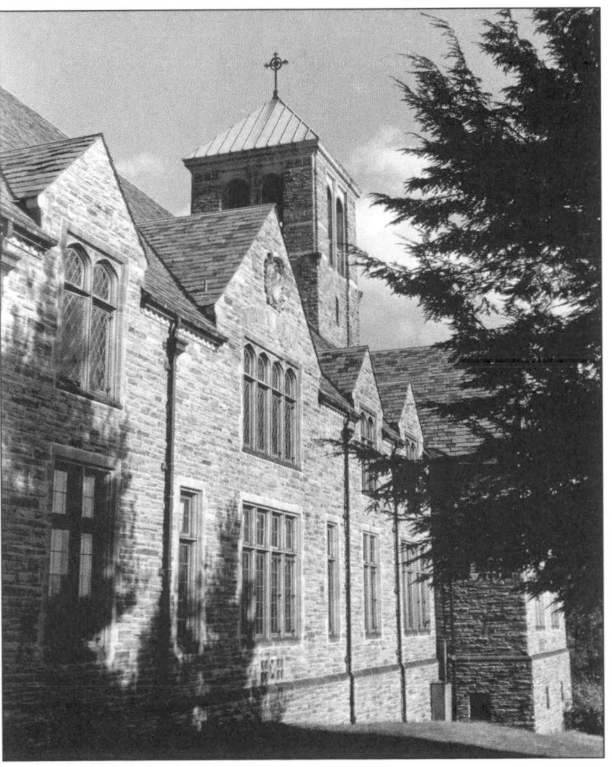

Loyola Blakefield moved to its current campus, on a beautiful hilltop overlooking Charles Street, in the mid-1930s. Since then, both the student body and the school's physical plant have grown. A recent addition made in the 1990s is virtually indistinguishable from its older counterparts. (Courtesy Loyola Blakefield.)

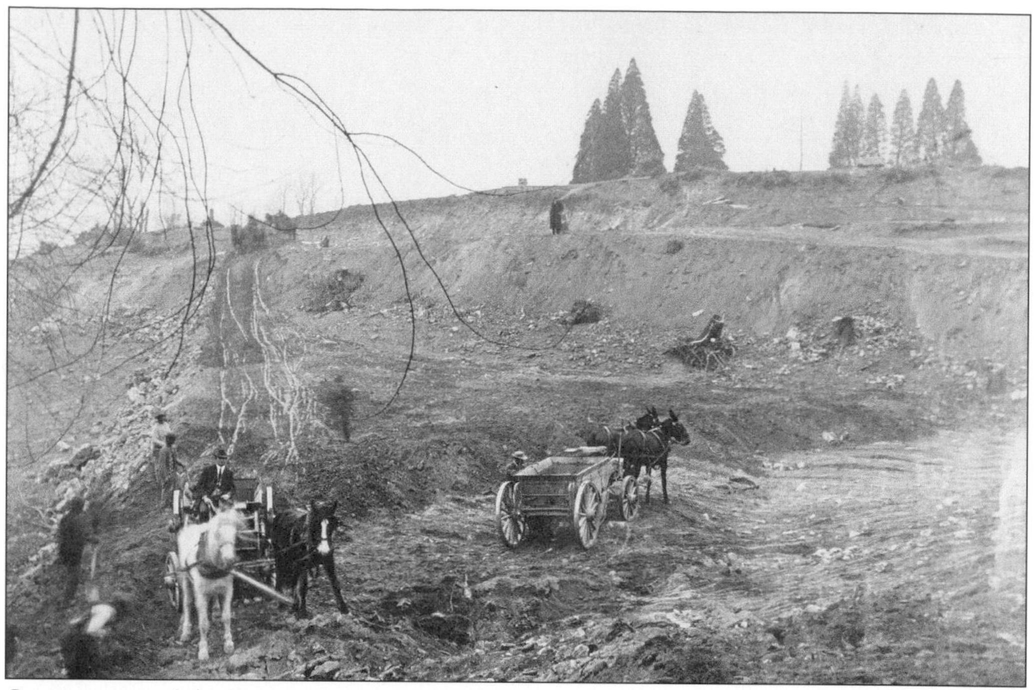

Construction of the Towson campus of the State Normal School began in 1913. Founded in January 1866 to train public school teachers, the school moved to its current site on York Road in 1915. (Courtesy Towson University Library.)

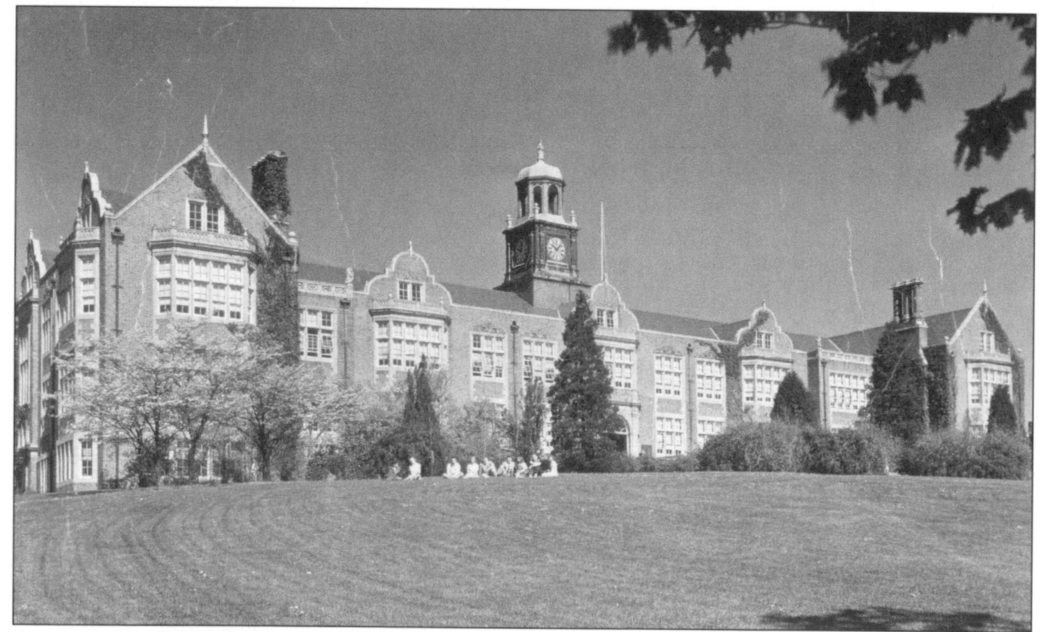

Stephens Hall, with its renowned clock tower, is part of Towson University. Since its founding in 1866 as the State Normal School, the school has undergone the following name changes: State Teachers College at Towson (1935), Towson State College (1963), Towson State University (1967), and, finally, Towson University (1997). (Courtesy Towson University Library.)

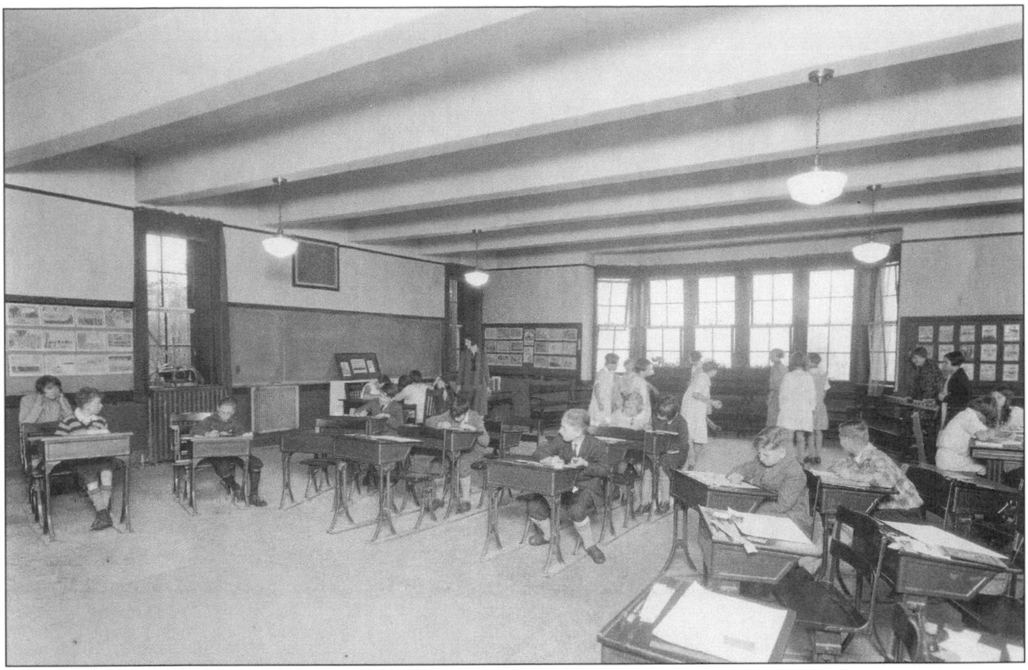

The Normal School, commonly referred to as the Model School, was located in Stephens Hall. This public school operated as a living "laboratory" for the training of future teachers. (Courtesy Towson University Library.)

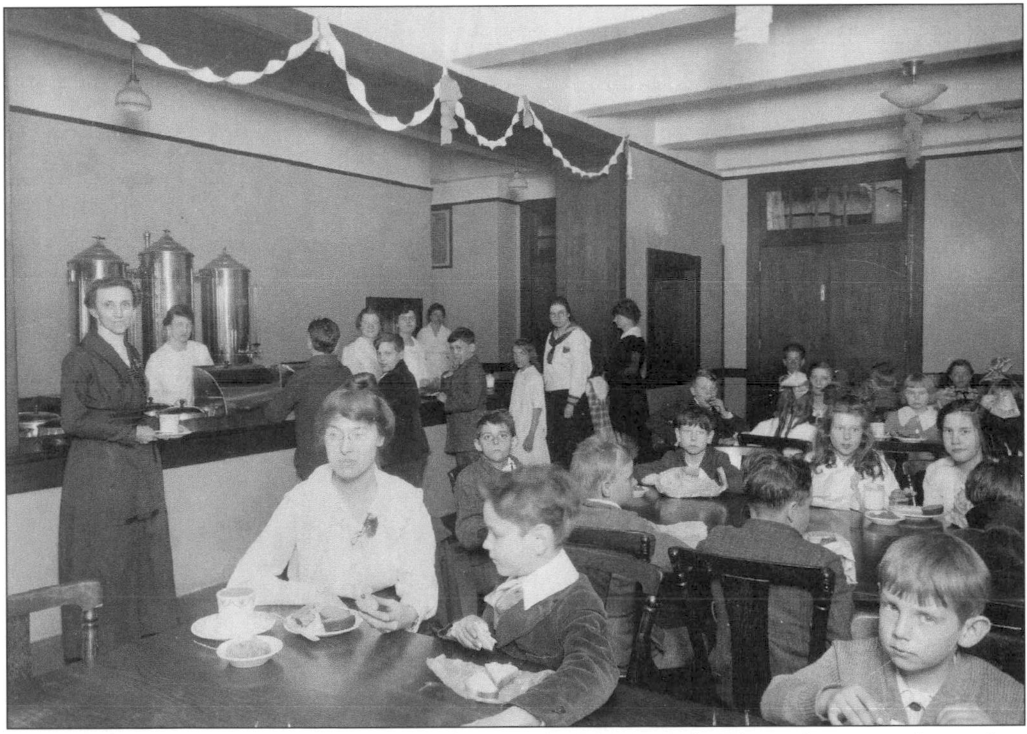

It is lunchtime for the Model School students in this photograph. This cafeteria was located in the basement of Stephens Hall. (Courtesy Towson University Library.)

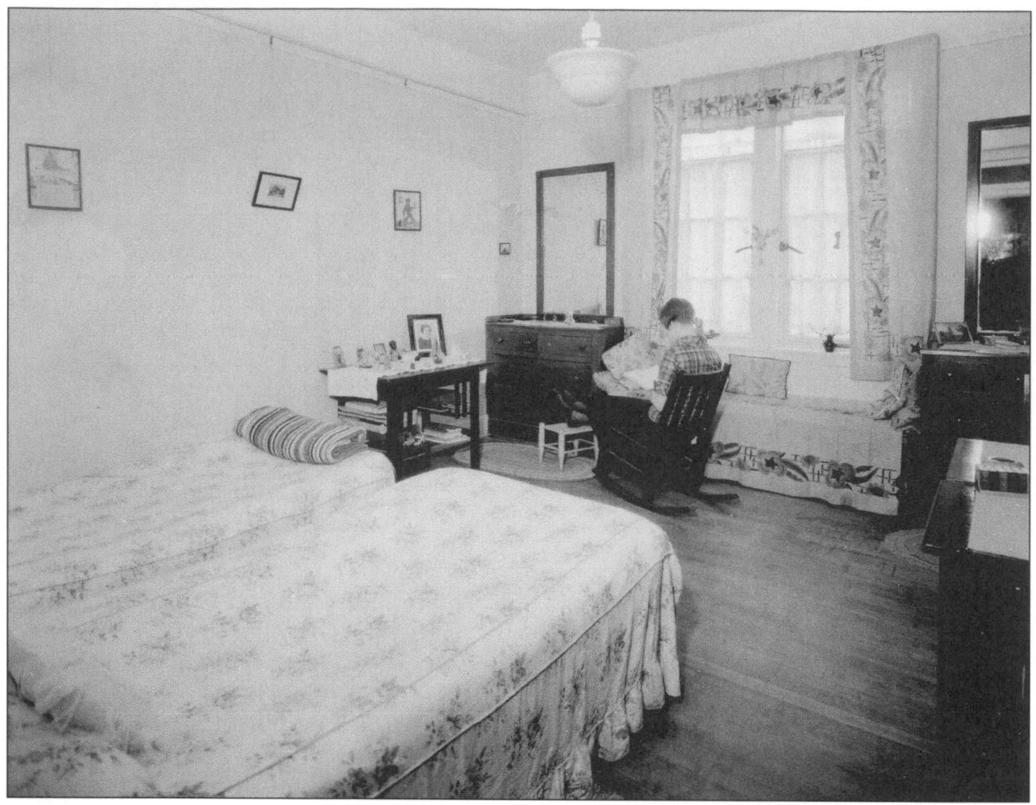

Note the pictures carefully hung from the picture rail in this c. 1925 image of a dorm room in Newell Hall. (Courtesy Towson University Library.)

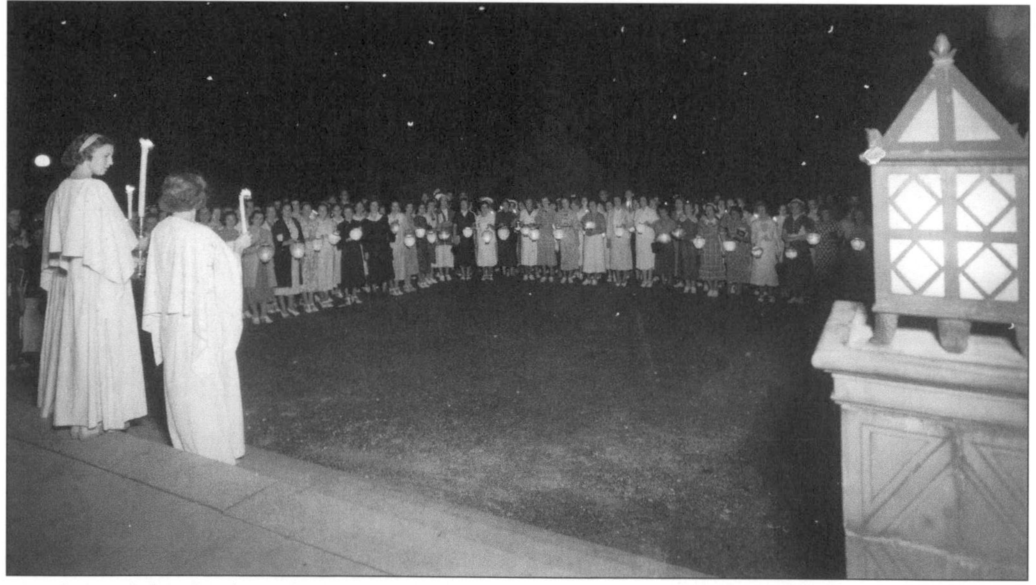

Members of the Student Government Association "light the way" for fellow students in this 1936 ceremony. (Courtesy Towson University Library.)

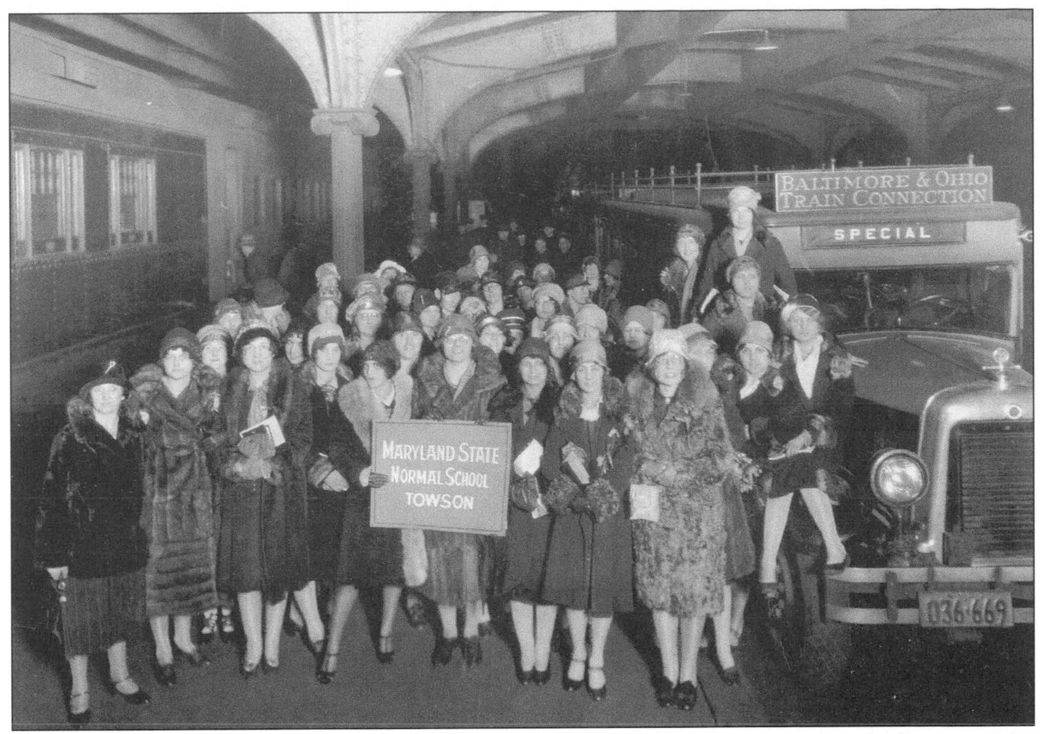

Fashionable 1920's coeds embark on a school trip. Note the short hemlines, cloche hats, and fur collars. (Courtesy Towson University Library.)

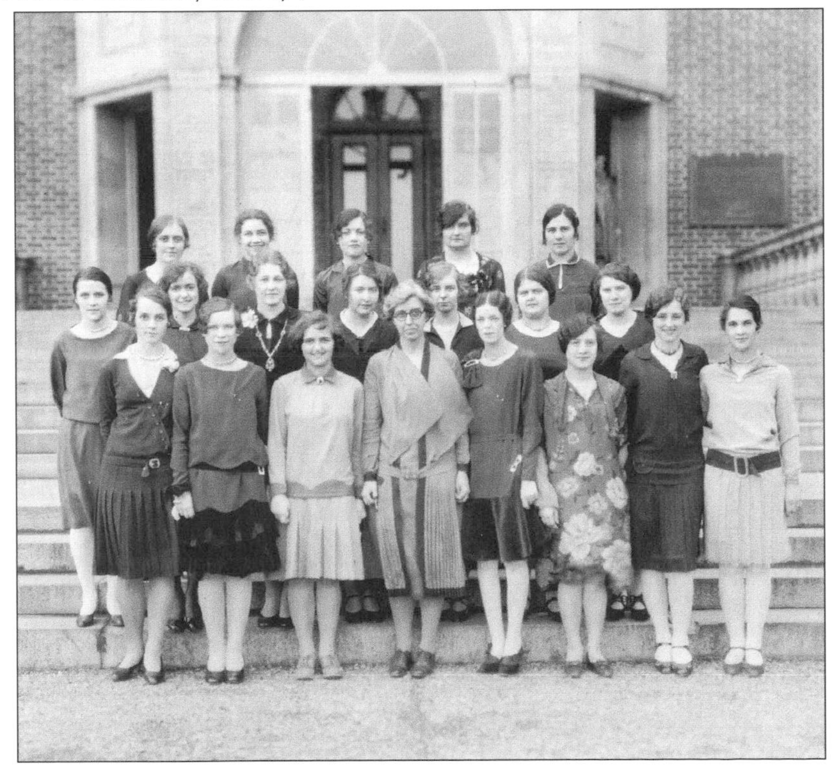

The League of Women Voters was a popular student organization. When this photograph was taken in 1928, women had held voting rights for only eight years. (Courtesy Towson University Library.)

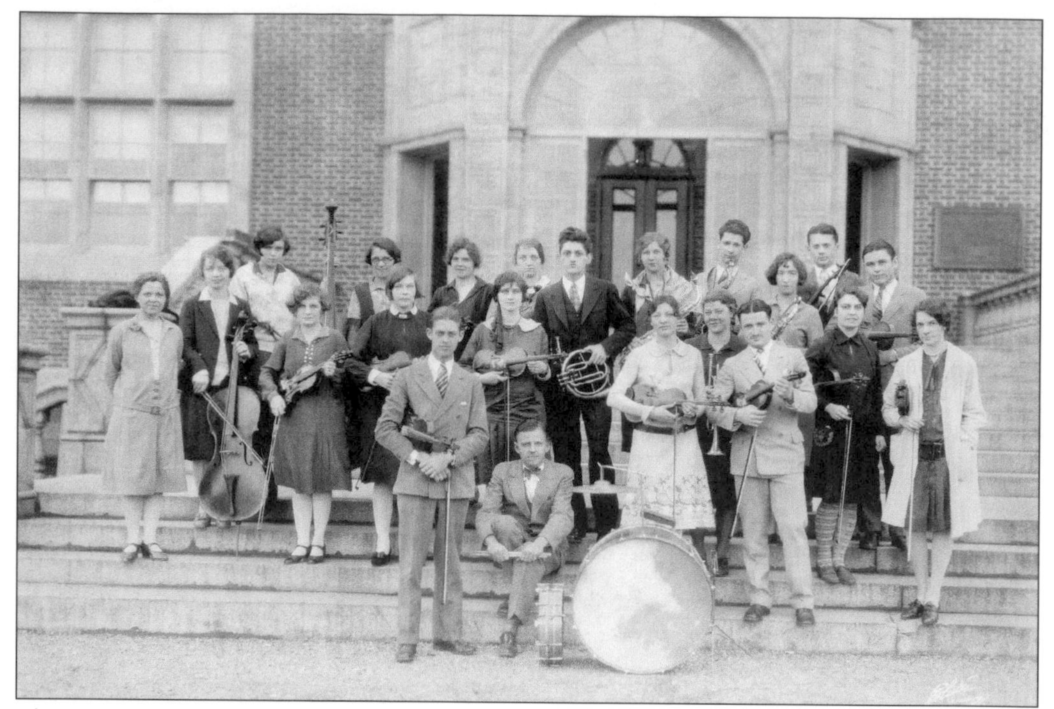

The campus orchestra is pictured here, c. 1930. (Courtesy Towson University Library.)

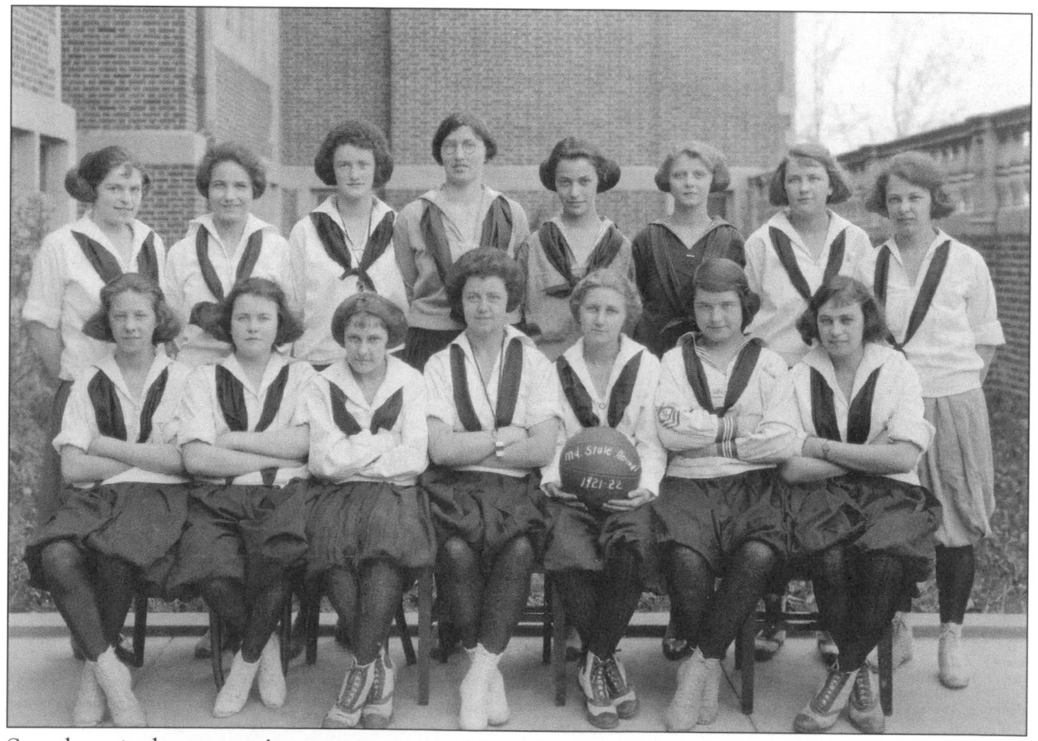

Seen here is the women's soccer team in 1922. (Courtesy Towson University Library.)

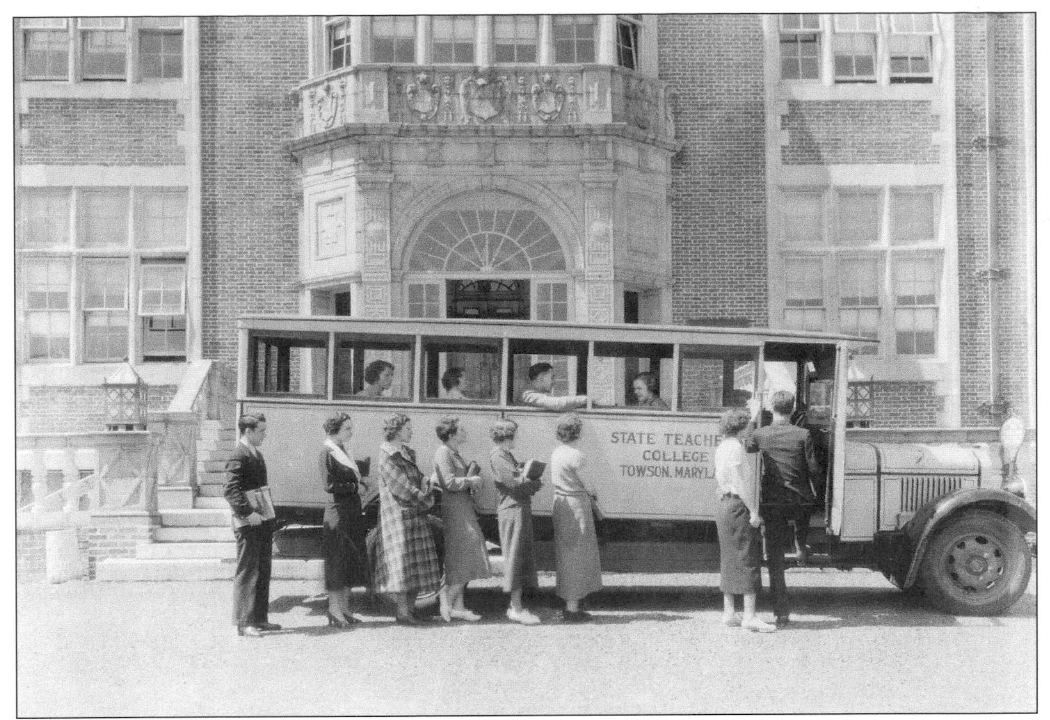

Students board the college bus in 1936. (Courtesy Towson University Library.)

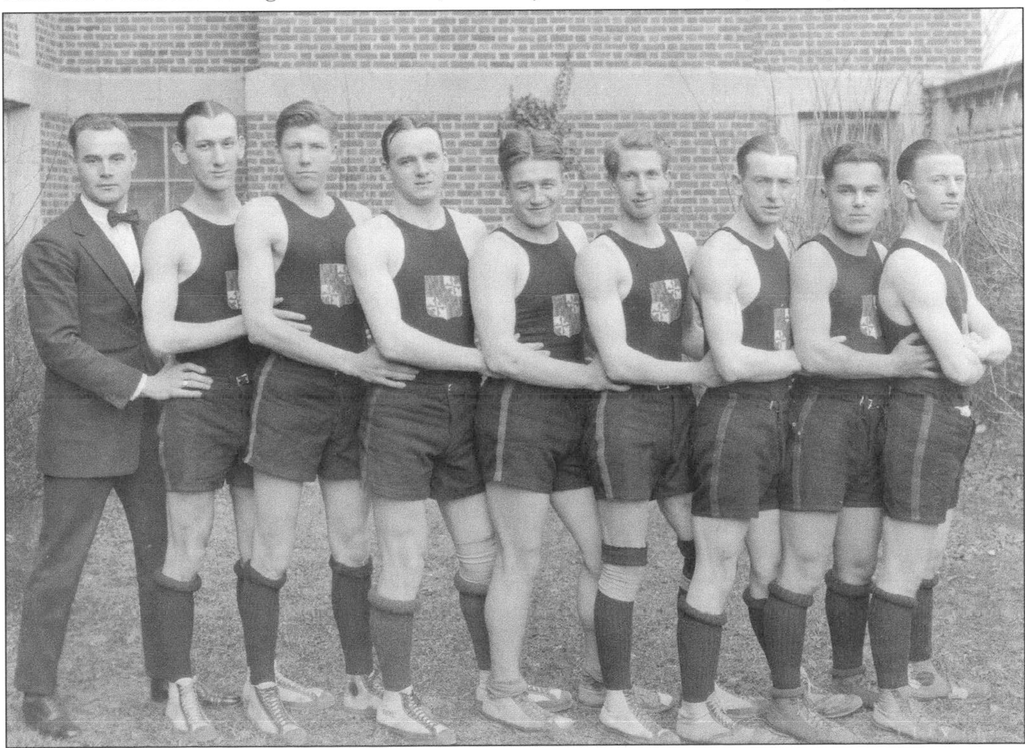

At the time of this 1924 men's basketball team picture, basketball was still a new sport, but one growing in popularity. (Courtesy Towson University Library.)

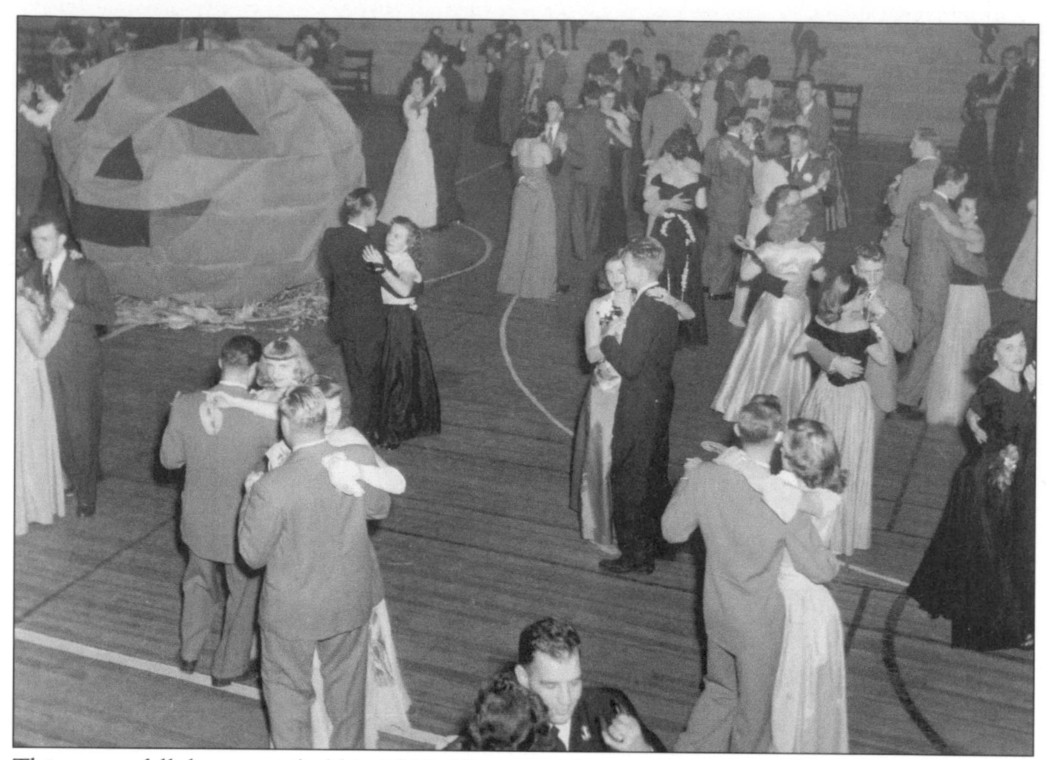

This senior fall dance was held in 1948. (Courtesy Towson University Library.)

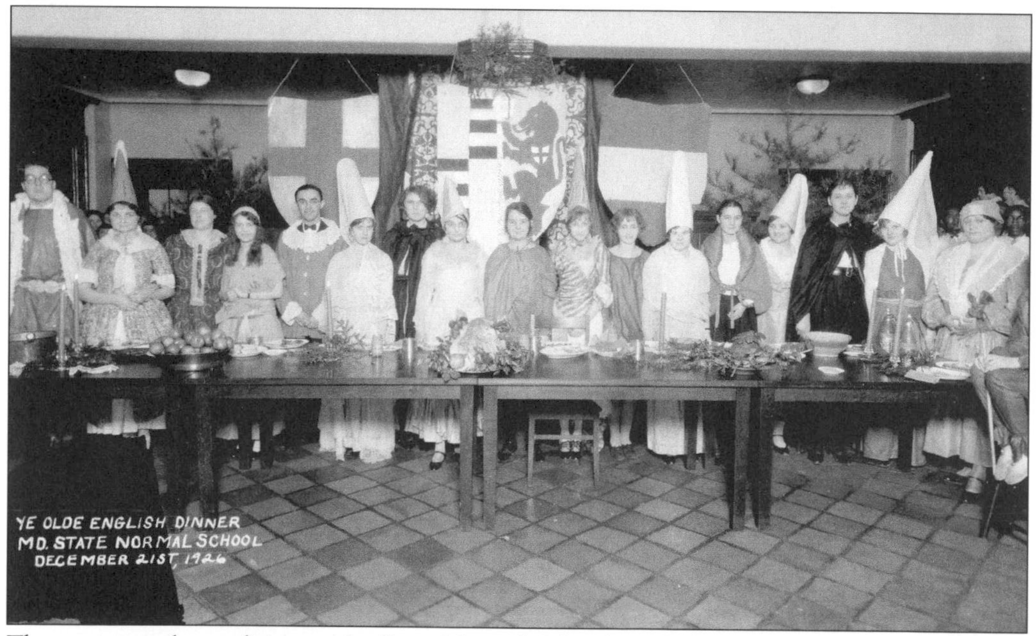

The most popular tradition at the State Normal School was held prior to the Christmas recess and was called "Ye Olde English Dinner." Students dressed as jesters, monks, ladies, and lords. This group posed in 1926. (Courtesy Towson University Library.)

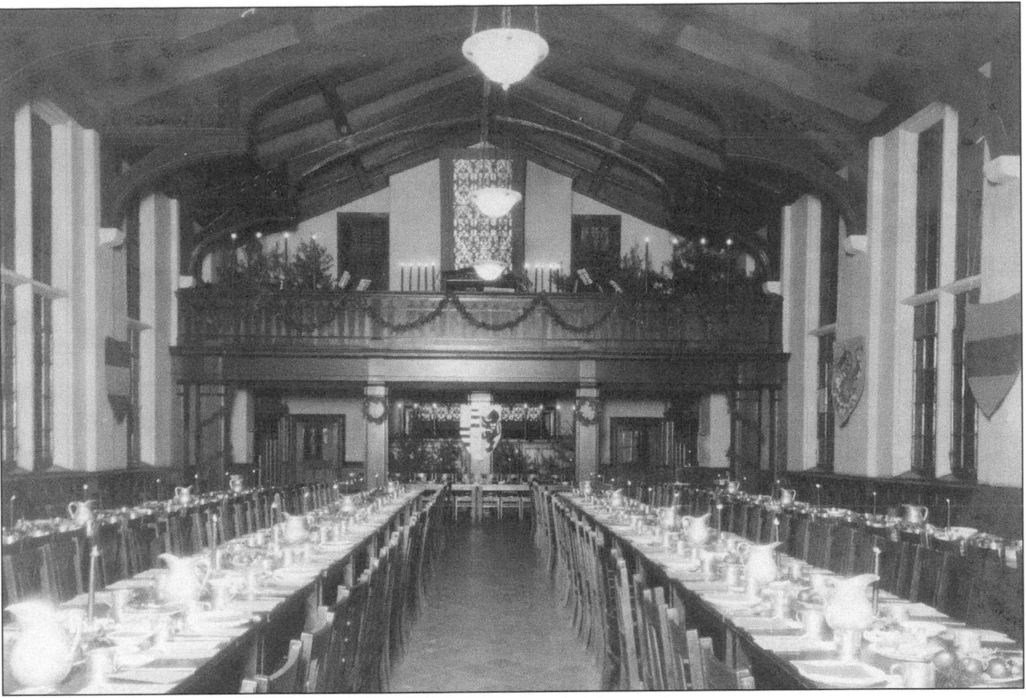

Newell Hall provided a marvelous setting for this evening of medieval merriment. Musicians seated in the balcony added to the ambiance. (Courtesy Towson University Library.)

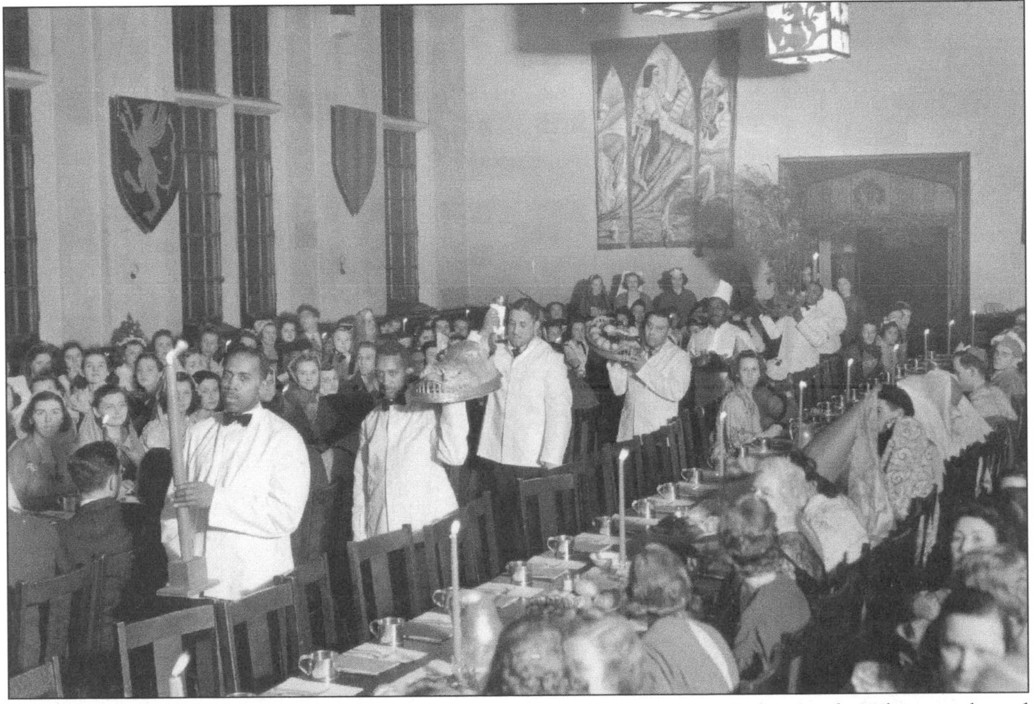

A highlight of this festive feast was the dramatic presentation of the food. White-jacketed waiters and cooks brought in special dishes, such as Peacock Pie (note the feathers), wassail, plum pudding, and, of course, the boar's head! (Courtesy Towson University Library.)

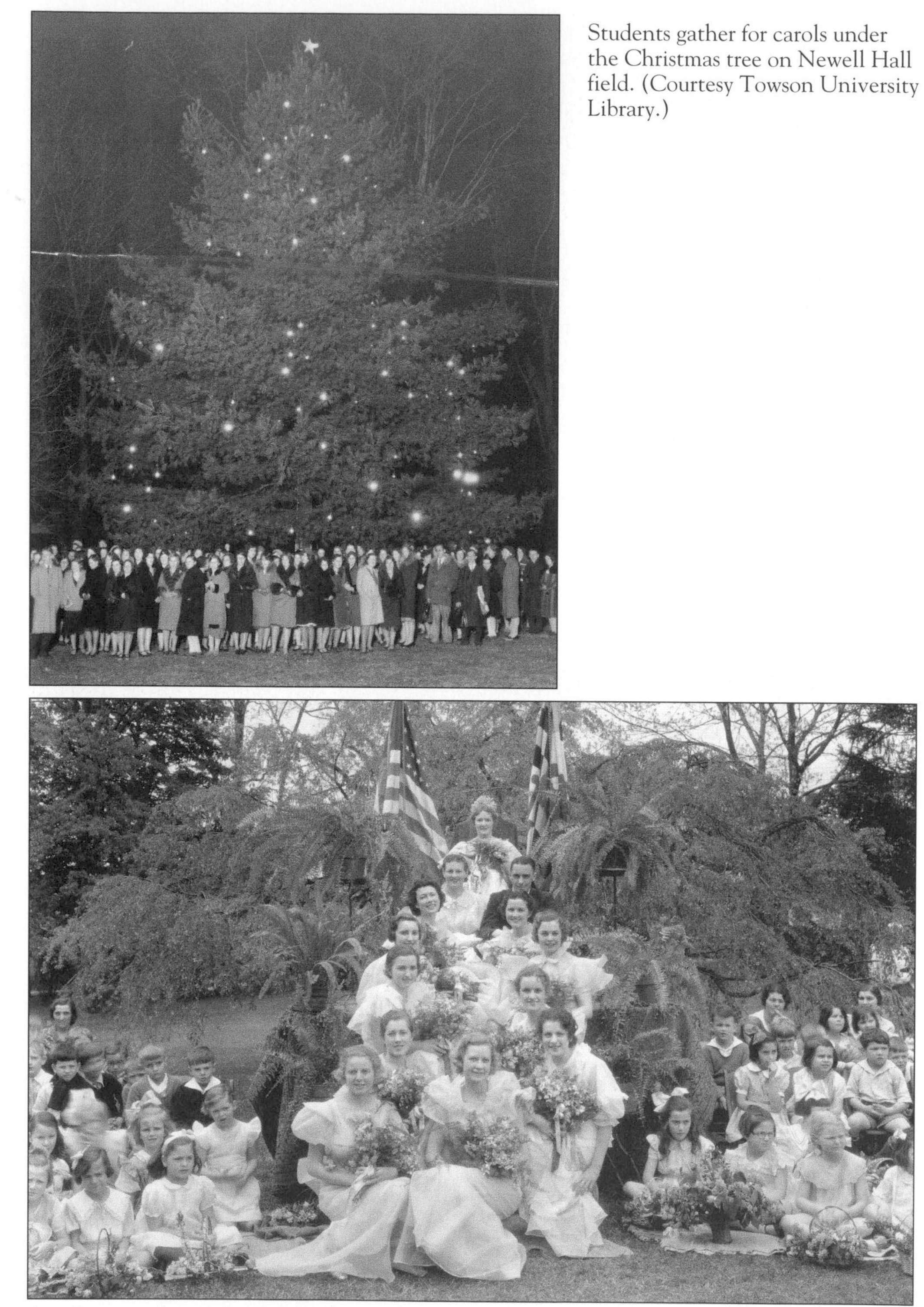

Students gather for carols under the Christmas tree on Newell Hall field. (Courtesy Towson University Library.)

Another popular tradition was the celebration of May Day, complete with a May court. Here are the 1934 May Queen, her king, and her attendants. (Courtesy Towson University Library.)

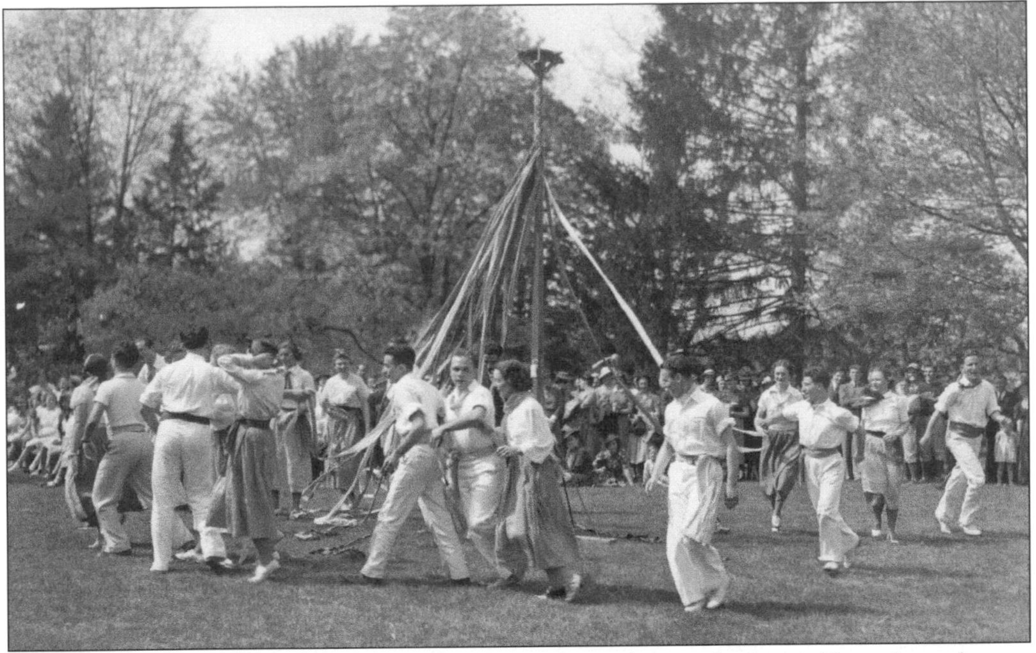

In 1937, May Day revelers participated in the traditional maypole dance. Note the sashes on both men and women. (Courtesy Towson University Library.)

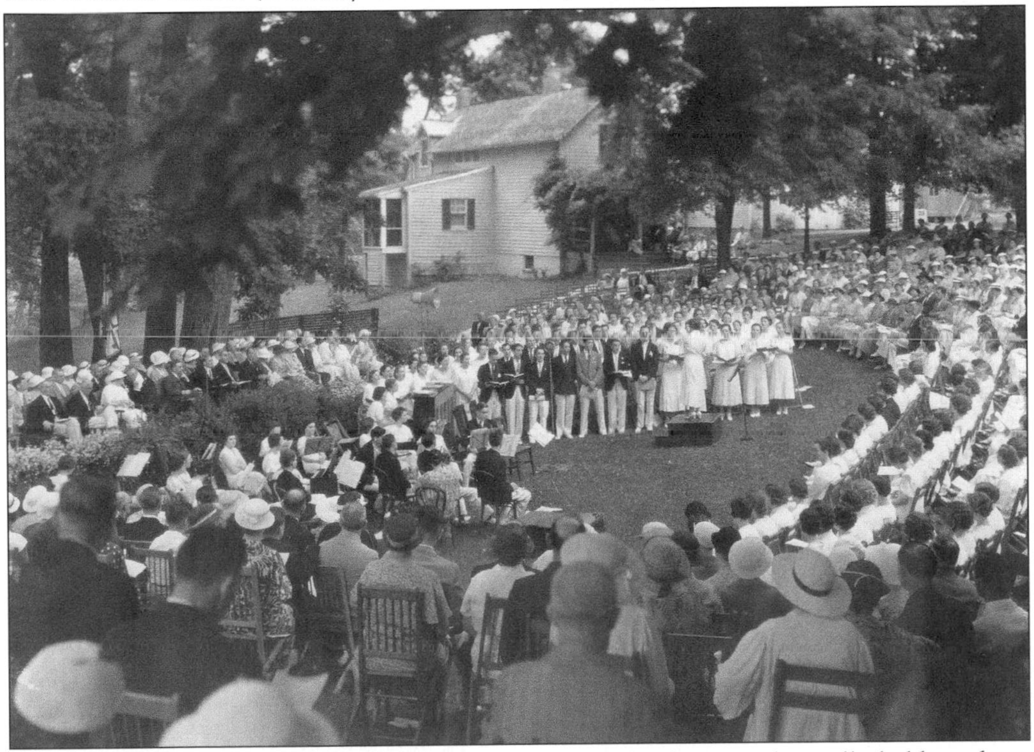

The commencement ceremony at the State Normal School was traditionally held outdoors near the president's house, which can be seen in the background of this 1934 ceremony. (Courtesy Towson University Library.)

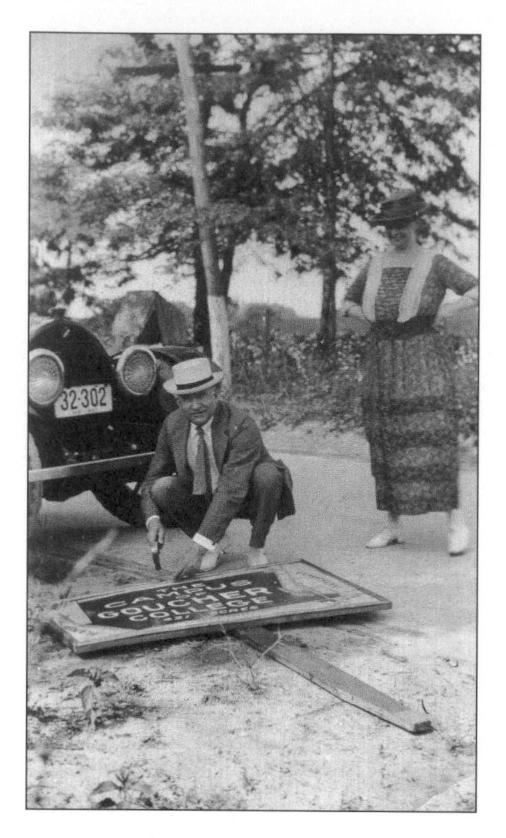

Goucher College acquired 421 acres in Towson for its new campus in 1921. Until its move north, the campus was located in Baltimore. (Courtesy Goucher College Archives, Julia Rogers Library.)

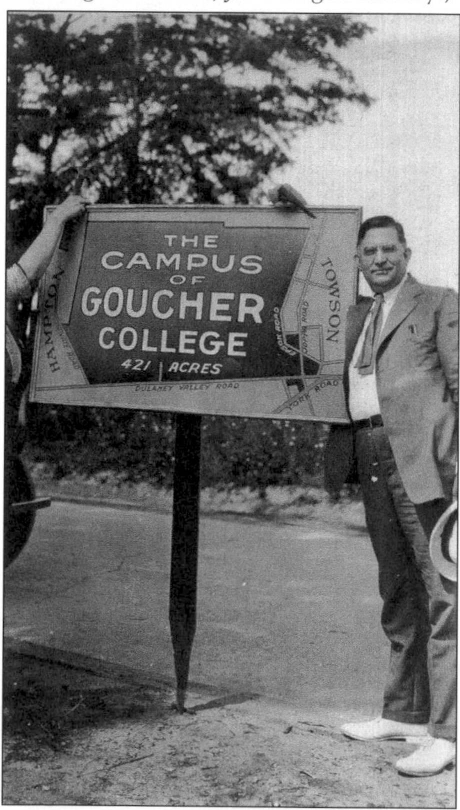

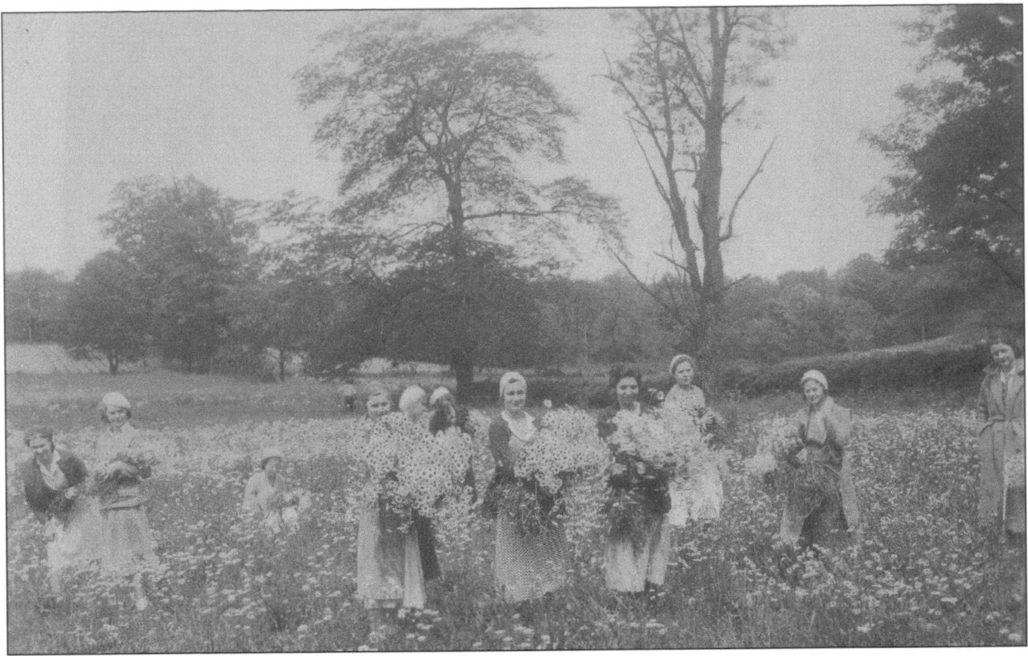

These winsome beauties are engaged in "fieldwork" for one of Goucher College's old traditions, the annual sophomore daisy chain, c. 1927. (Courtesy Goucher College Archives, Julia Rogers Library.)

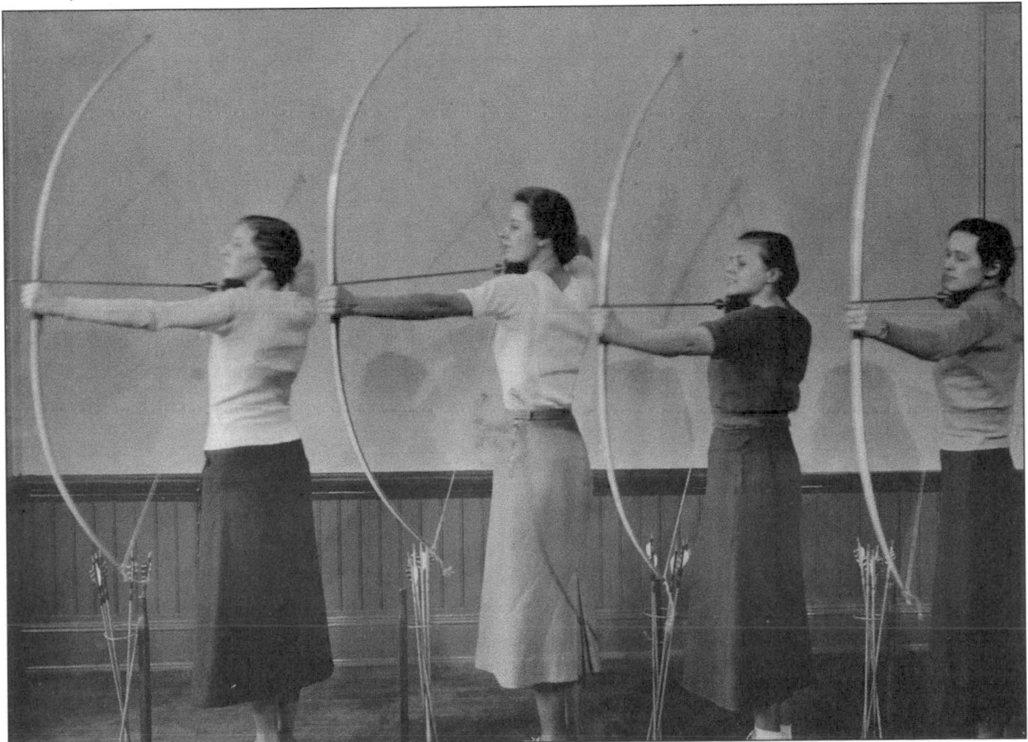

Watch out William Tell! The women in this archery class are on the mark. (Courtesy Goucher College Archives, Julia Rogers Library.)

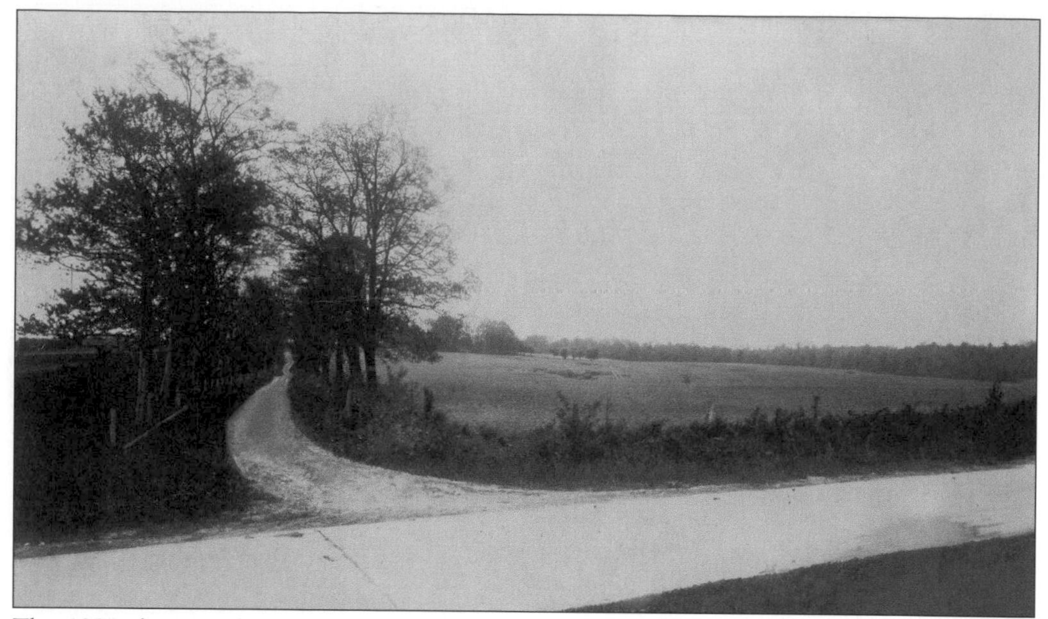

This 1921 photograph shows the campus entrance from Dulaney Valley Road. Today, that road is six lanes wide and intersects with the beltway immediately after passing the college. (Courtesy Goucher College Archives, Julia Rogers Library.)

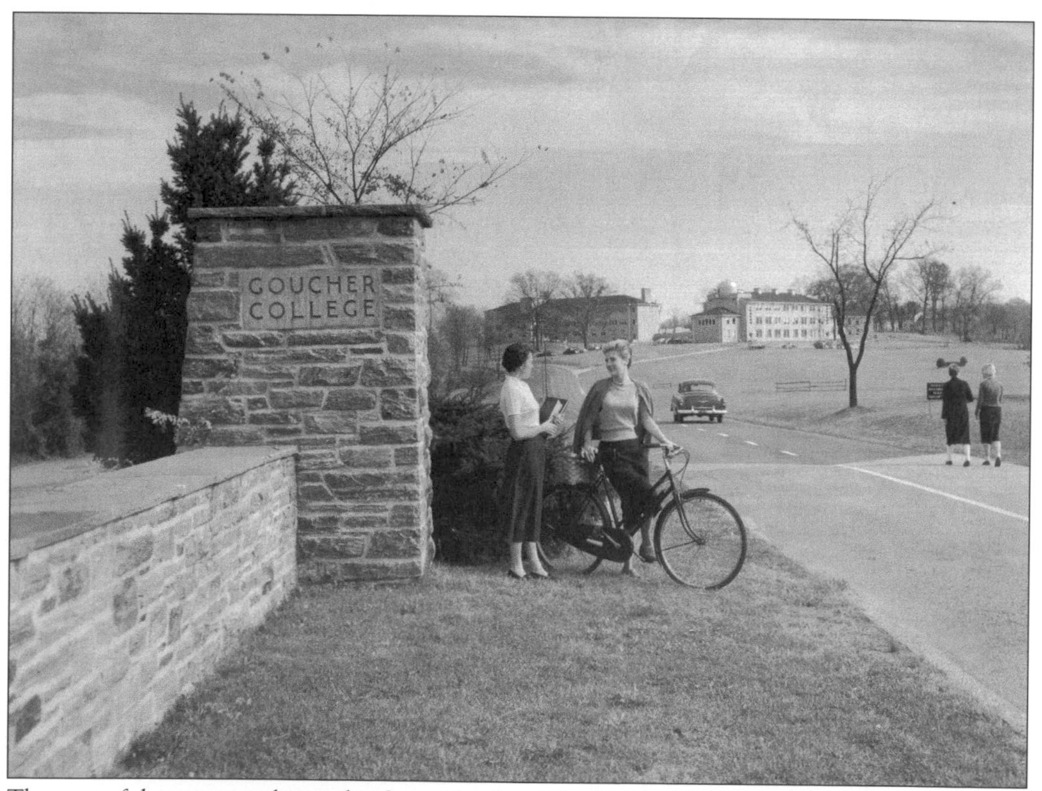

The peaceful campus is located a few miles from the bustle of the city, providing the best of both worlds. (Courtesy Goucher College Archives, Julia Rogers Library.)

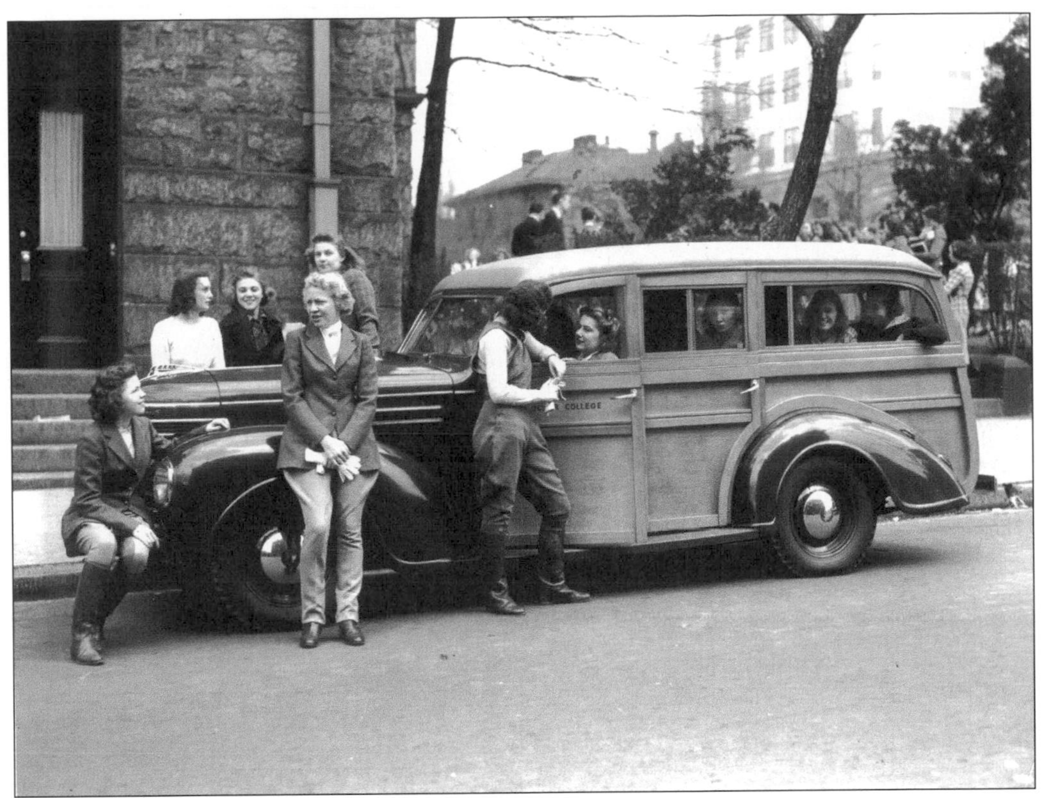

Some of the women in this 1937 photo are obviously off to the stables, while others seem content with a more modern mode of transport, one of the college cars. (Courtesy Goucher College Archives, Julia Rogers Library.)

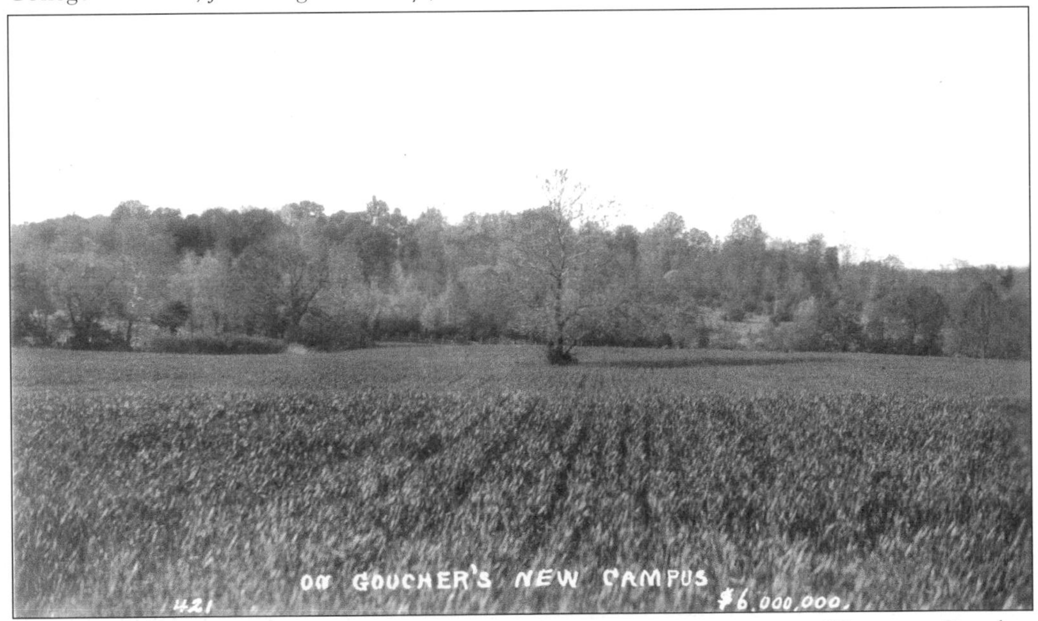

This is how Goucher's new campus looked in 1921, upon its acquisition. (Courtesy Goucher College Archives, Julia Rogers Library.)

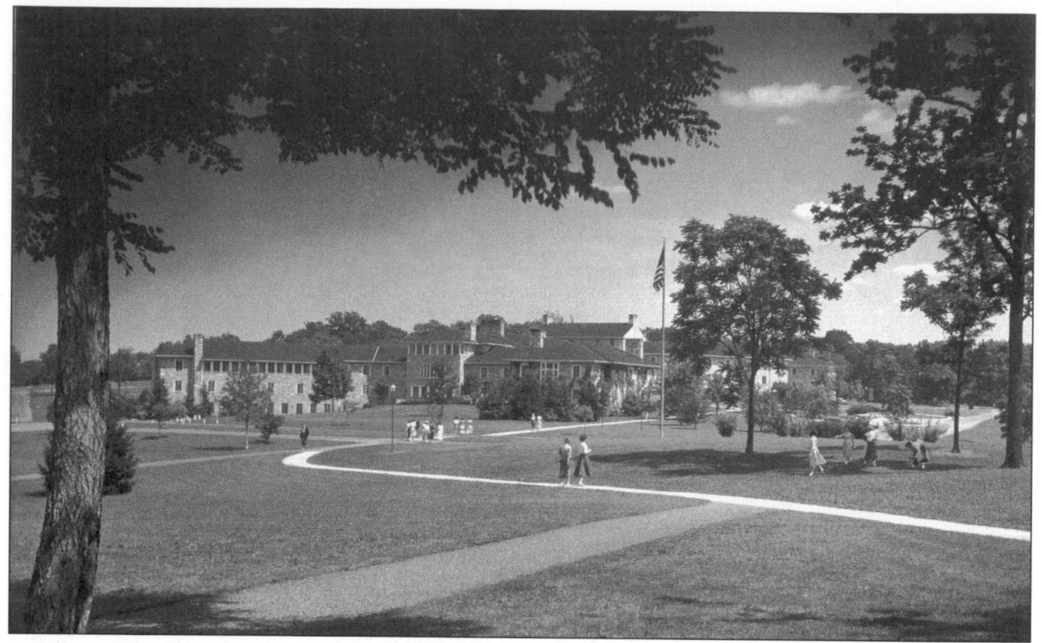

A view of the Goucher campus shows Mary Fisher Hall in the background. (Courtesy Goucher College Archives, Julia Rogers Library.)

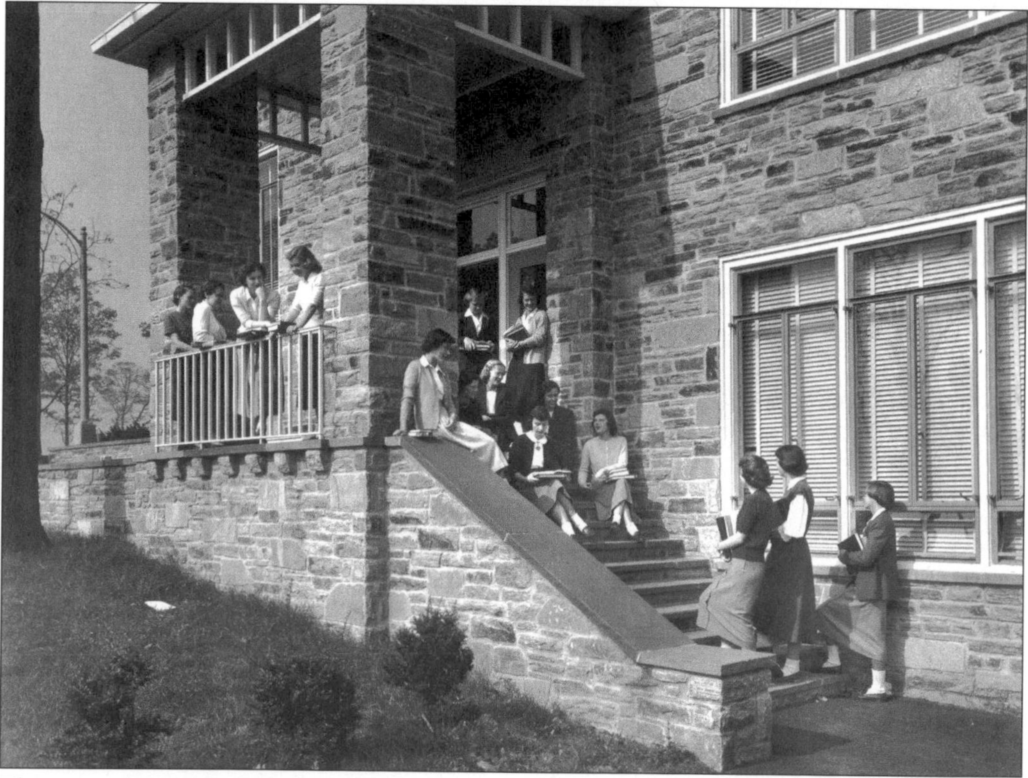

The steps of Van Meter Hall provide a popular setting for students to relax. (Courtesy Goucher College Archives, Julia Rogers Library.)

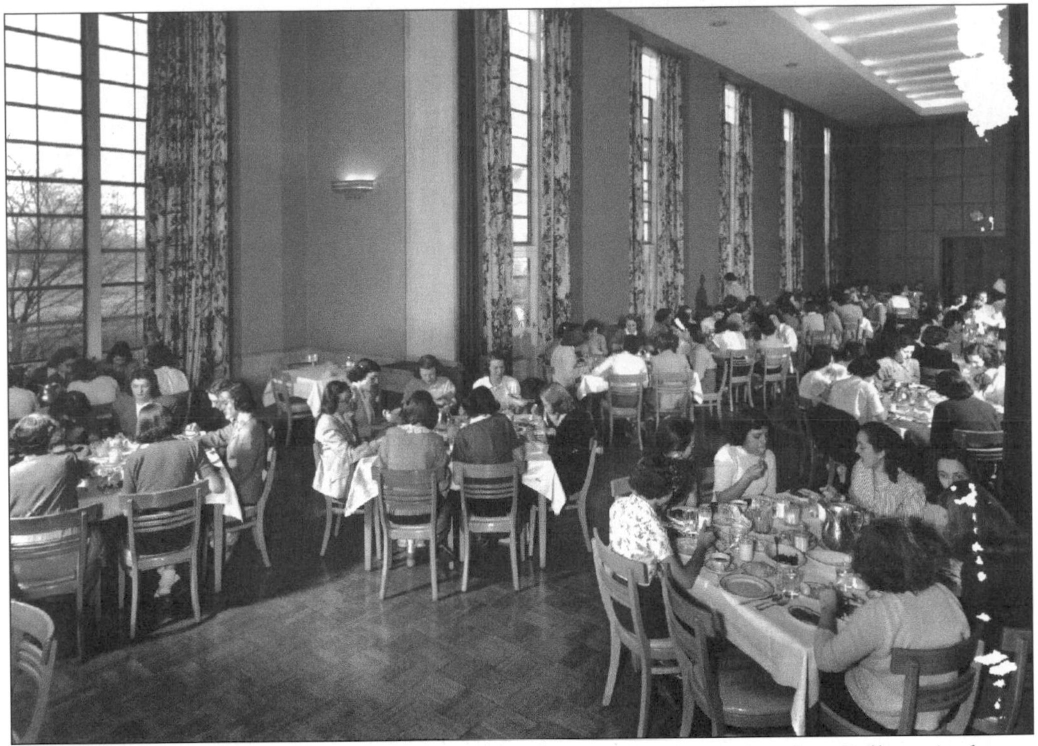

The dining room at Mary Fisher Hall is pictured here. (Courtesy Goucher College Archives, Julia Rogers Library.)

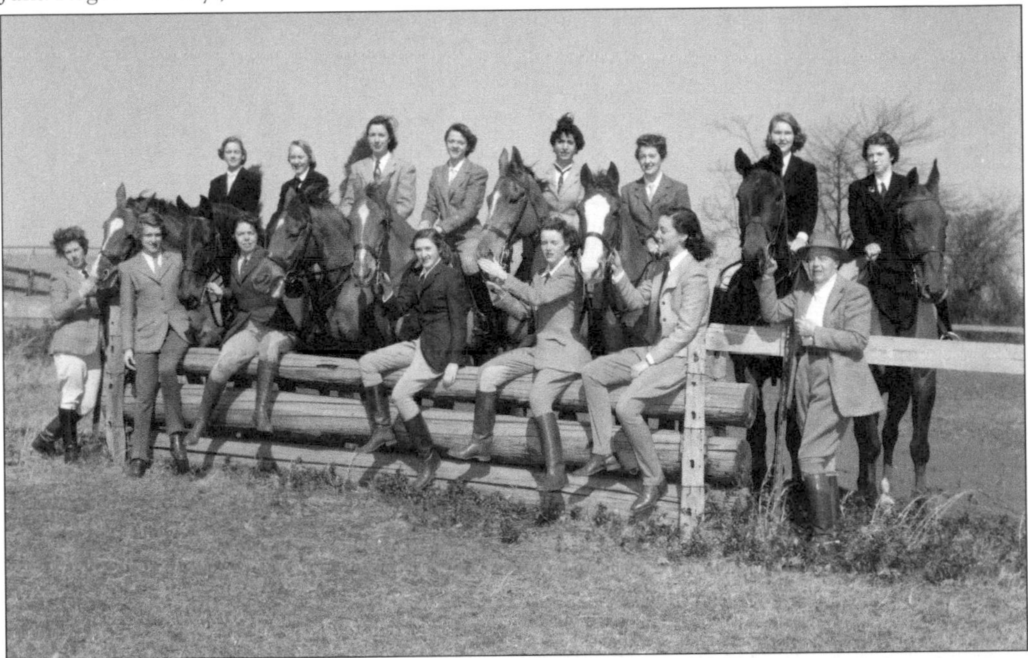

Miss Eline von Borries and some of her students are shown c. 1956. Goucher's equestrian program has been widely renowned for many years. The college boasts its own stables and riding trails, all within the Beltway. (Courtesy Goucher College Archives, Julia Rogers Library.)

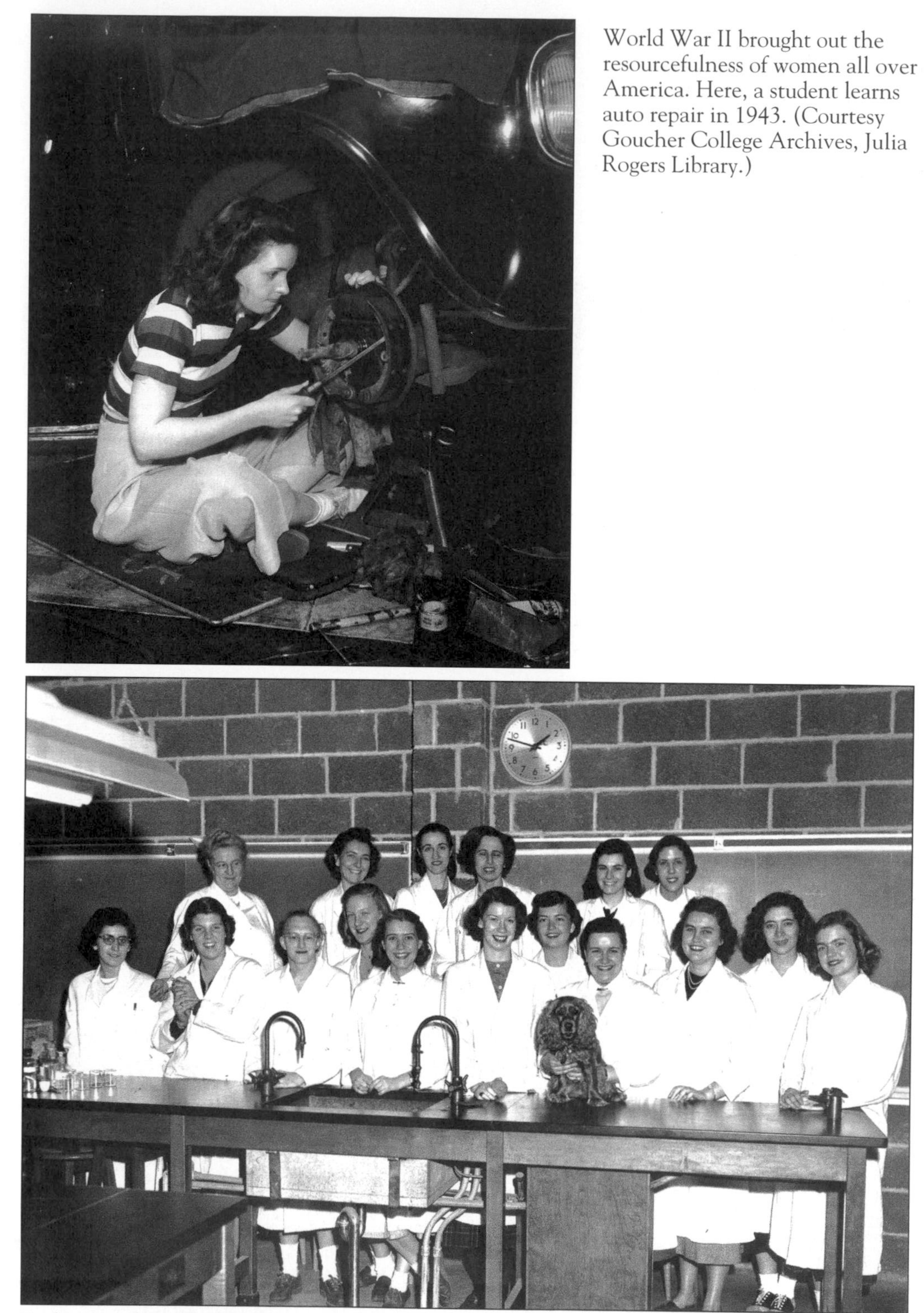

World War II brought out the resourcefulness of women all over America. Here, a student learns auto repair in 1943. (Courtesy Goucher College Archives, Julia Rogers Library.)

Biology students and professors pose with their mascot (at least we hope it is the mascot). (Courtesy Goucher College Archives, Julia Rogers Library.)

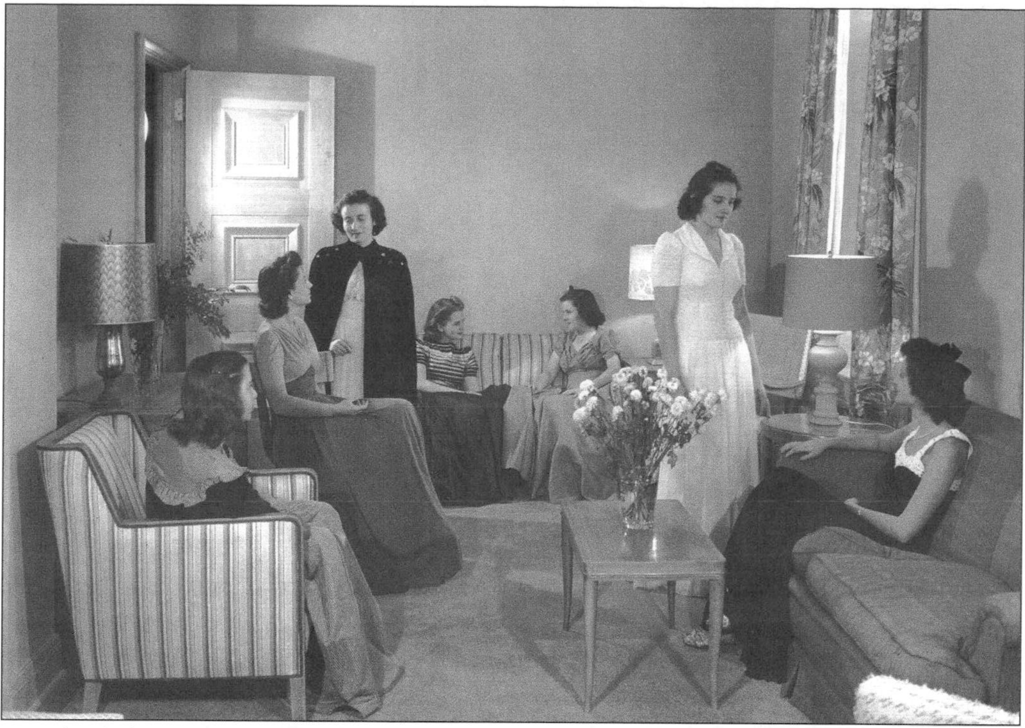

Goucher ladies strike an elegant pose in the lounge before a dance in 1942. (Courtesy Goucher College Archives, Julia Rogers Library.)

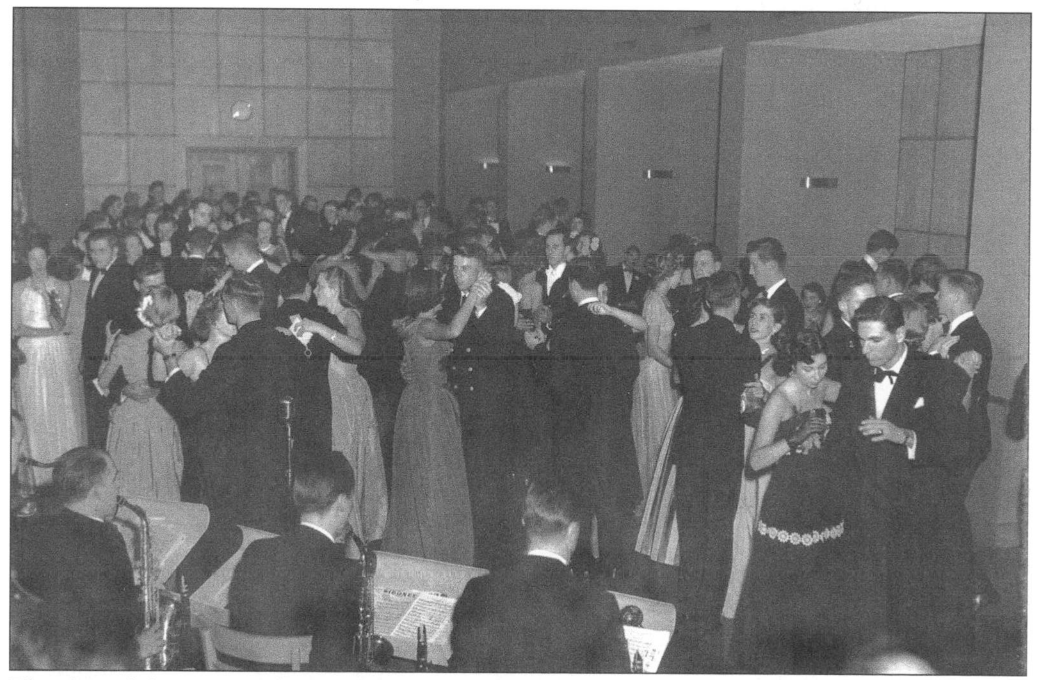

This formal dance, complete with swing band, was held in Mary Fisher Hall, *c.* 1950. Note that flowers in the hair and wrist corsages appear to be popular. (Courtesy Goucher College Archives, Julia Rogers Library.)

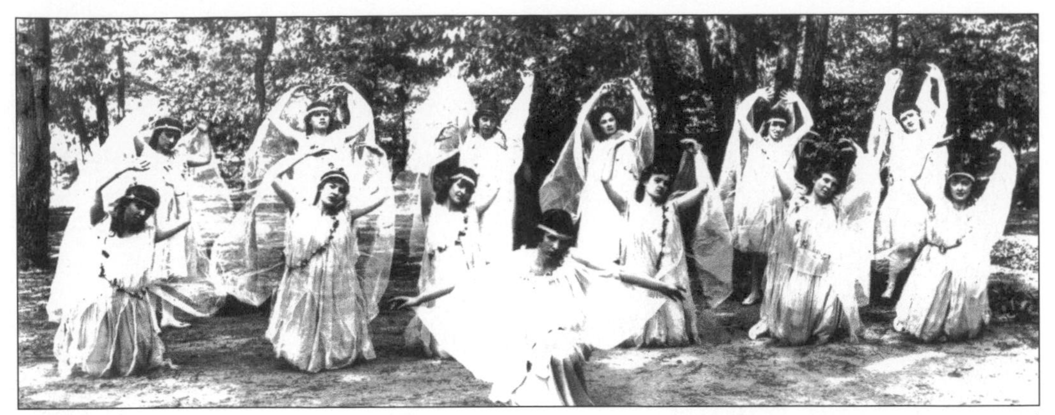

The May Day pageant was a popular tradition at Goucher. Many hours of preparation ensured its success. (Courtesy Goucher College Archives, Julia Rogers Library.)

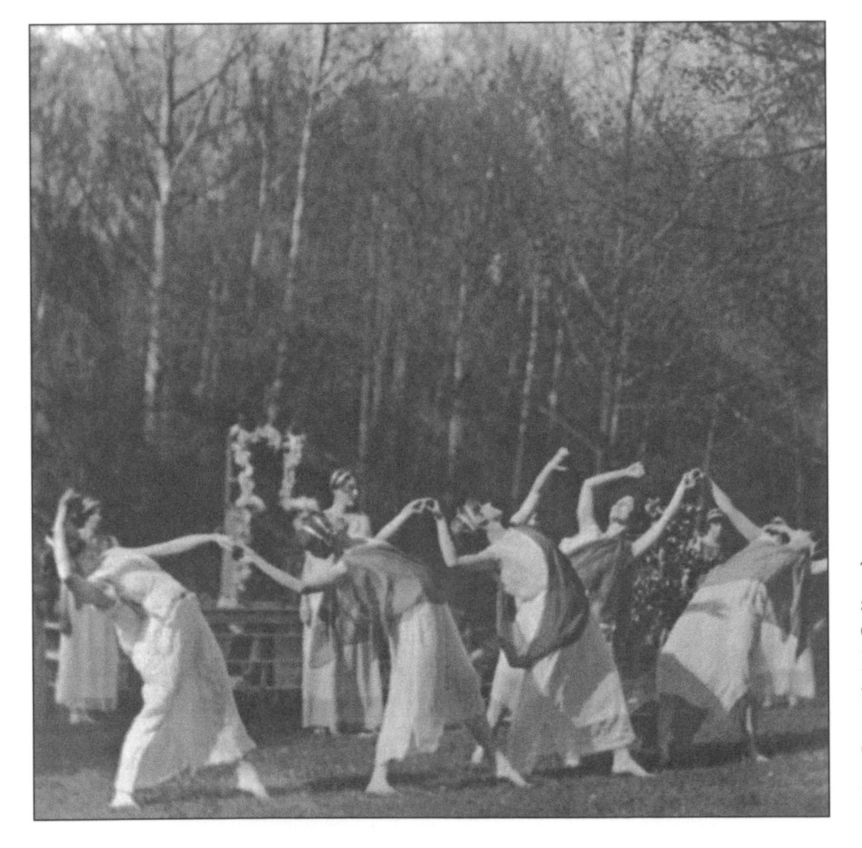

This tableau shows part of Goucher's 1927 May Day festivities. (Courtesy Goucher College Archives, Julia Rogers Library.)

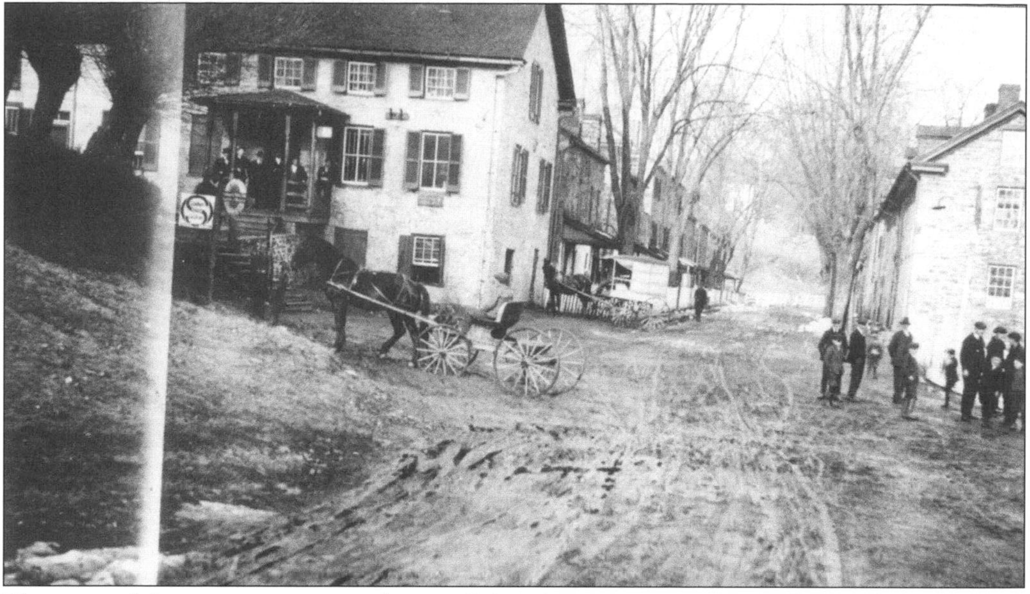

This view of the company store and part of Main Street in Warren was taken at the turn of the century. By November 1922, the entire town had been razed. It was flooded soon thereafter to create an expanded Loch Raven Reservoir. (Courtesy Baltimore County Historical Society.)

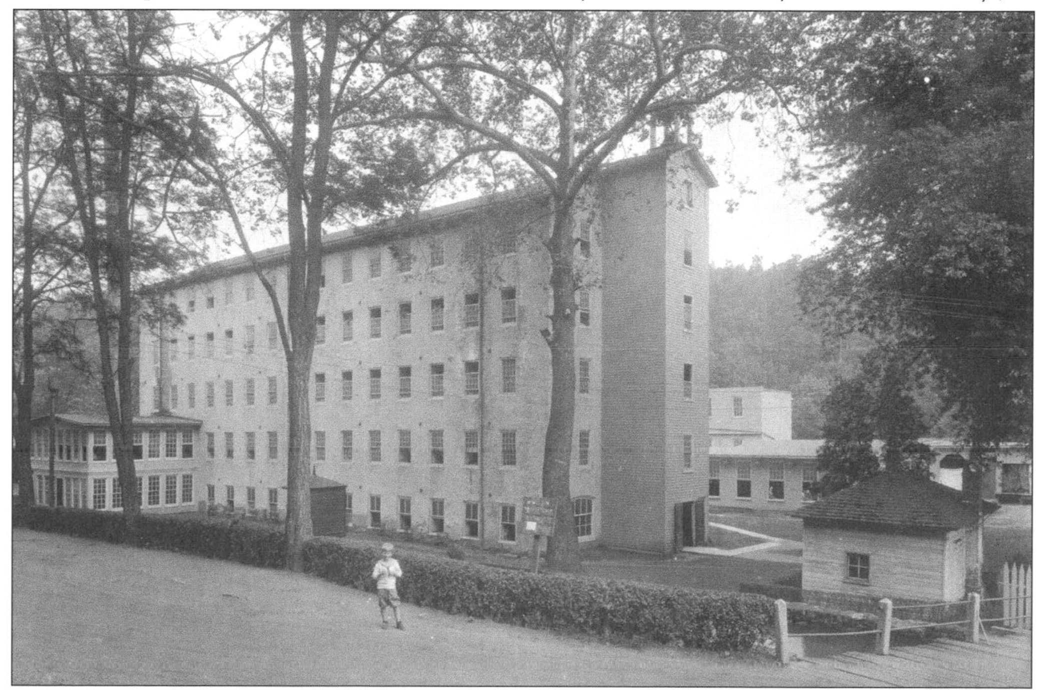

The Warren Manufacturing Company produced cotton in mills powered by the Gunpowder River. During the time Baltimore City was arranging to purchase the land and all structures, from the smallest shack to these large millhouses, the *Baltimore Sun* caught wind of a scandal regarding a "private arrangement" between the owners of the Warren and the Phoenix Mills and city officials. The scandal resulted in a delay of 13 years before the Loch Raven Dam project was completed. (Courtesy Baltimore County Historical Society.)

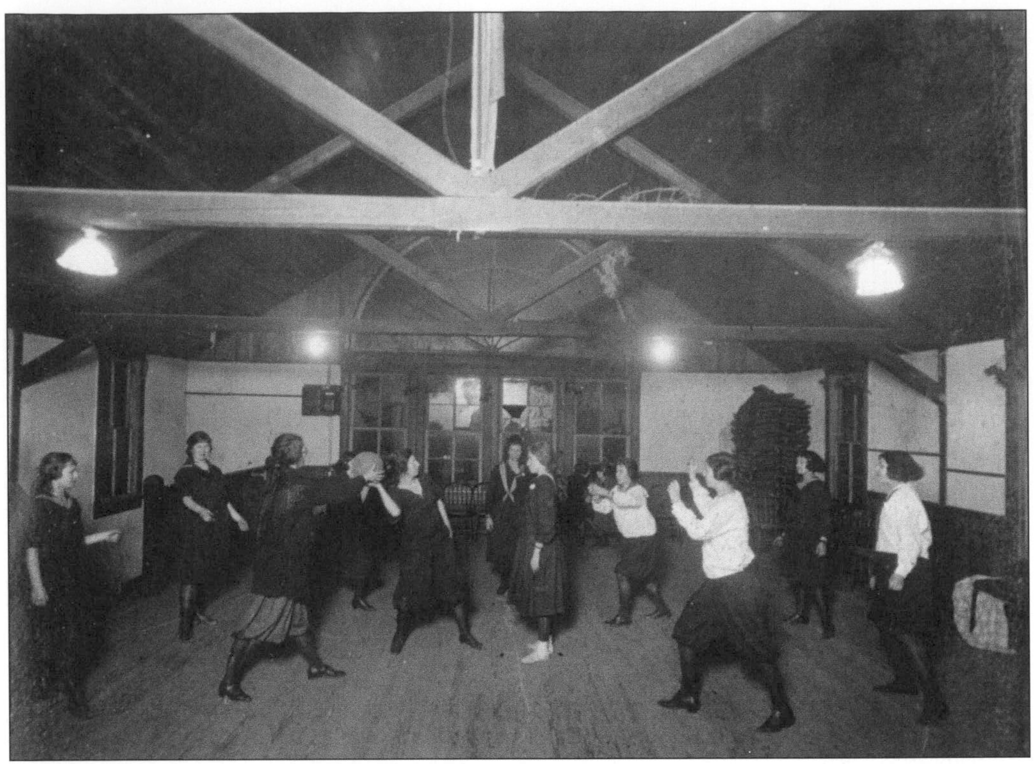

These young women were probably among the 200 townspeople employed by the Warren Manufacturing Company. They are enjoying a lively game of end ball in a large room above the company's offices. (Courtesy Baltimore County Historical Society.)

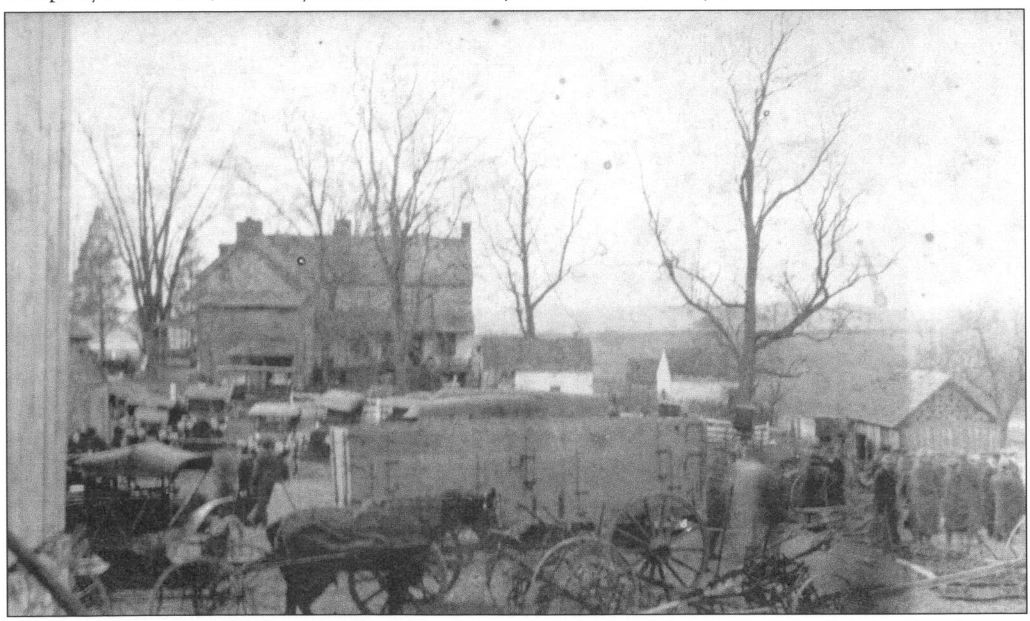

The Jessop Farm, or Hickory Hill, held a farm sale on December 15, 1915. The farmlands were submerged as part of the reservoir project in the early 1920s. (Courtesy Baltimore County Historical Society.)

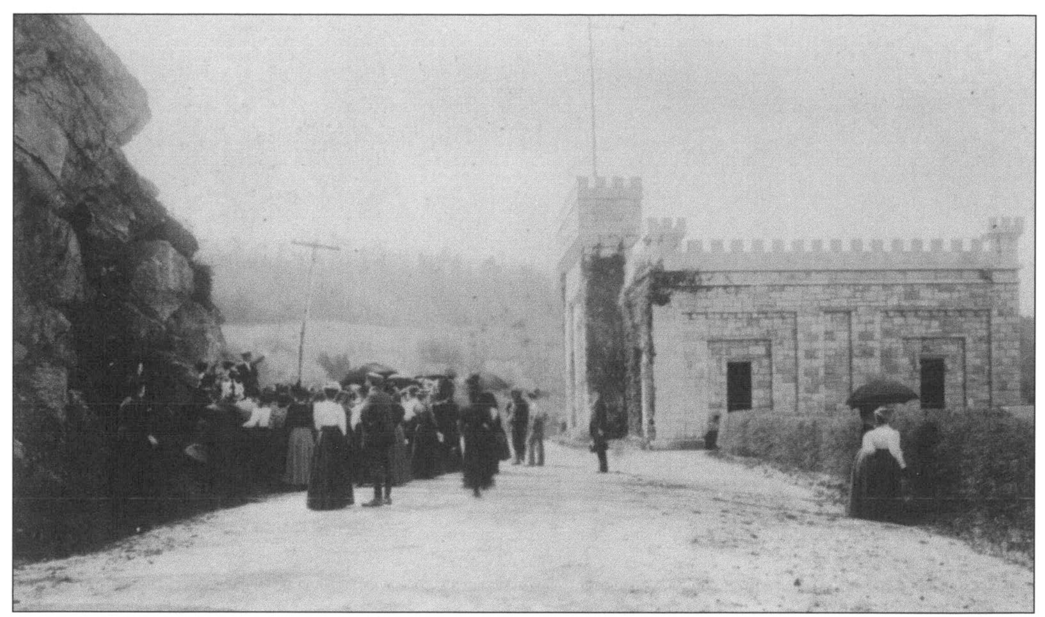

A group from Johns Hopkins University on a field trip enjoy Loch Raven's scenic shore. Increasing pollution in Lake Roland compelled Baltimore City to seek a new water source, so in 1881, a dam and a tunnel to Lake Montebello were completed for $4.5 million. The tunnel is still in use, so you could say the city got its money's worth! (Courtesy Baltimore County Historical Society.)

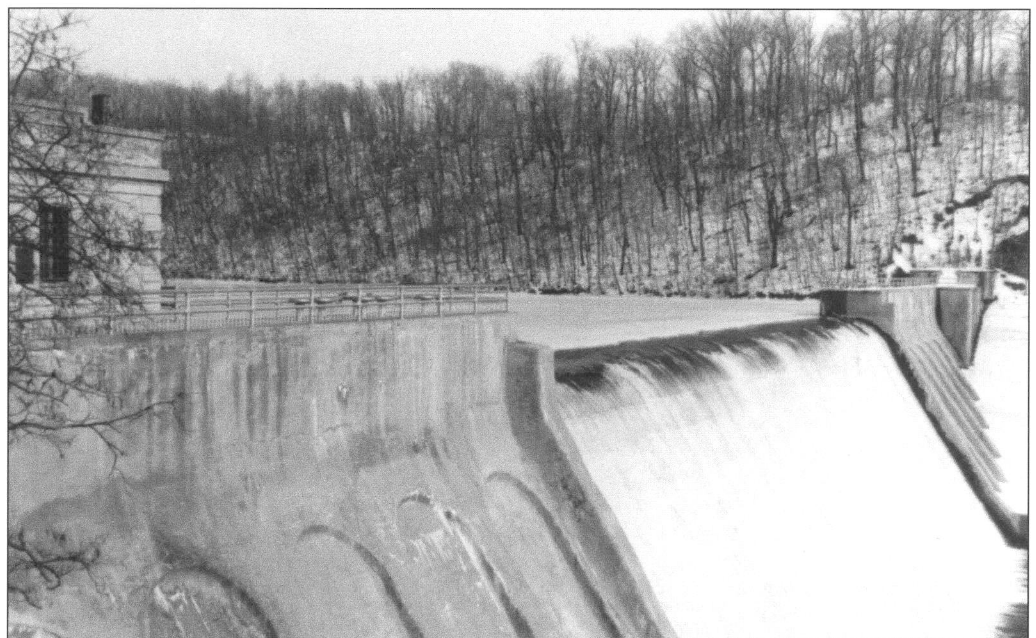

Baltimore City rebuilt the dam in 1912. After the Warren scandal was resolved, the dam's height was increased to 240 feet. The Loch Raven Watershed was an attraction for many locals. Although hundreds of people had to relocate as a result of the organized flooding of the valley, the reservoir project has proven to be an invaluable resource for the entire community. (Courtesy Baltimore County Historical Society.)

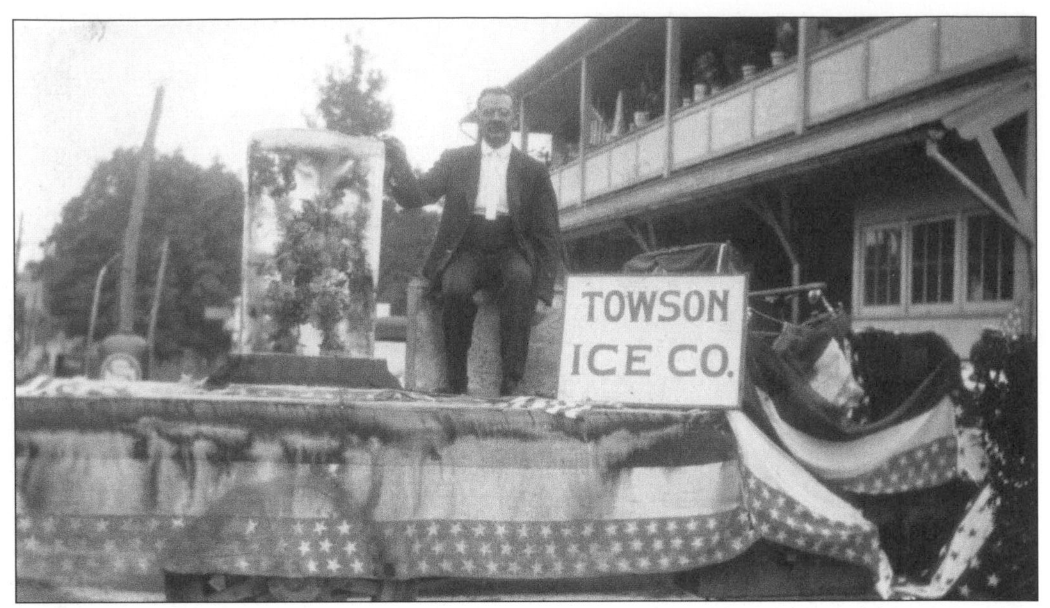

The annual Towson Fourth of July parade is over a century old and has long been a major celebration for the community. Here, Mr. S.C. Seitz poses on one of the Independent Ice Company wagons, with a bouquet of flowers preserved in a block of ice. (Courtesy Baltimore County Historical Society.)

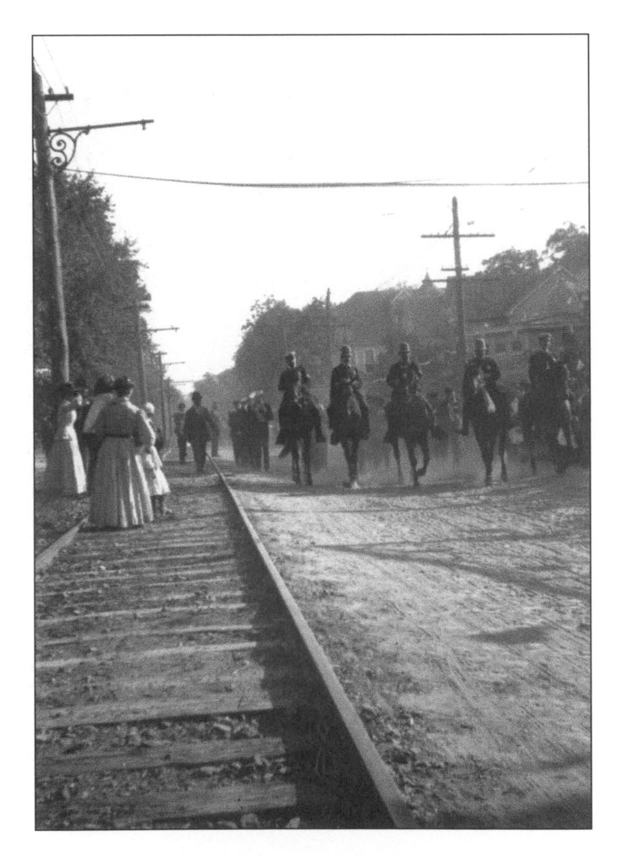

Mounted police march in the Fourth of July parade, *c.* 1900. (Courtesy Baltimore County Historical Society.)

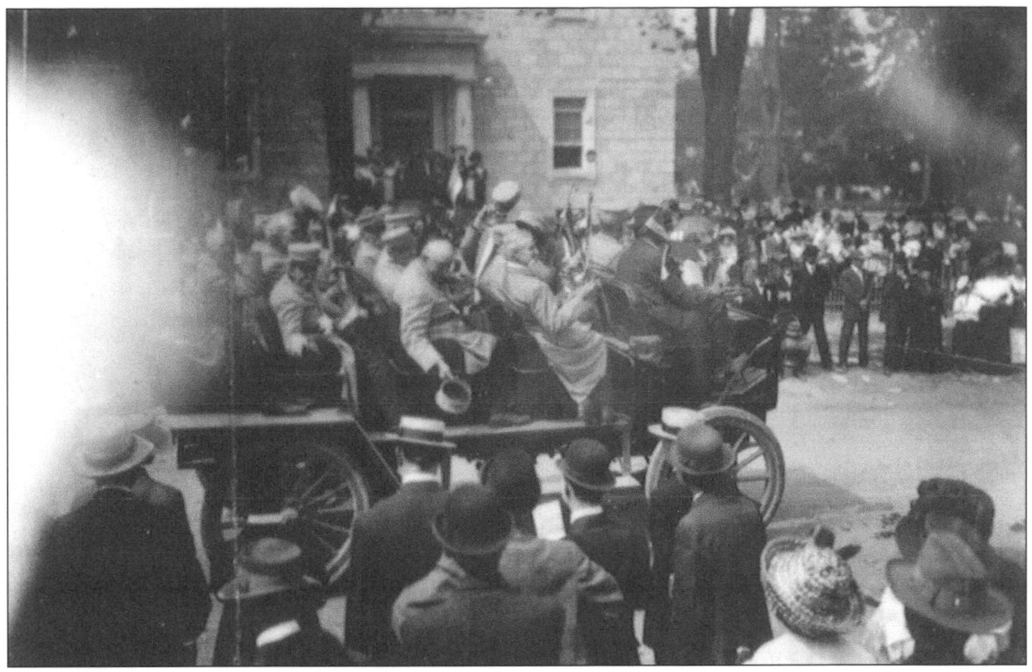

These gentlemen are probably Civil War veterans from the Confederate side. While Maryland was officially on the Union side of the war, many in Towson leaned strongly toward the Confederacy, so these Southern gentlemen probably received an enthusiastic response. (Courtesy Baltimore County Historical Society.)

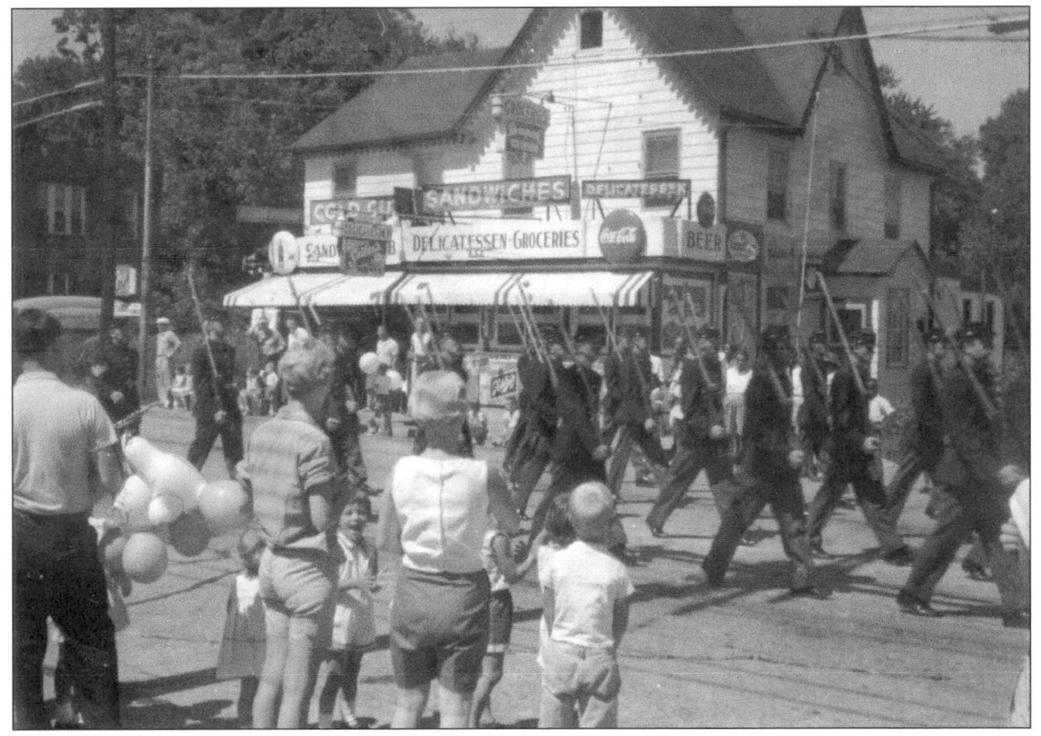

The "Sharpsburg Rifles" march in the 1959 parade. (Courtesy John W. McGrain.)

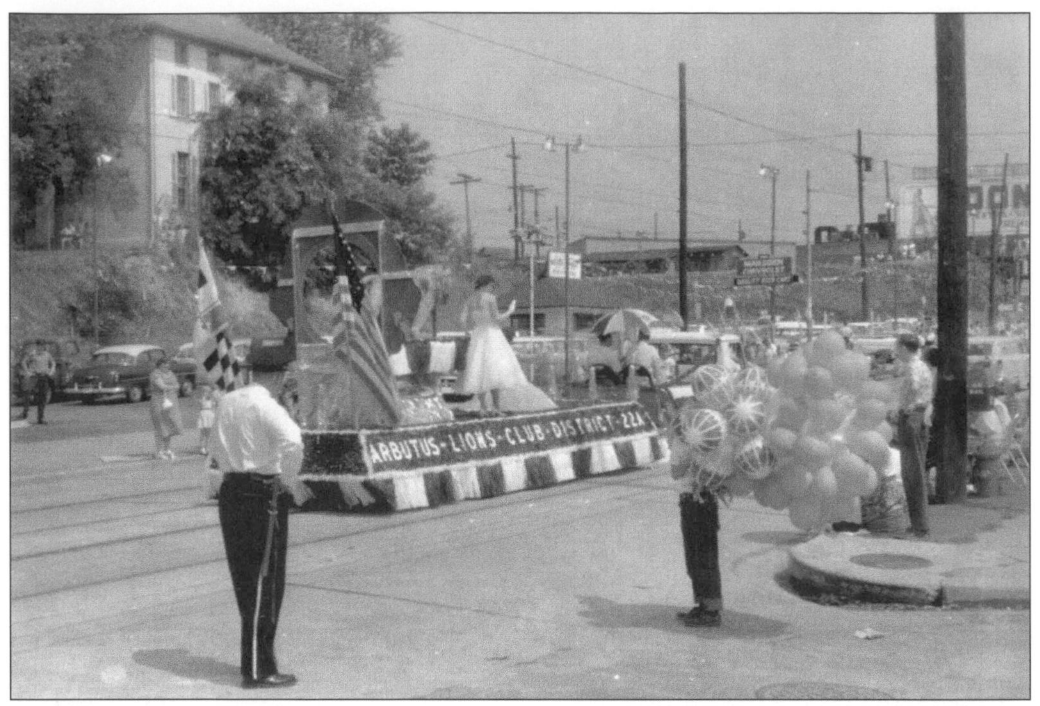

Other communities are invited to help Towson celebrate the Fourth. This group from Arbutus is passing the old YMCA. (Courtesy John W. McGrain.)

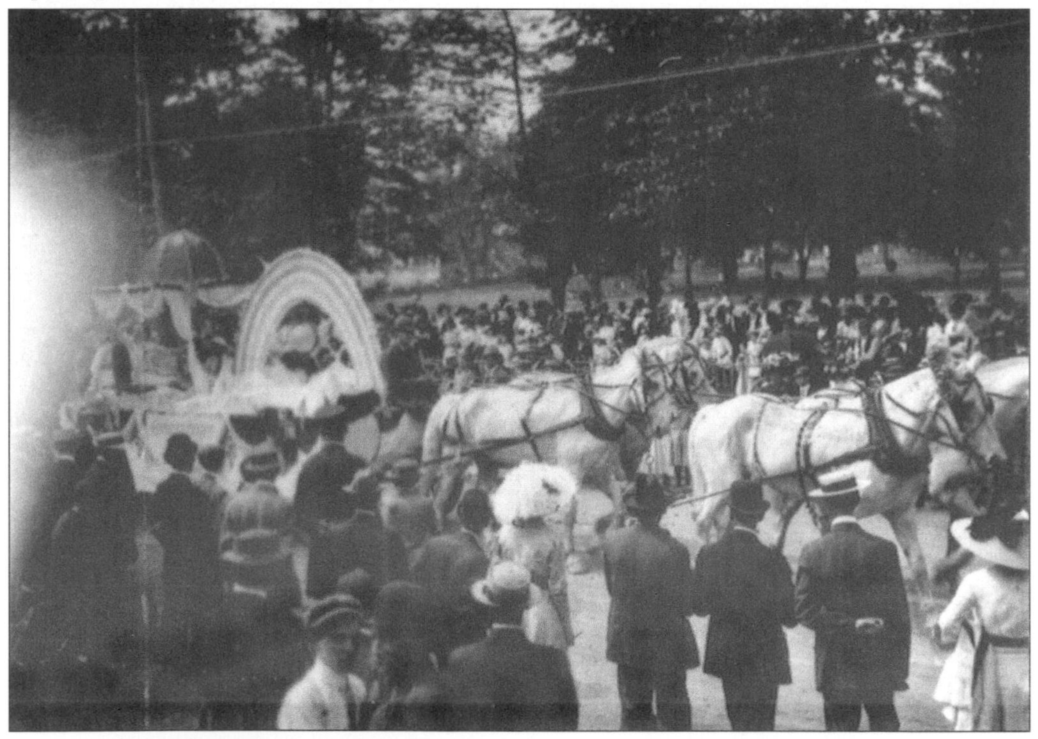

You can almost hear the harnesses ringing on these proud white steeds. (Courtesy Baltimore County Historical Society.)

Two

RUXTON

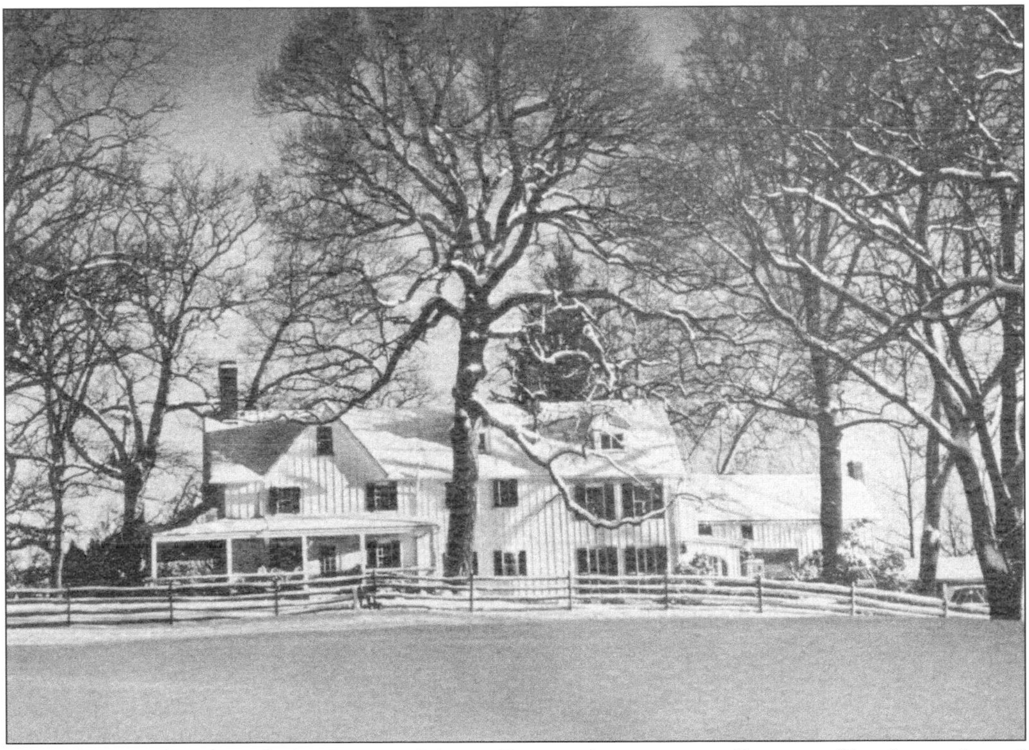

Named for Colonel Nicholas Ruxton Moore, Ruxton began as a collection of land parcels and small farms. Until the late 1800s, Ruxton remained largely an agricultural area, dotted with mills. Baltimoreans, eager to escape the city, moved northward, as landowners divided their property into smaller building lots. While retaining a rural sensibility, Ruxton began to grow into a community, which offered residents not only a bucolic setting in which to live, but also practical resources for transportation, shopping, recreation, and worship. (Courtesy Mrs. Beatrice Hooker Marty.)

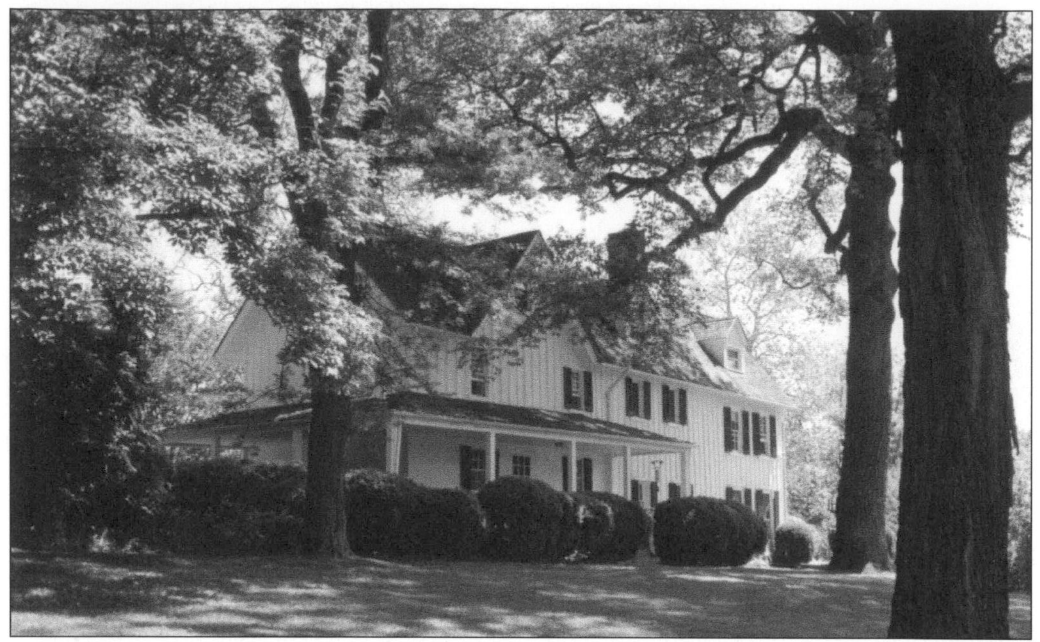

Carr's Pleasure was purchased by Samuel Bowen in 1752. It is thought that the left side of the house dates back to the 1690s. The significant additions were built in the 1720s. (Courtesy Mrs. Beatrice Hooker Marty.)

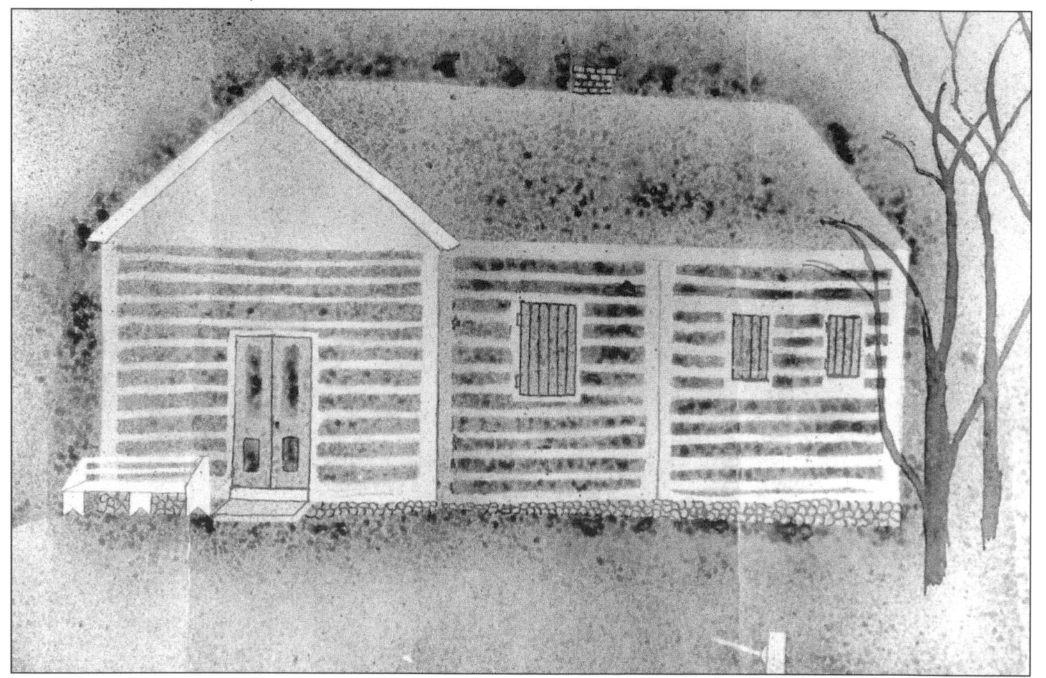

Eliza Hawkins's 1835 drawing depicts the St. John's AME Church on Bellona Avenue. The .75-acre property was sold in 1833 to five men, both free men and slaves, by landowner Elijah Fishpaw. This venture may have been one of the earliest efforts to ensure freedom of religious expression in pre-emancipation Maryland. The log structure was built in 1835 and destroyed by fire in 1876. (Courtesy Mrs. Charles O'Donovan III.)

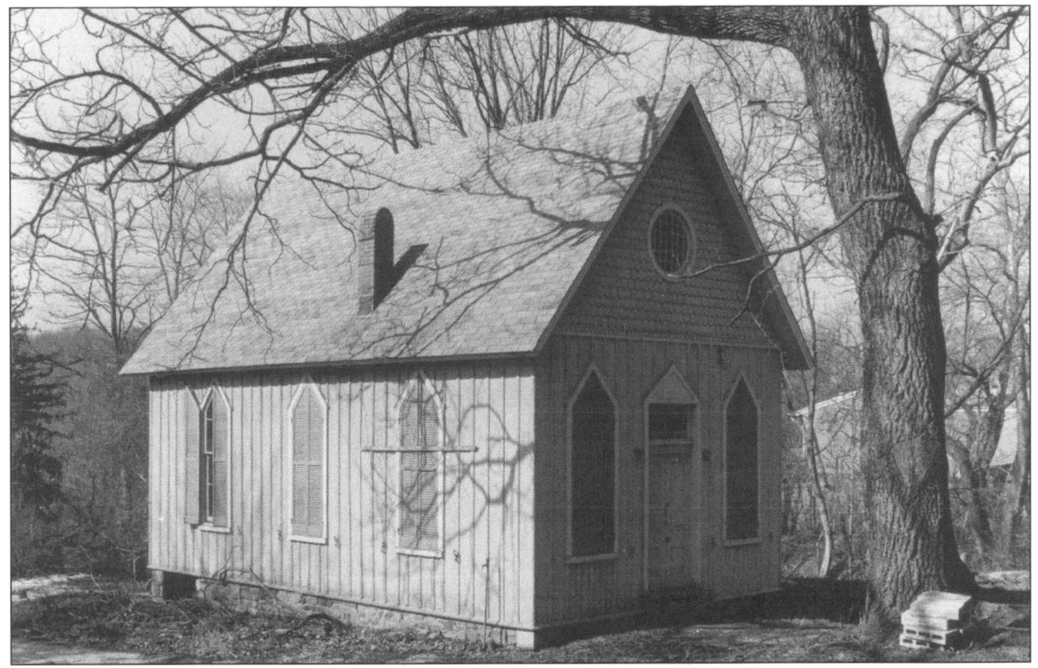

The gothic-revival structure was built on the original site of St. John's AME in 1886. The oldest black parish in Baltimore County, St. John's AME served the surrounding community until the 1950s. In 1981, the church and the parsonage were put under the protection of the Baltimore County Historical Trust. (Courtesy Mrs. Charles O'Donovan III.)

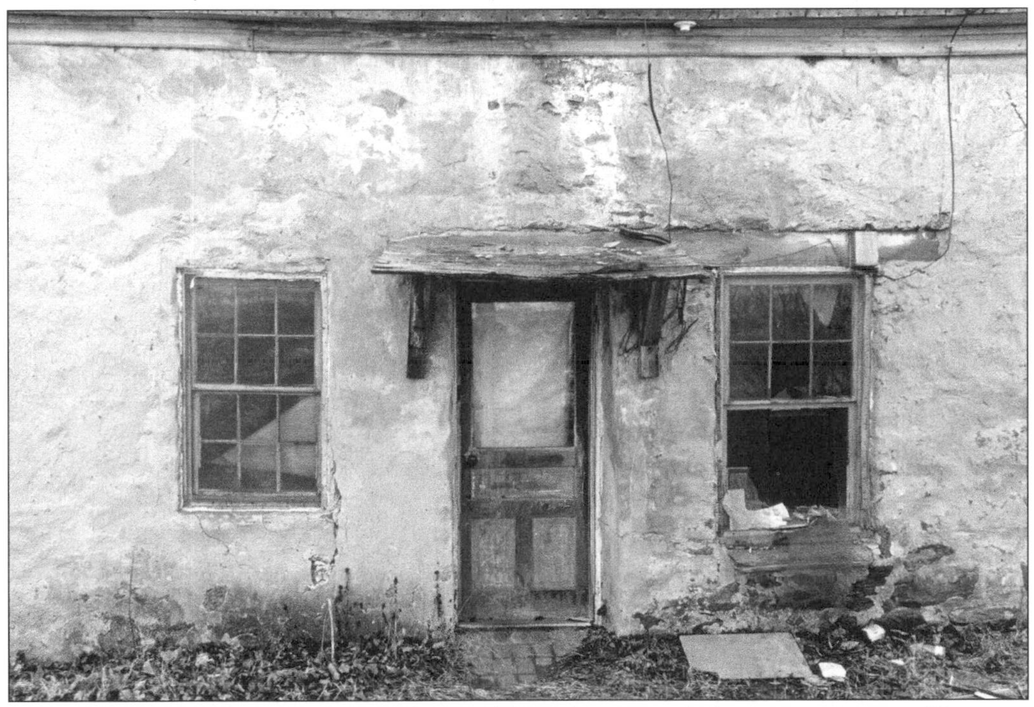

The parsonage had become a target for vandals and arsonists before its restoration. (Courtesy Mrs. Charles O'Donovan III.)

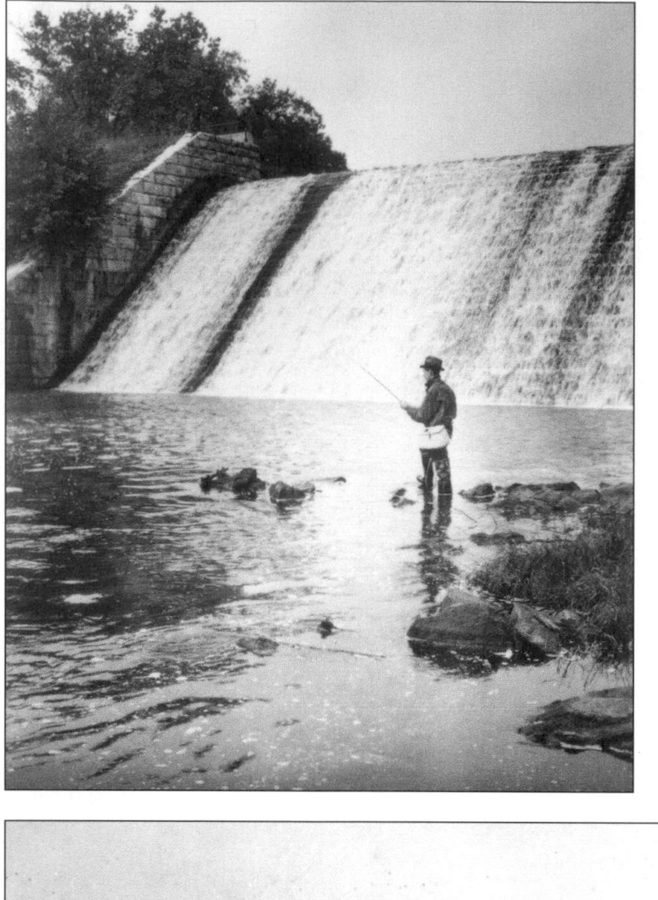

In an effort to meet Baltimore City's increasing demand for water, the Roland Run was dammed in 1860 to create Lake Roland. (Courtesy Baltimore County Public Library.)

The Northern Central Line, connecting Baltimore and York, Pennsylvania, had several depots in Ruxton. They included Ruxton, Riderwood, Brightwood, and Lake stations. Here, the *Liberty Limited* steams across the trestle over Lake Roland. (Courtesy Baltimore County Historical Society.)

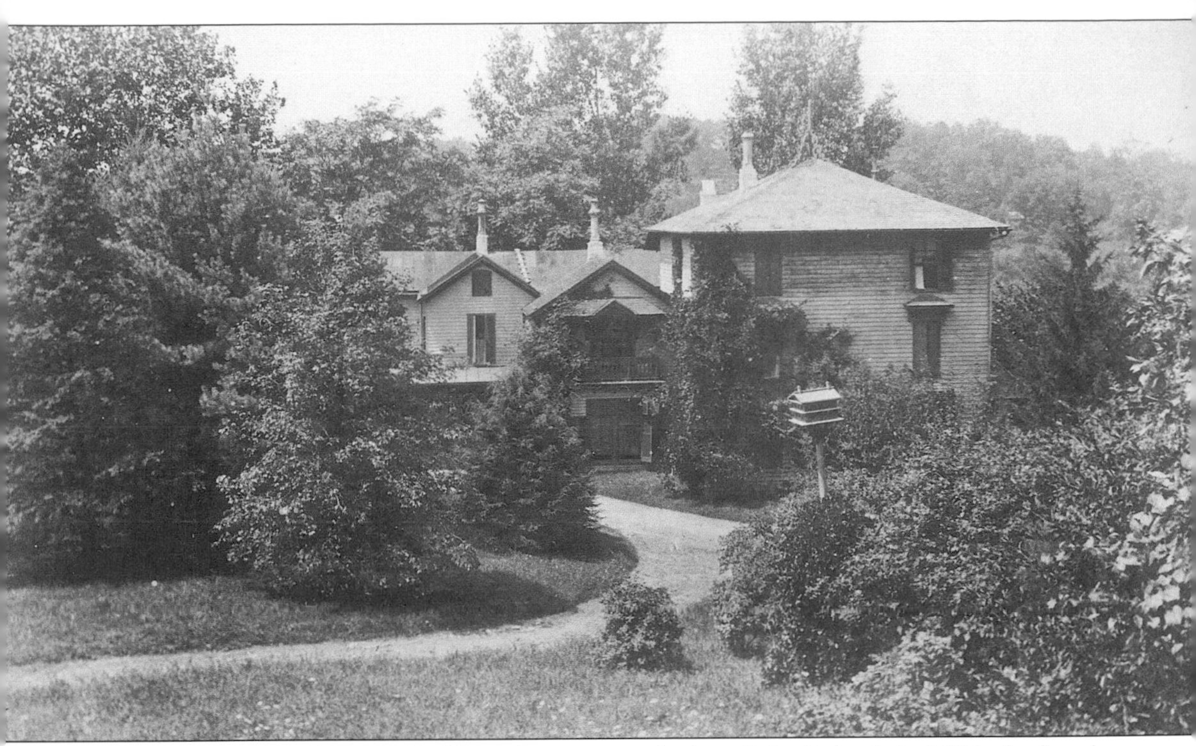

Brightside was situated west of Bellona Avenue, overlooking Lake Roland. In 1886, the hotel was operated by the Poseys as a summer escape for Baltimoreans. Shortly after being purchased by W. Kennedy Cromwell, the building burned on February 8, 1913. (Courtesy Baltimore County Public Library.)

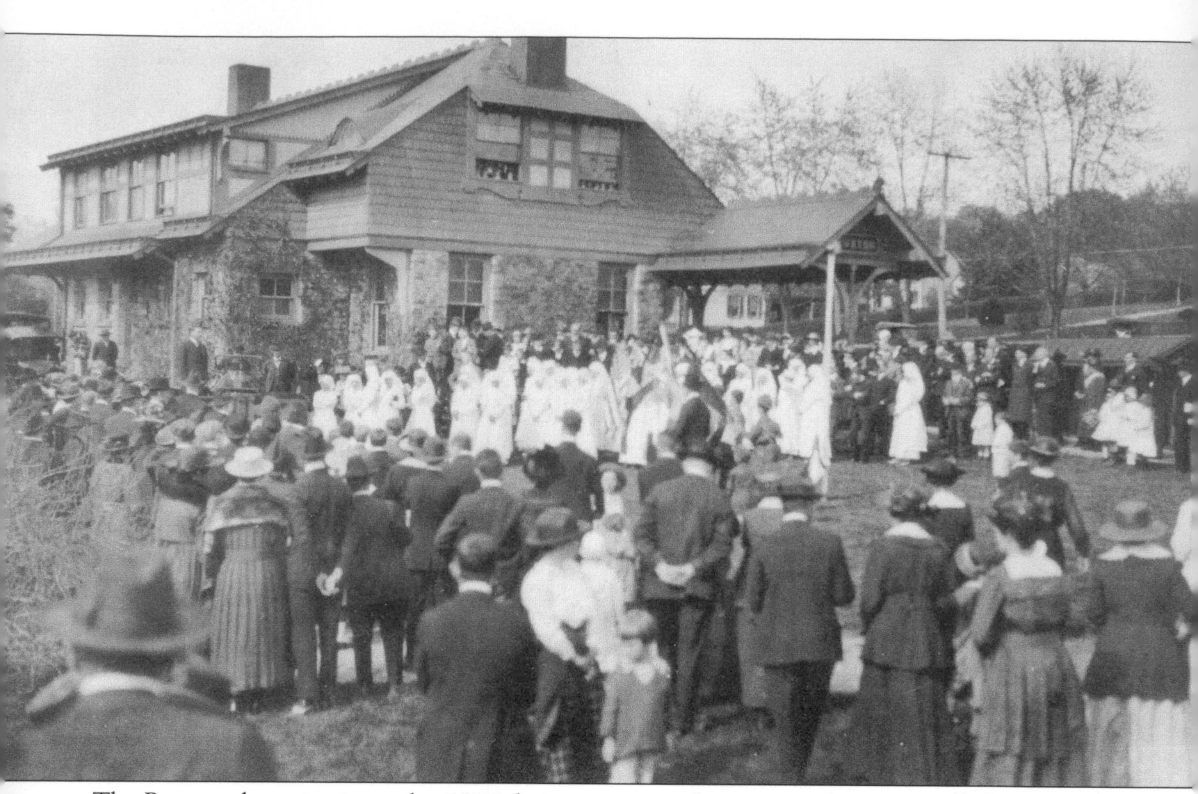

The Ruxton depot is pictured *c.* 1910 during an event that attracted an unusually large crowd. The presence of nurses (the figures in white) suggests a rally to gather support for a foreign war. The Northern Central Railroad (N.C.R.) Line saw several events of note (a dreadful train wreck occurred in 1856, President Lincoln's train traveled through on his way to Gettysburg in 1863, and sadly, his funeral cortege passed through in 1865). (Courtesy Collection of the late Samuel W. Wiley Jr.)

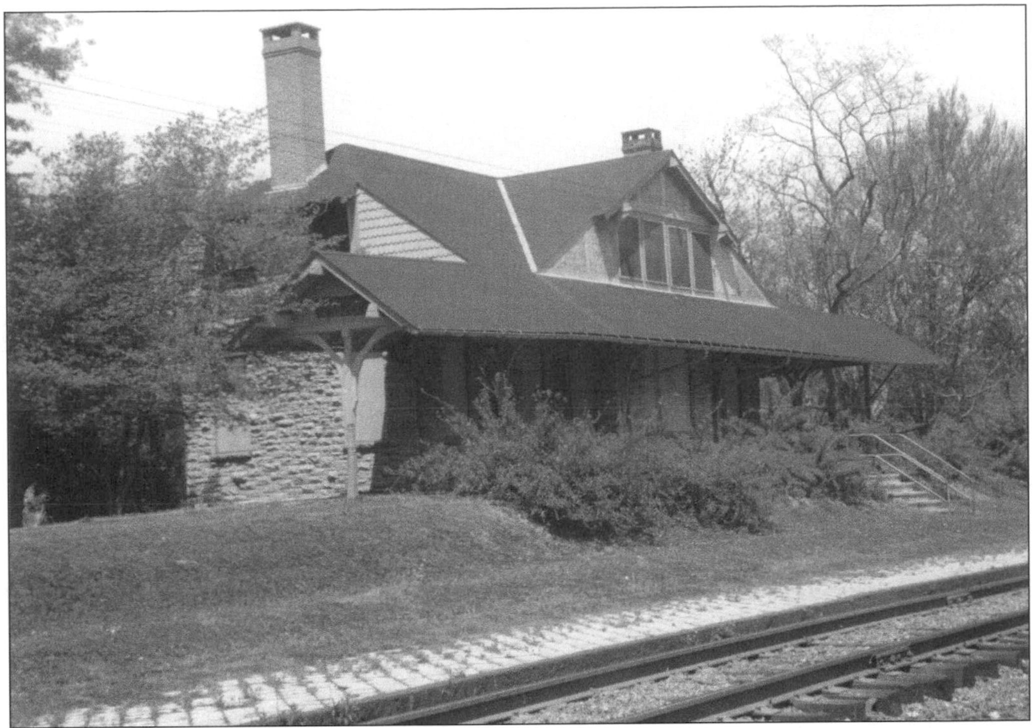

The charming Ruxton Station was built in 1885. It was razed in 1963 to clear the way for the Ruxton Township townhouses. (Courtesy Baltimore County Historical Society.)

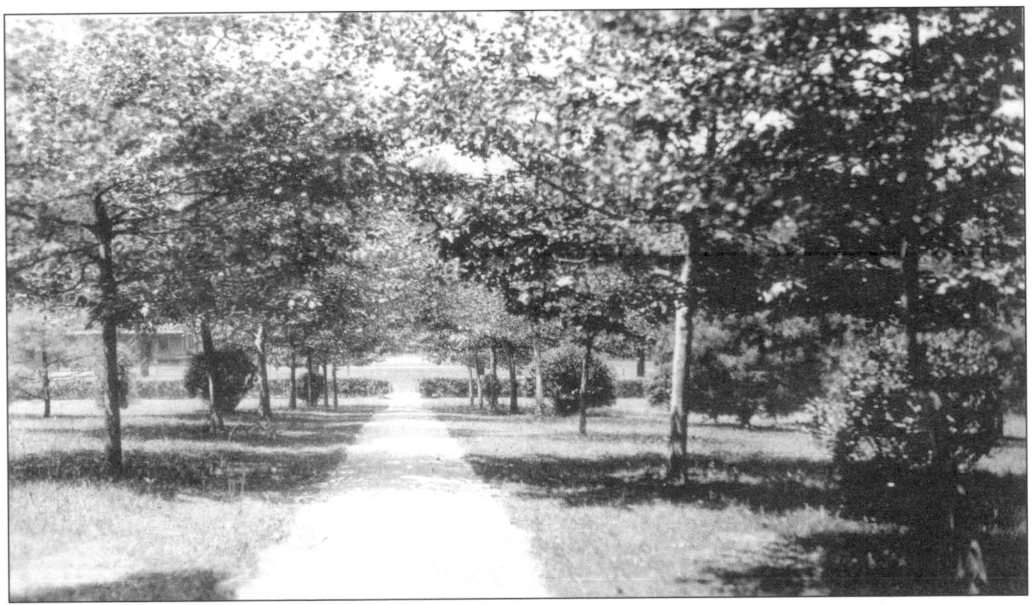

This grassy plot, known as Wiley's Park, eventually became the Graul's parking lot. (Courtesy collection of the late Samuel W. Wiley Jr.)

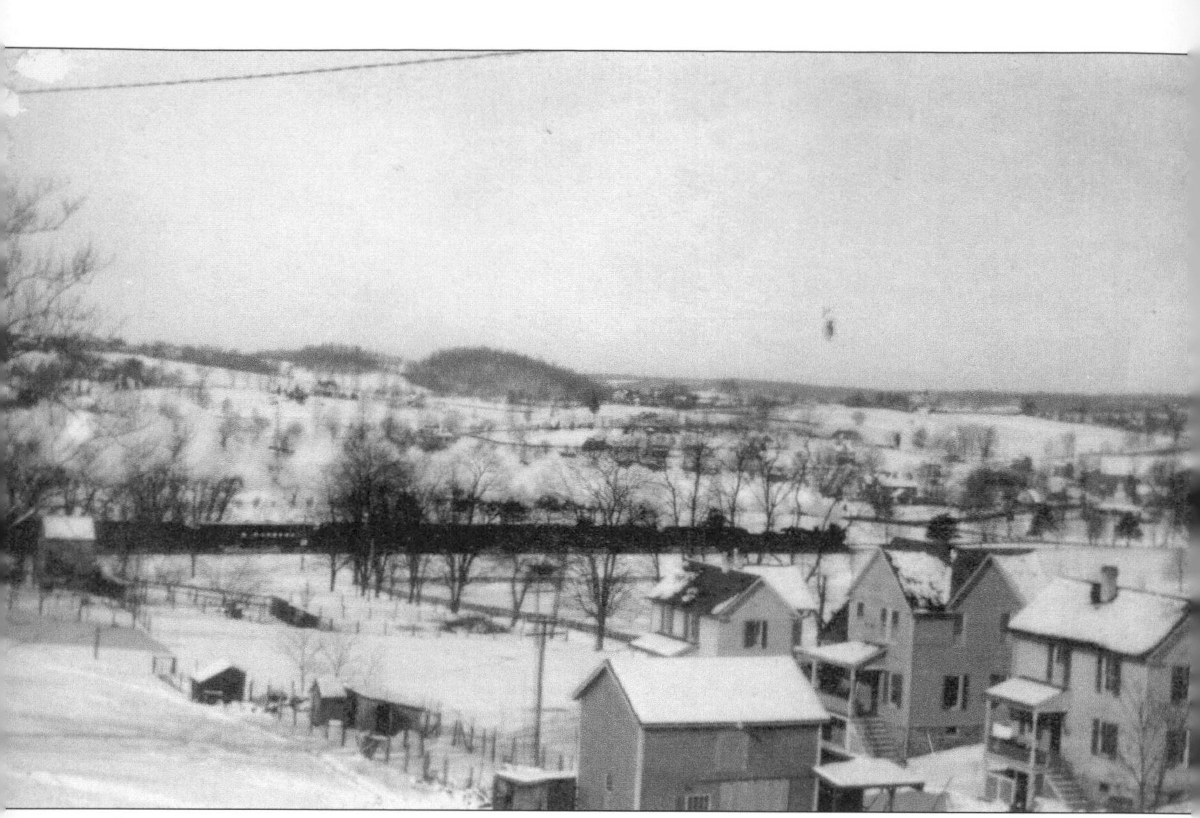

This is a westward view across Ruxton from Ruxton Heights. In the early 1900s, Ruxton was still largely undeveloped on the west side of the N.C.R. Line (The line can be recognized by the train roaring through the scenery.). (Courtesy collection of the late Samuel W. Wiley Jr.)

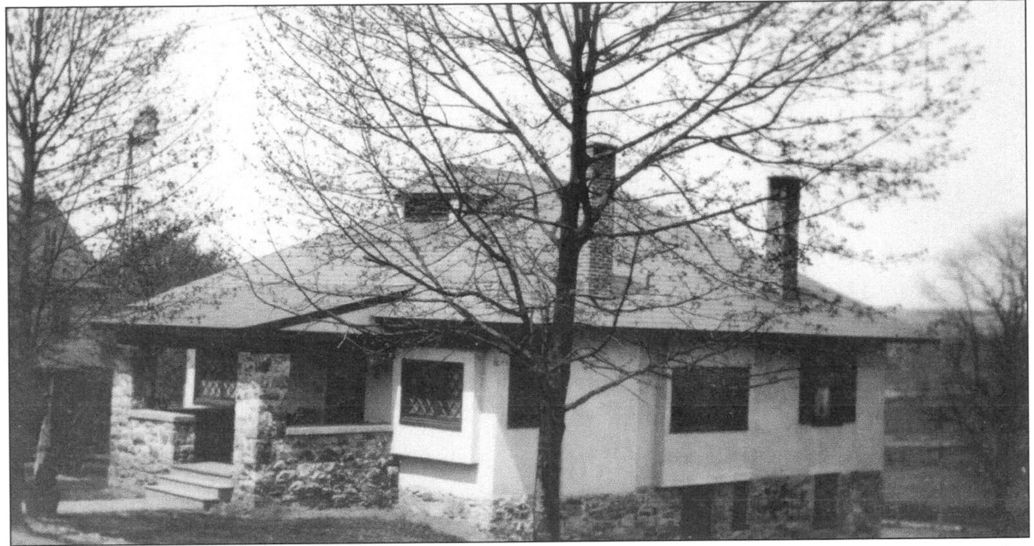

Ruxton Heights, the hillside immediately east of Bellona Avenue, was developed in 1894. The lovely Arts and Crafts house on Berwick Avenue was typical of the homes built here. (Courtesy collection of the late Samuel W. Wiley Jr.)

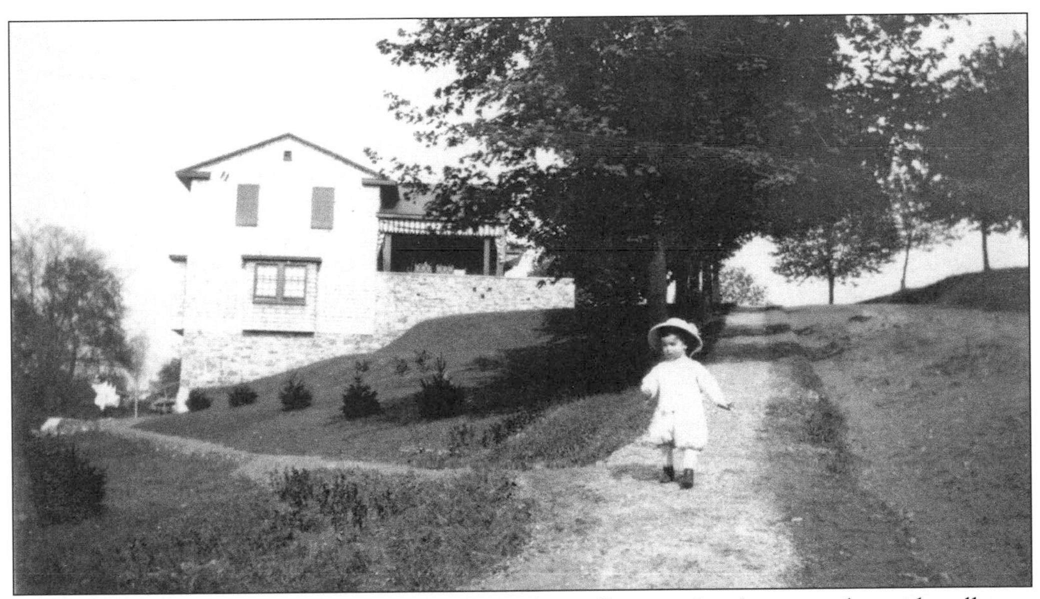

A young Samuel Wiley makes his way down the walking paths that served as sidewalks on Ruxton Heights. (Courtesy collection of the late Samuel W. Wiley Jr.)

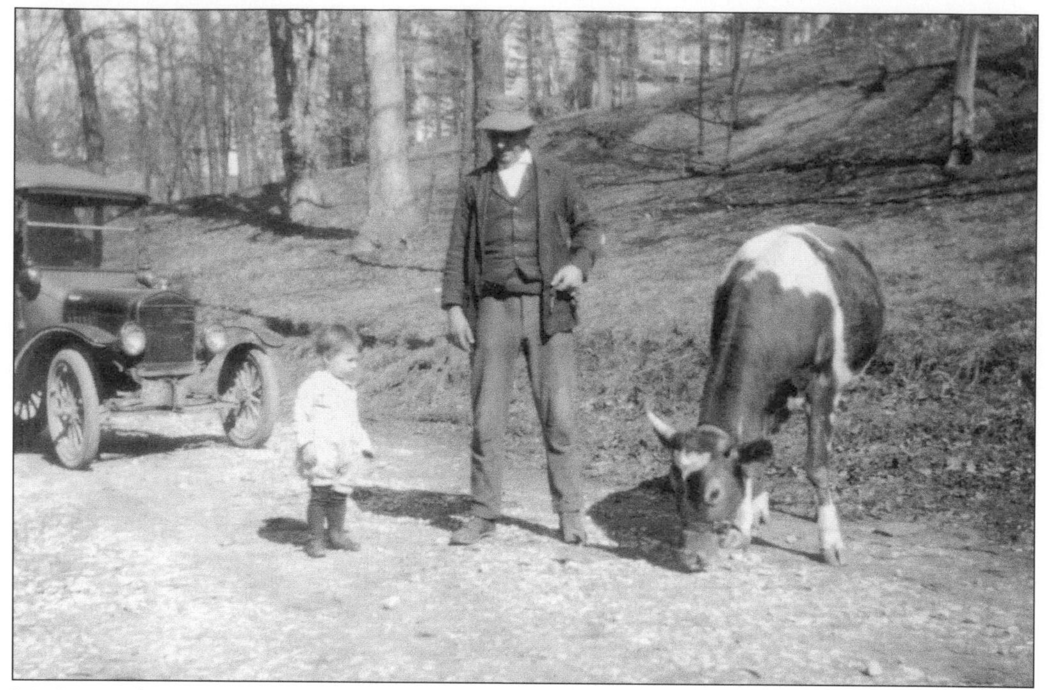

Mr. Bernard Tiepe, caretaker, poses with his grandson, Lyman Anderson, and a friendly cow on the Finney estate in 1924. The area is now Circle Road, and the house, barely visible in the background, is still standing. (Courtesy Mrs. Joan Kaltenbach.)

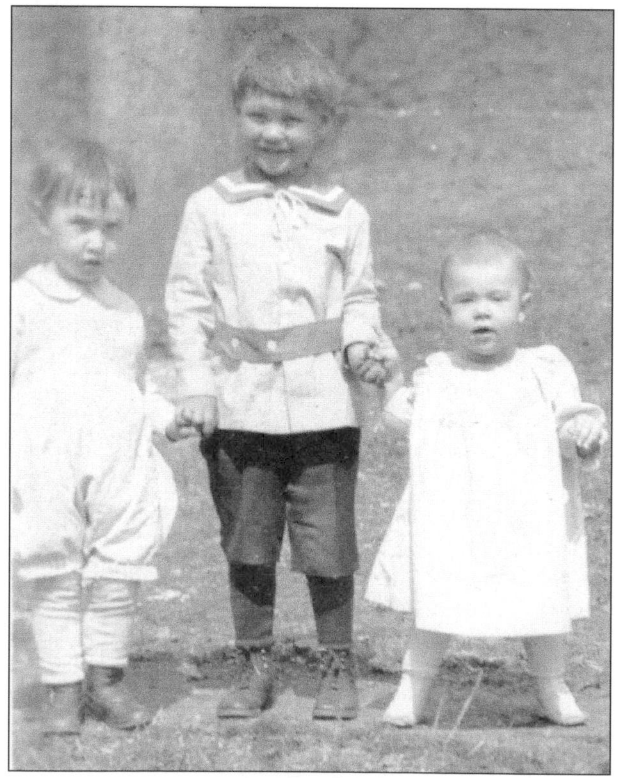

Sidney Mash is pictured in between his cousins, Lyman and Joan Anderson, in Ruxton, *c.* 1923. (Courtesy Mrs. Joan Kaltenbach.)

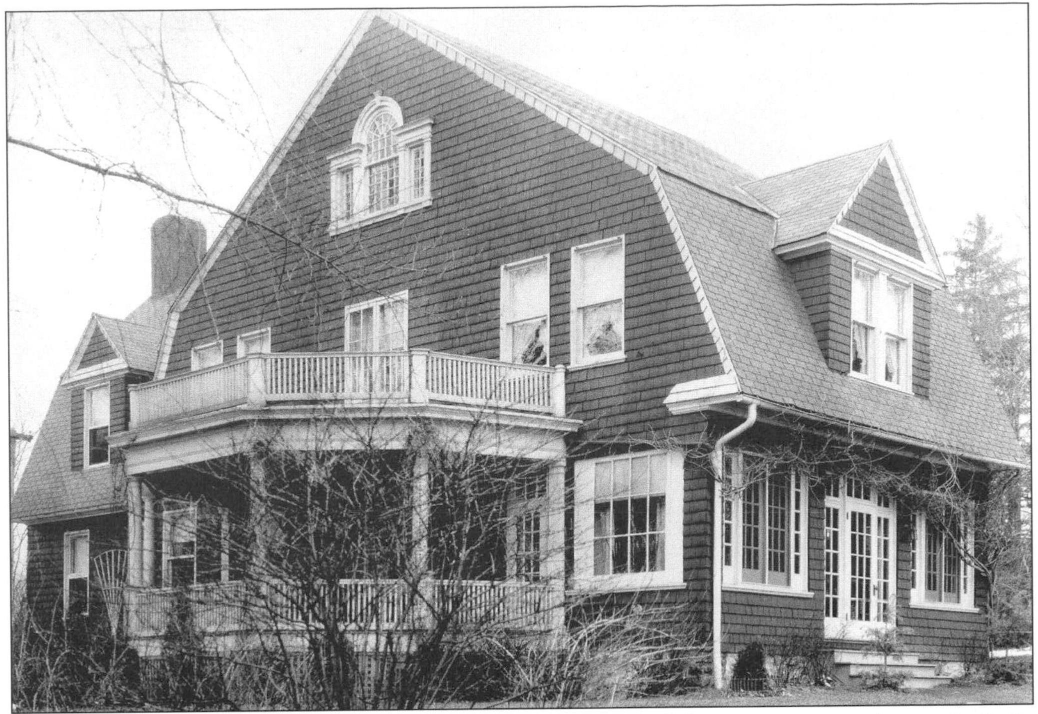

This classic shingle-style home on Wagner Road is typical of the larger summer homes built in Ruxton at the turn of the century. (Courtesy Mr. and Mrs. Raleigh Brent III.)

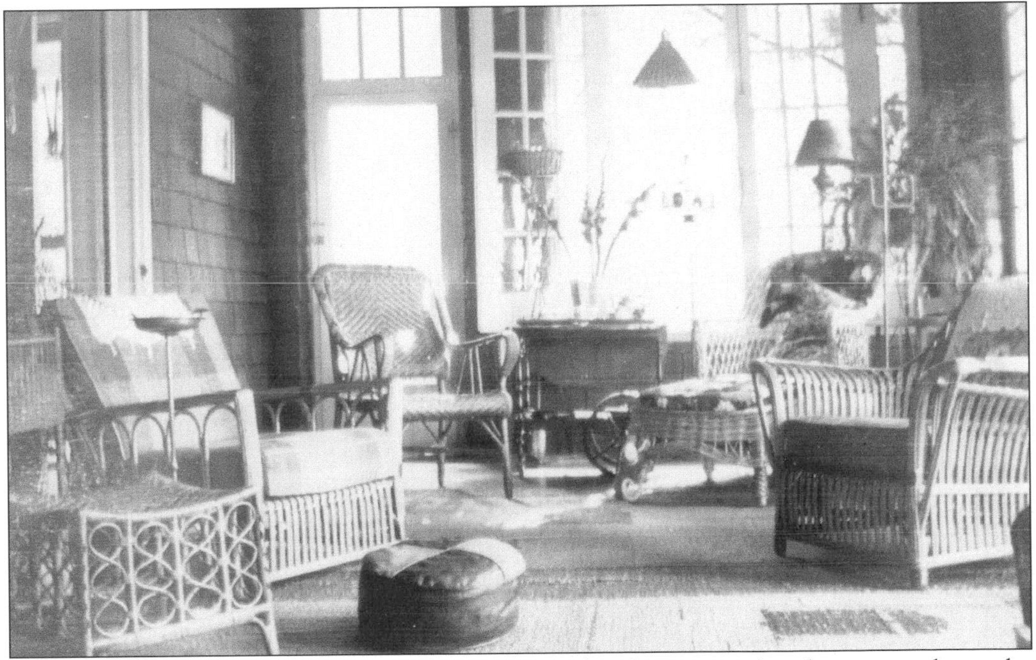

The porch of the home pictured above was decorated with rattan and sisal rugs, popular at the turn of the century. It is easy to imagine the lady of the house being roused from a good book by the sound of the train pulling into the Lake Station, alerting her that her husband had returned from a busy week in town. (Courtesy Mr. and Mrs. Raleigh Brent III.)

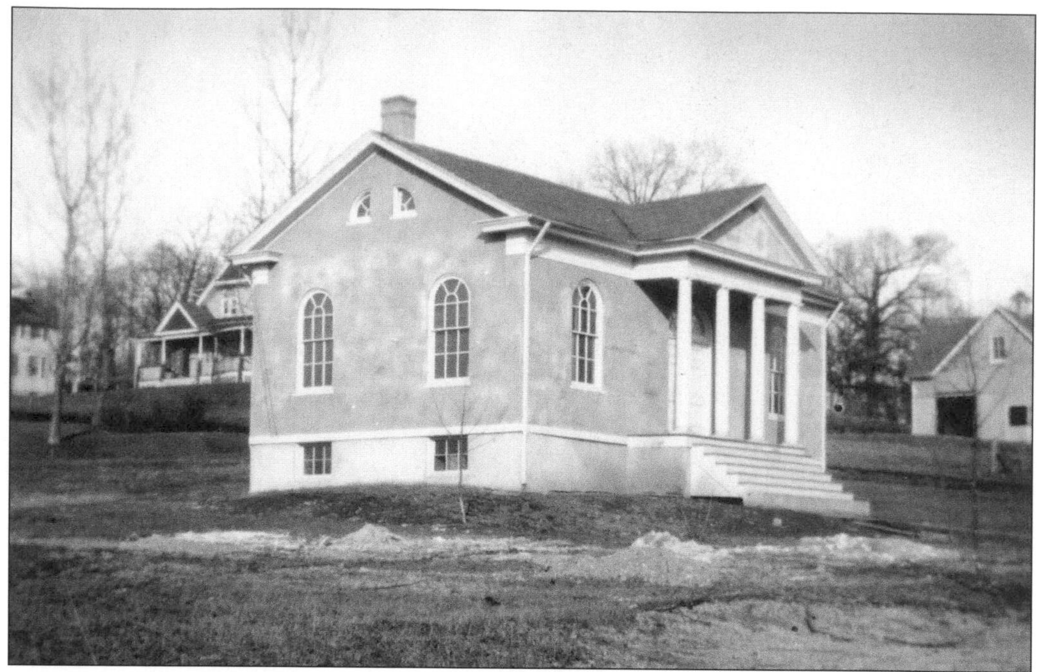

Built on property purchased in 1906, this 1910 photo shows the Chapel of the Good Shepherd, which was built as a Sunday school. Good Shepherd's congregation included many community leaders, such as the Hoffs, the DeFords, and the Hoopers. (Courtesy Mr. and Mrs. Douglas Brinkley.)

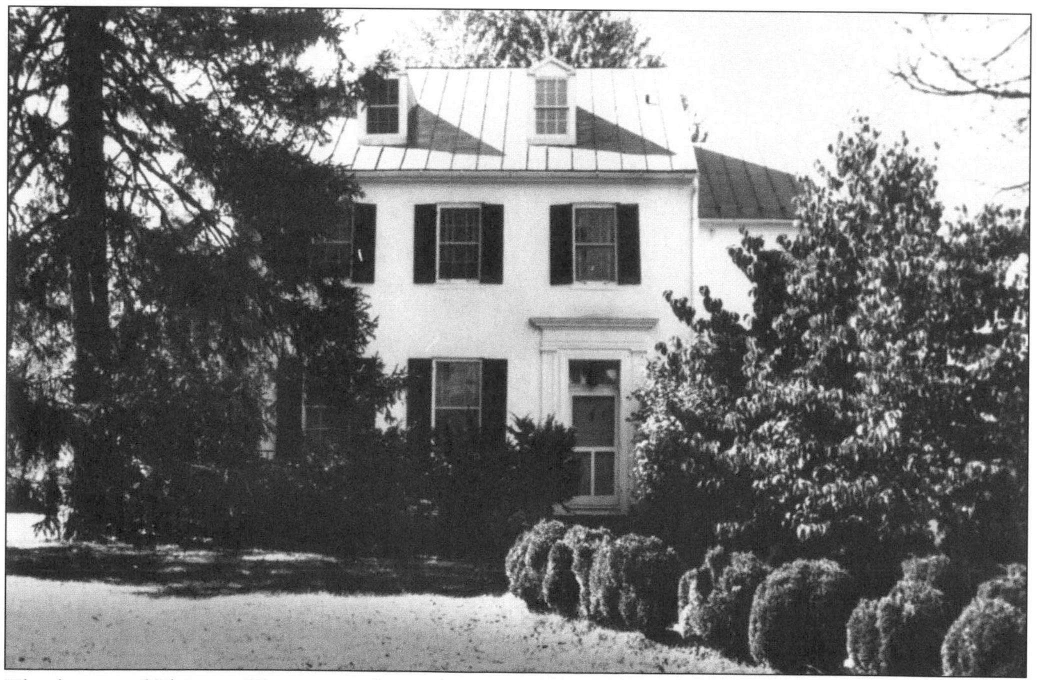

The home of Phineas Hunt was where devout Methodists attended lay services until the 1780 construction of Hunt's Church. The original log structure stood on Joppa Road at the site of the present day Hunt's Church. (Courtesy Baltimore County Historical Society.)

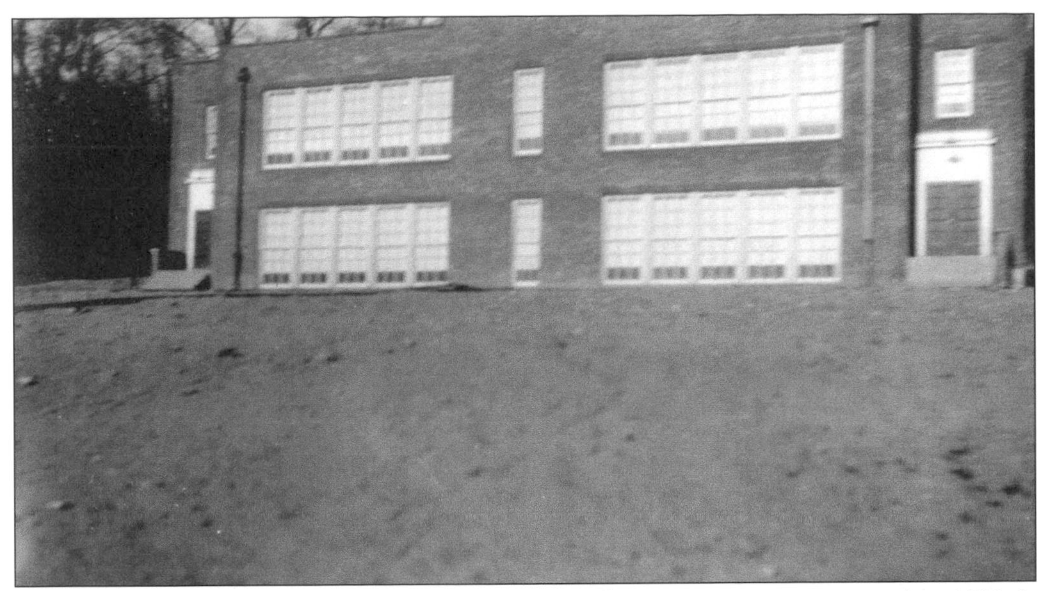

This is the original Riderwood School, located on Bellona Avenue, as it appeared in 1920. It was torn down in 1999. (Courtesy Baltimore County Historical Society.)

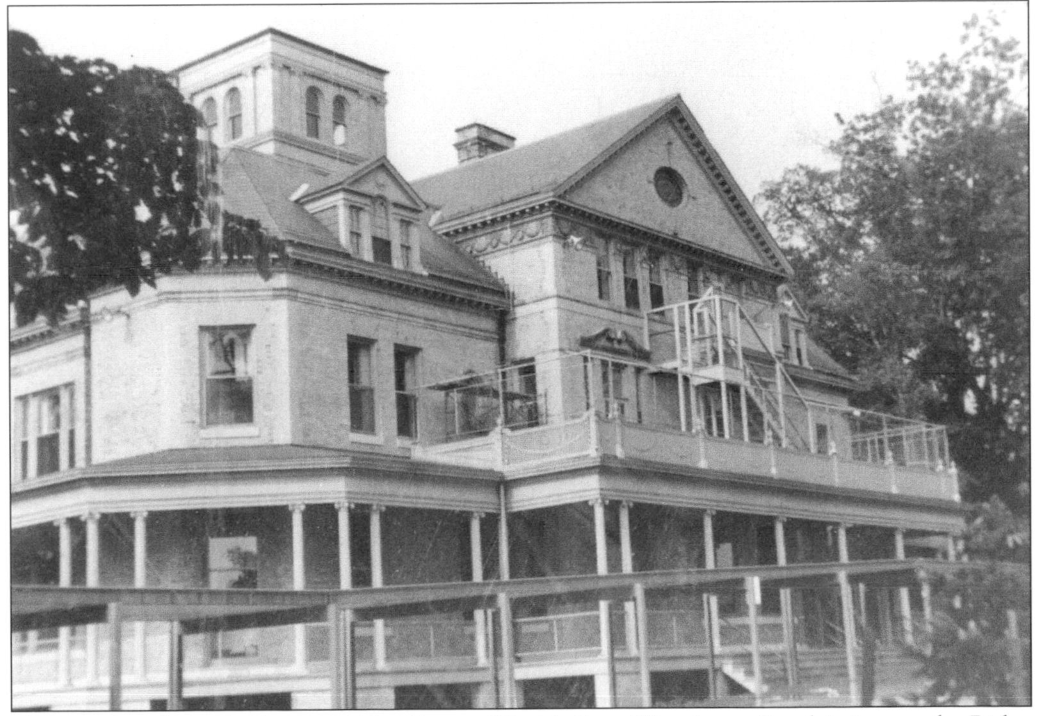

Sherwood Park was built in 1894 by George W. Abell on West Joppa Road. It is now the Ridge School. (Courtesy Baltimore County Historical Society.)

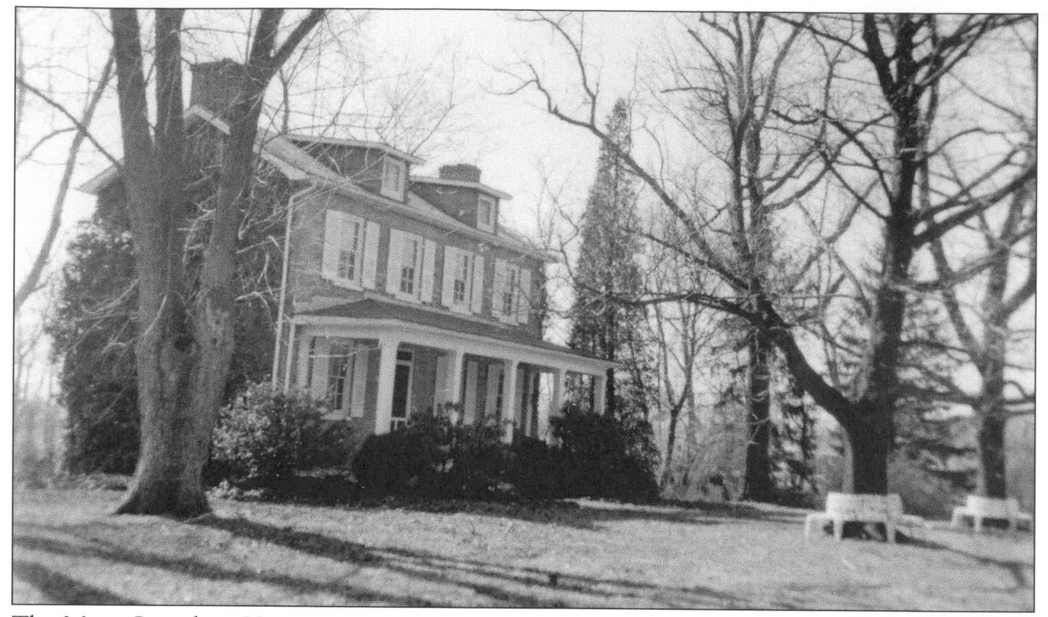

The Mary Creaghan House, construction date unknown, was preserved when a development, The Willows of Ruxton, was built. (Courtesy Baltimore County Public Library.)

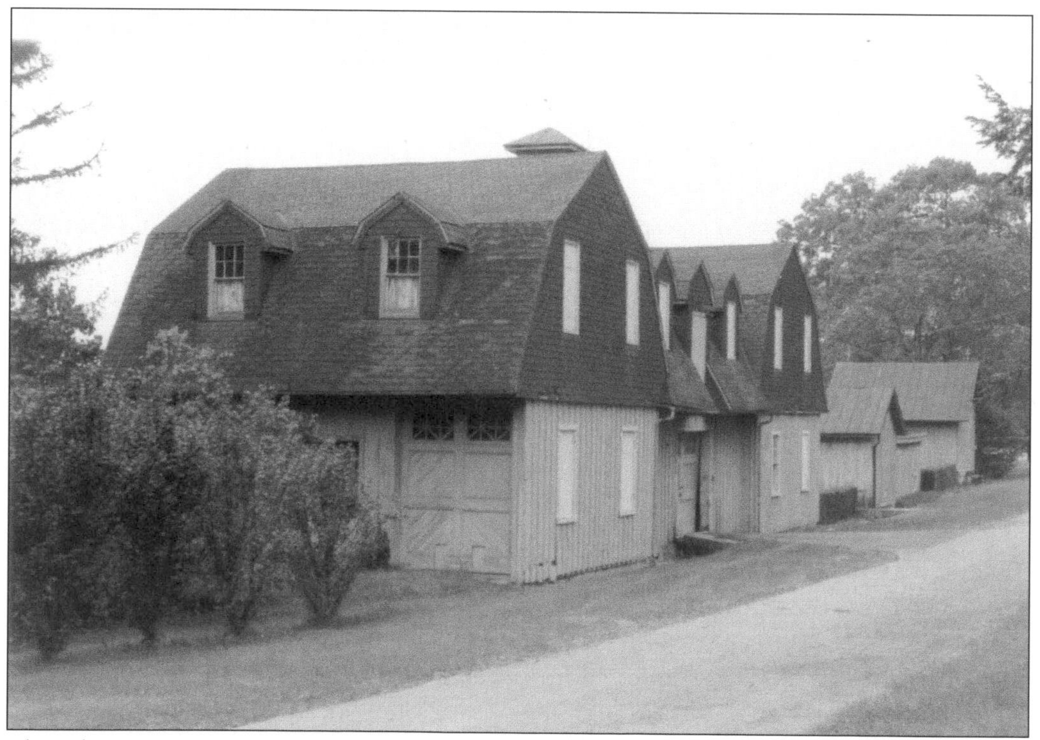

These barns were once a part of Greenwood, the DeFord estate. One of the barns has been restored and is currently used as a hobby shop for Blakehurst Assisted Living. (Courtesy John W. McGrain.)

Three

LUTHERVILLE

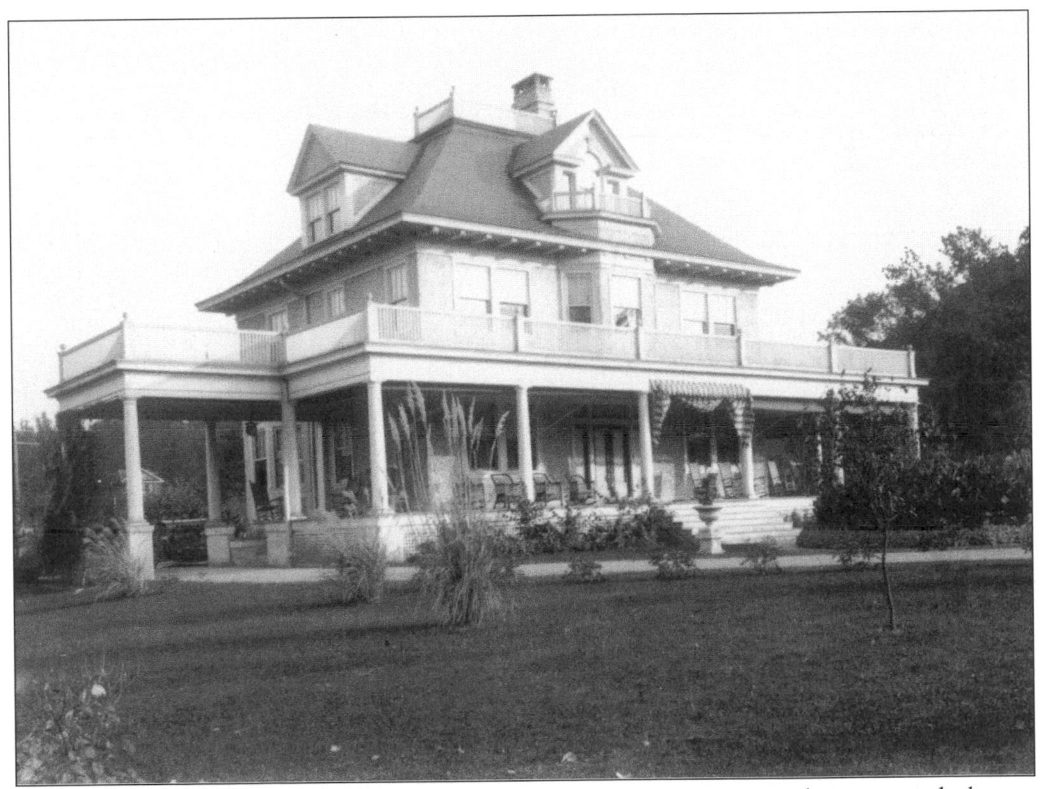

The Gelston House, which still stands at 1603 Franke Avenue, is a charming and elegant example of the architectural delights and surprises discovered by a first-time visitor to Lutherville. The combination of comfort and affluence, with a dash of the exotic (note the roofline), transforms this home from the mundane to the marvelous. (Courtesy Baltimore County Historical Society.)

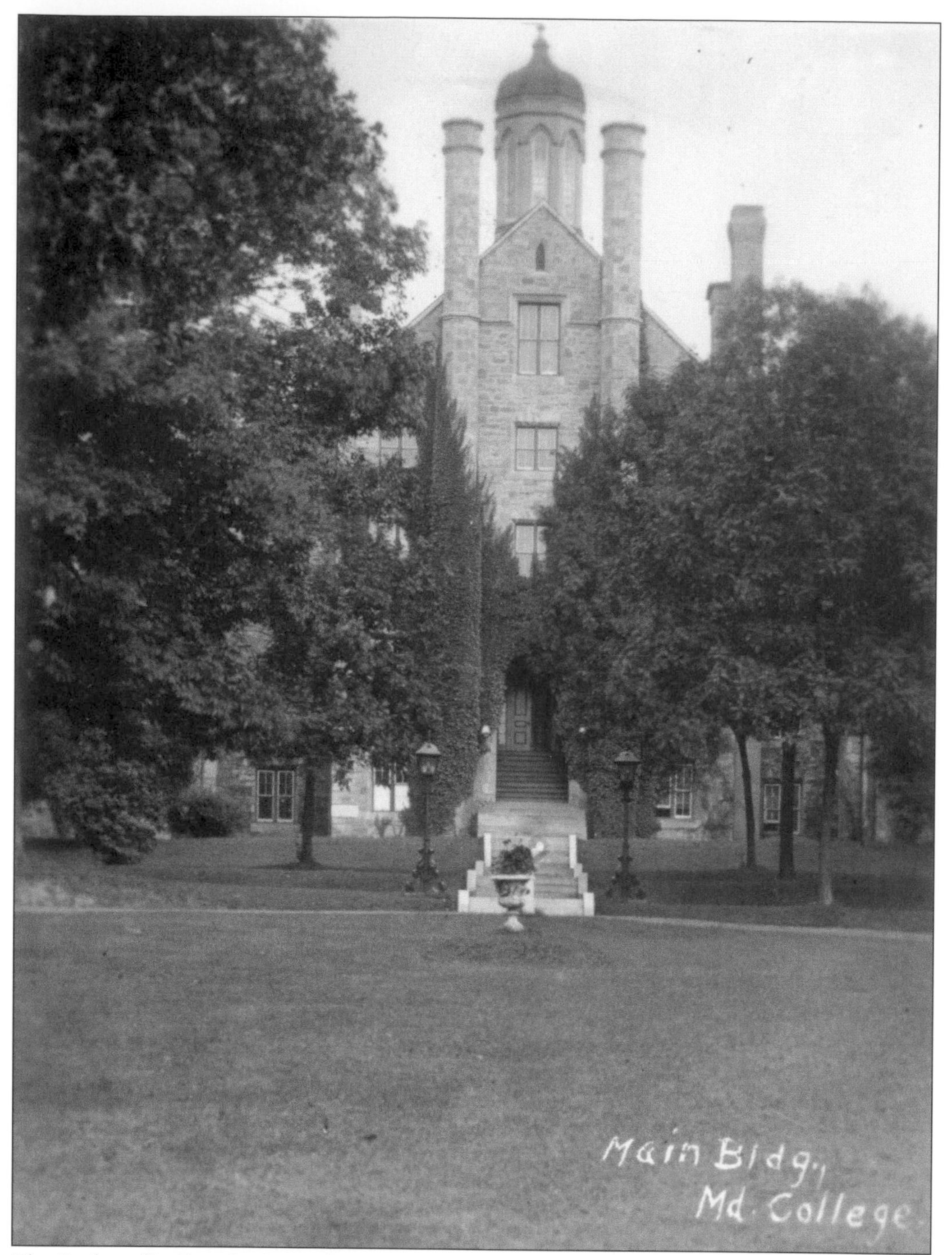

The Lutherville Female Seminary, founded in 1854 by two Lutheran ministers named Dr. Benjamin Kurtz and Dr. John Gottlieb Morris, was the town's raison d 'être. Over the years, the school's focus and name were changed to the Maryland College for Young Ladies and School for Music in 1895, and finally to the Maryland College for Women. The school closed in 1952. It then became a nursing home, suitably named College Manor. One may well wonder if any of its residents were former students. (Courtesy Baltimore County Historical Society.)

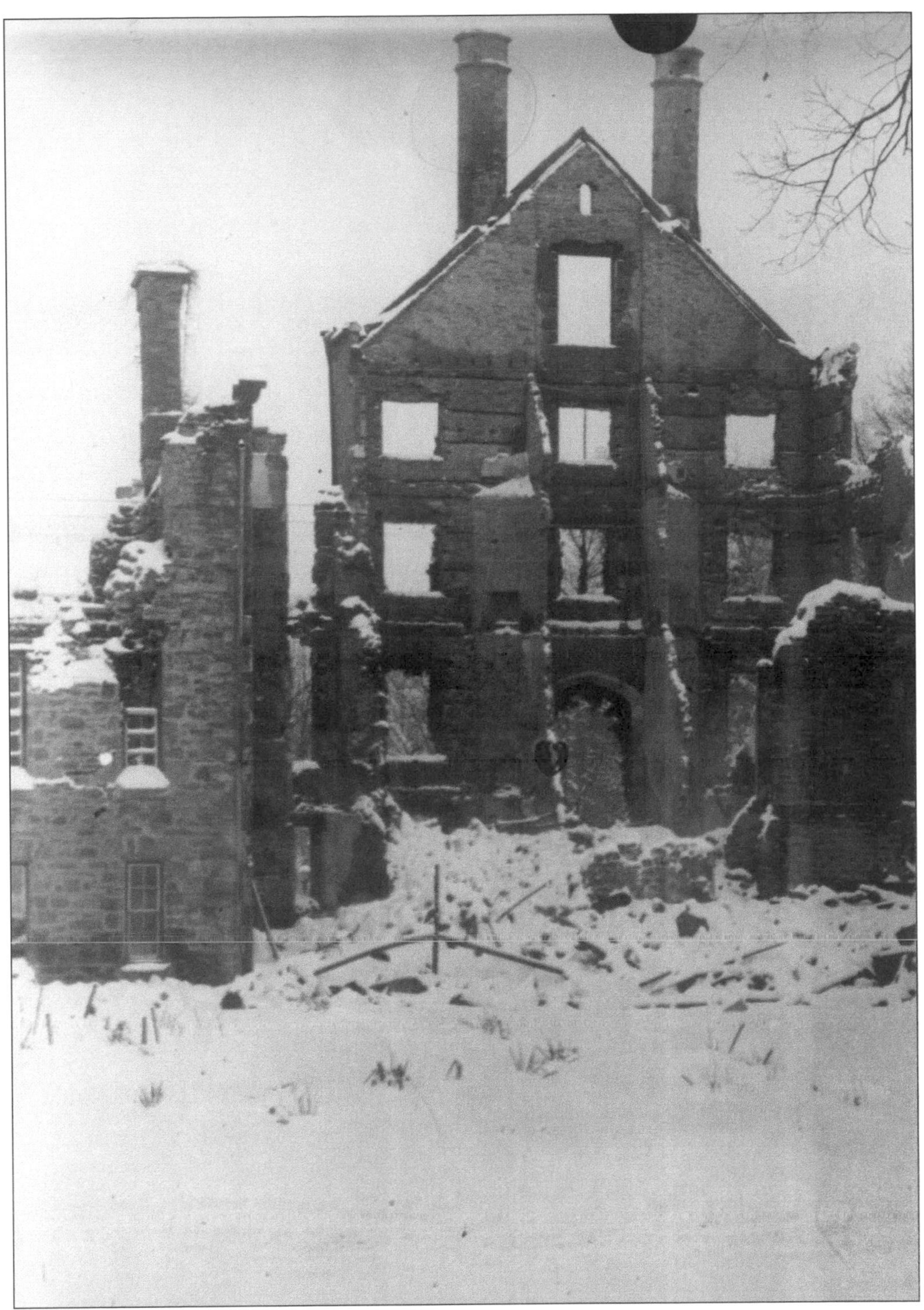

The Maryland College for Women was destroyed by fire on January 31, 1911. The disastrous results were thought to have been caused by one of the young ladies ignoring the ban on smoking. The school was later rebuilt. (Courtesy Baltimore County Historical Society.)

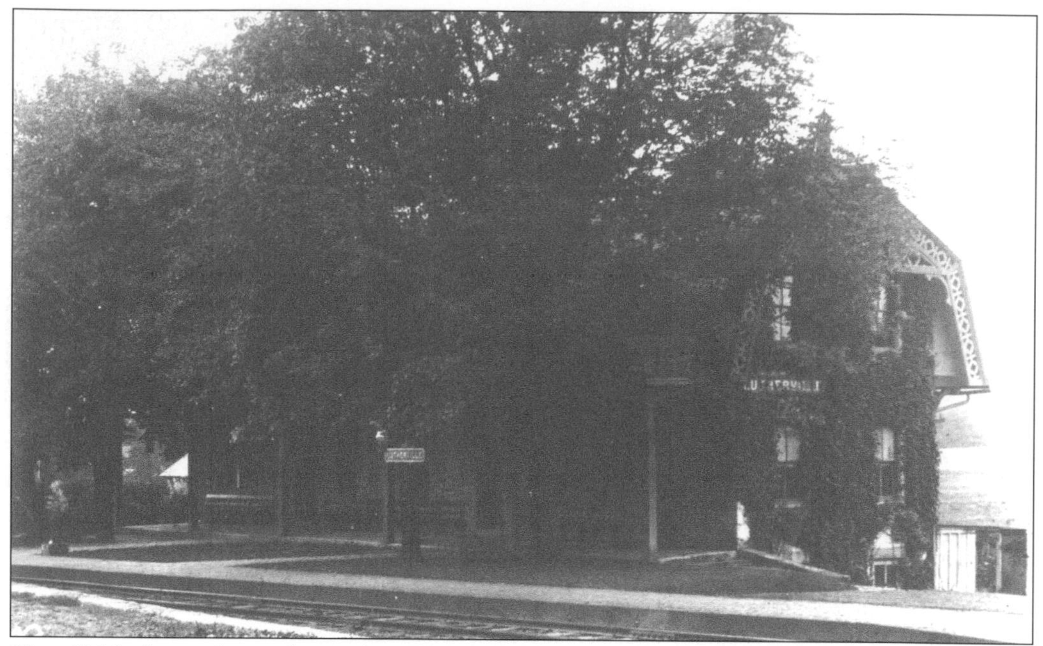

This 1915 photo shows the Lutherville Station of the Northern Central Railroad. Privately built in 1873, the structure was later sold to the railroad. After many years of commercial use, it was turned into a private residence. (Courtesy Baltimore County Historical Society.)

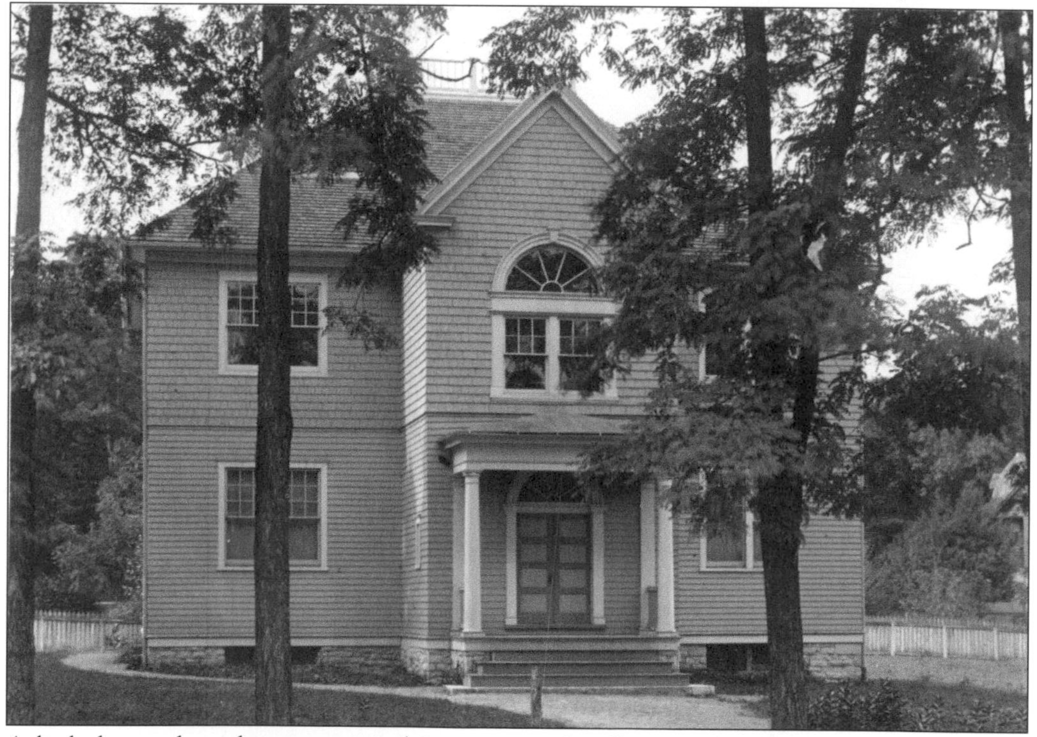

A little larger than the stereotypical "one-room schoolhouse," this building served for many years as Lutherville's elementary school. The building was later enlarged and divided into apartments. (Courtesy Baltimore County Historical Society.)

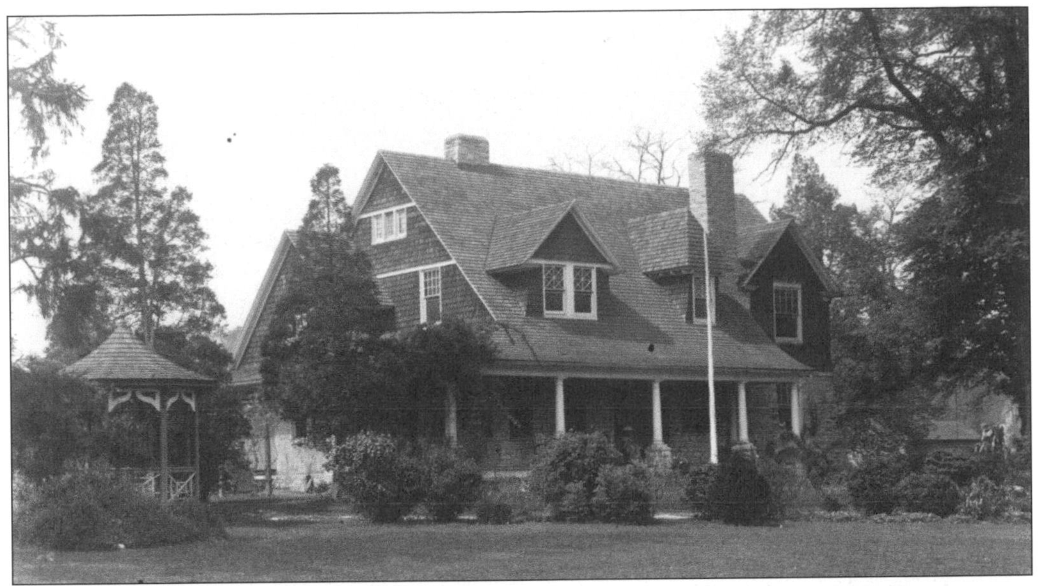

Gazebos were a popular addition to many properties. They were equally conducive to quiet, shaded reading and reflection, or to convivial gatherings fueled by food and chatter. Of course, most were located close enough to the house for a father to keep a protective eye out for any possible shenanigans where courting couples were concerned. (Courtesy Baltimore County Historical Society.)

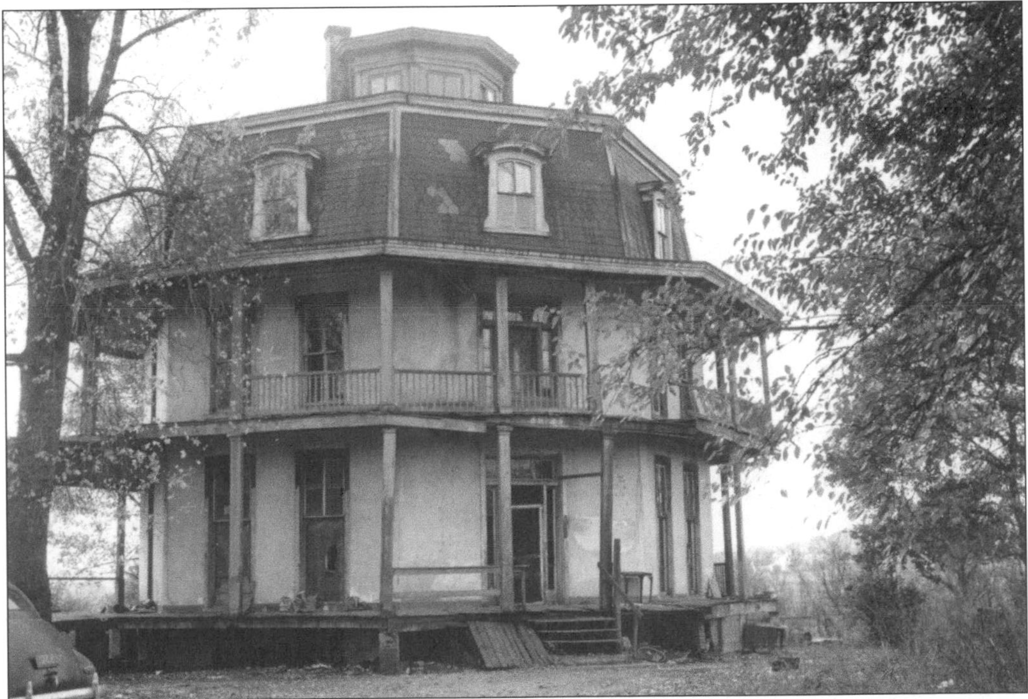

The well-known Octagon House at 1708 Kurtz Avenue was built in 1856 by the Reverend William Heilig. This photo, taken in 1946, shows the house prior to the dramatic renovations, made the following year, which involved the removal of the home's top two stories. (Courtesy Baltimore County Historical Society.)

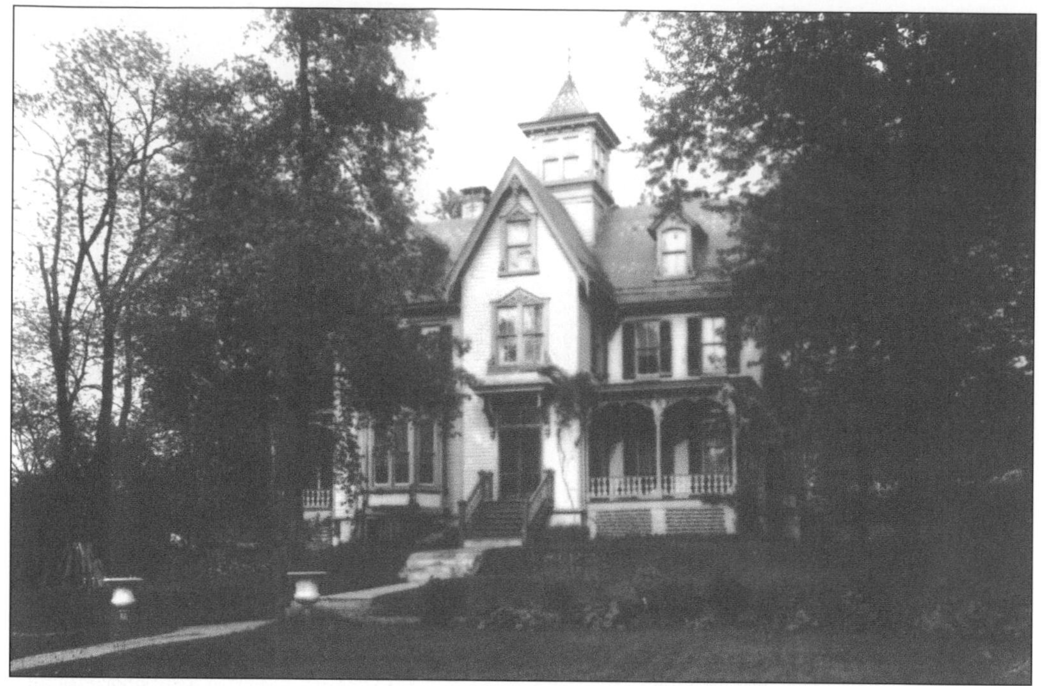

This finely detailed Downing-Vaux home is one of many which no longer stands. Known as the Woods-Littleton House, its manicured gardens and tree-shaded porches give a glimpse of Lutherville's glory days. (Courtesy Baltimore County Historical Society.)

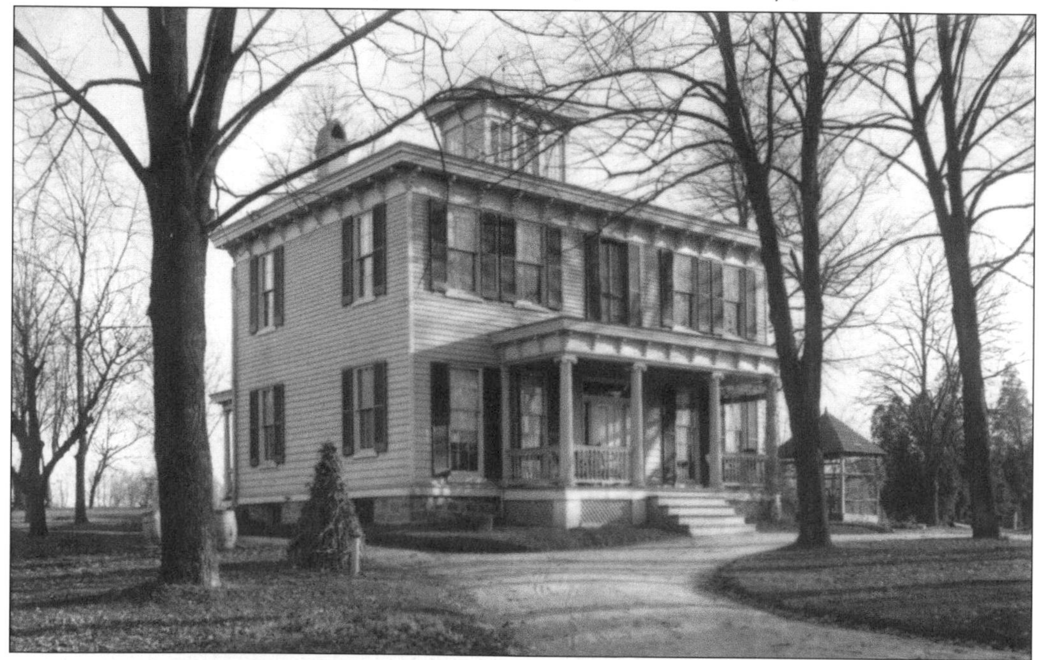

This imposing home, built in 1855 and known as Eldon, was destroyed in 1965. The large windows helped keep it cool in the years before air conditioning. Note the elaborate cupola, which surely had a commanding view of the area. (Courtesy Baltimore County Historical Society.)

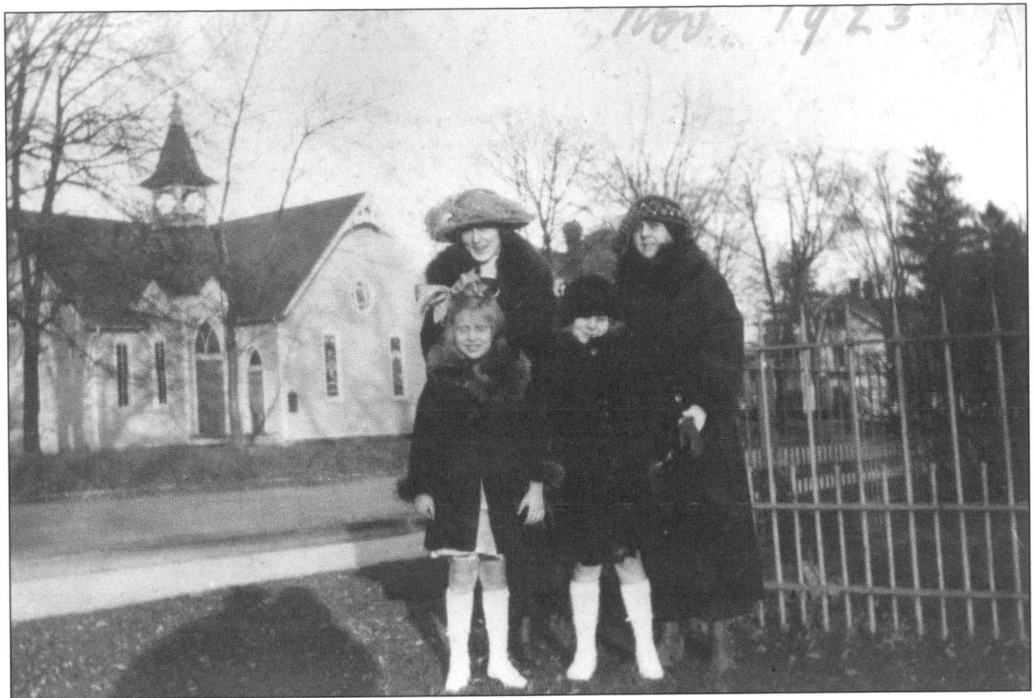

Although fashionable, the shorter hemlines of 1923 might have made this foursome long for warmer weather. In the background, note the Church of the Holy Comforter, a Lutherville landmark, which stands at Seminary and Bellona Avenues. (Courtesy Baltimore County Historical Society.)

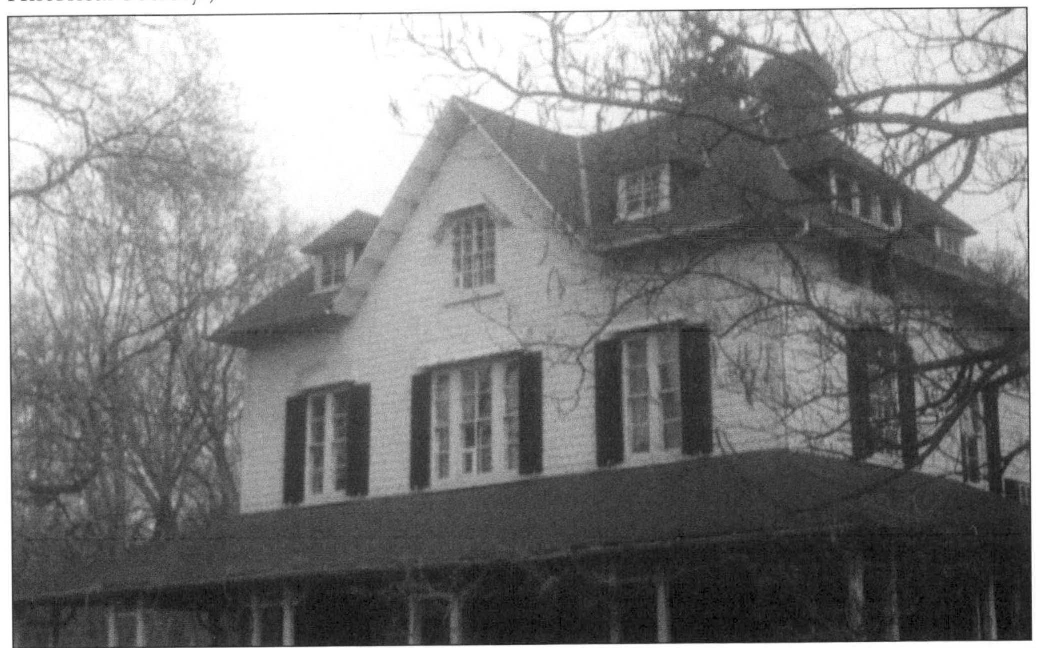

Long, shaded porches were a crucial component for keeping cool during the hot and humid summer weather. Many houses in Lutherville were used, originally, only as summer retreats. (Courtesy Baltimore County Historical Society.)

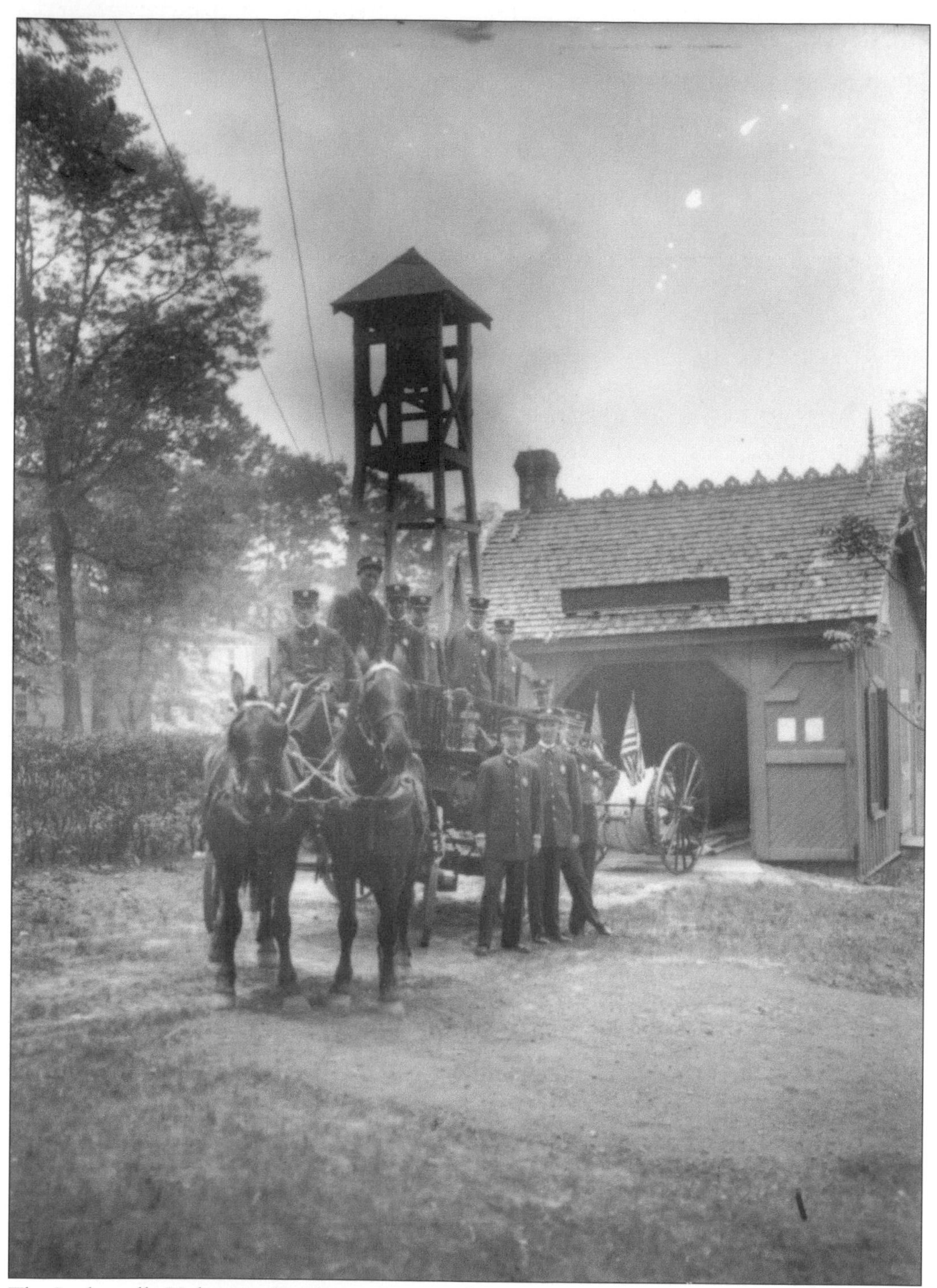

The Lutherville Volunteer Fire Department is shown in its finery as it heads out for the annual Fourth of July parade. These photos were taken in 1912, several years after the formation of the department. Note the bell tower, with its sizable bell, which was used to sound the alarm. (Courtesy Baltimore County Historical Society.)

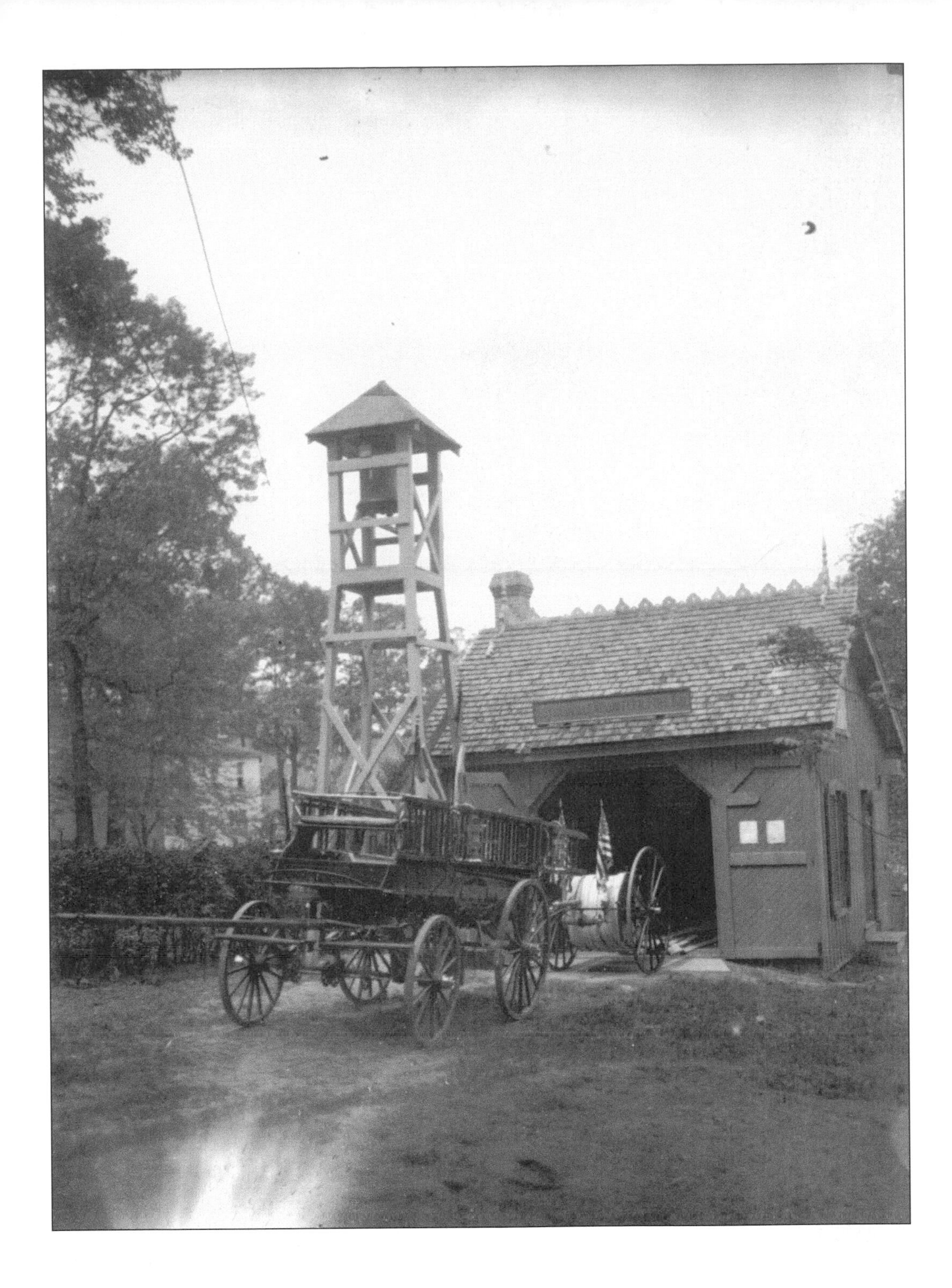

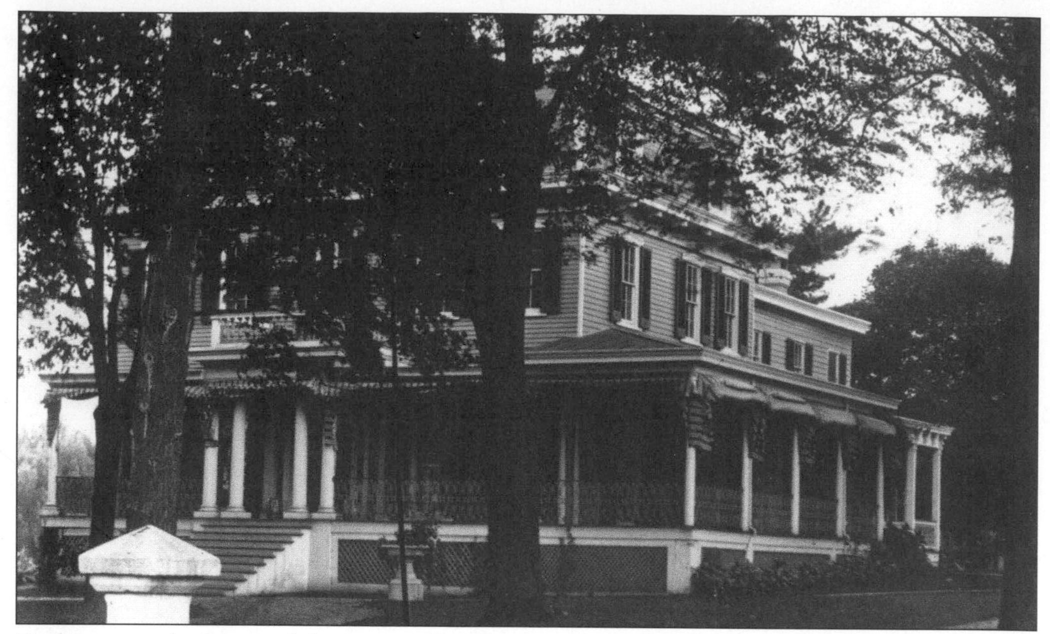

Keyburn was the home of democratic Congressman J. Frederick C. Talbott. Upon his election in 1878, Talbott represented Maryland's second district. During "the recent unpleasantness," as the Civil War was frequently referred to by southern sympathizers, Talbott had ridden in the Confederate cavalry. Known as a hands-on politician, constituents had an open invitation to air issues at his home on Sundays. Sadly, the house was torn down many years ago. (Courtesy Baltimore County Historical Society.)

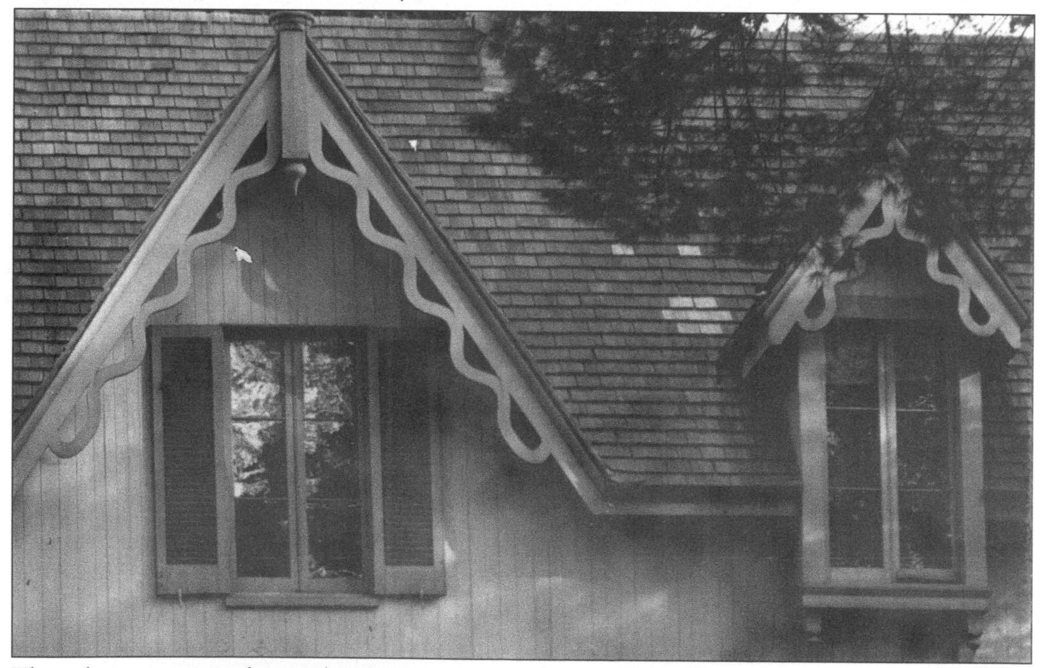

This close-up view shows the fine craftsmanship of the open-scalloped trim on Dr. John Gottlieb Morris's home named Oak Grove. Built in 1852, it set the tone for gracious homes in his planned community. (Courtesy Baltimore County Historical Society.)